Negotiating Tribal Water Rights

D1571298

Negotiating Tribal Water Rights

Fulfilling Promises in the Arid West

Bonnie G. Colby

John E. Thorson

Sarah Britton

FOREWORD BY David Getches, Dean

University of Colorado School of Law

The University of Arizona Press   Tucson

The University of Arizona Press
© 2005 The Arizona Board of Regents
All rights reserved

♾ This book is printed on acid-free, archival-quality paper.
Manufactured in the United States of America

10 09 08 07 06 05   6 5 4 3 2 1

Library of Congress Cataloging-in-Publication Data
Colby, Bonnie G.
Negotiating tribal water rights : fulfilling promises in the arid
west / Bonnie G. Colby, John E. Thorson, and Sarah Britton ;
foreword by David Getches. — 1st ed.
p. cm.
Includes bibliographical references and index.
ISBN 0-8165-2455-6 (pbk. : alk. paper)
1. Indians of North America — Legal status, laws, etc. — West
(U.S.) 2. Indians of North America — West (U.S.) — Claims.
3. Water rights — West (U.S.) I. Thorson, John E. II. Britton,
Sarah, 1976– III. Title.
KF8210.N37C65 2005
346.7304′32 — dc22
                                        2004023865

Publication of this book is made possible in part by the proceeds
of a permanent endowment created with the assistance of a
Challenge Grant from the National Endowment for the
Humanities, a federal agency.

DEDICATIONS

Bonnie Colby dedicates her contribution to her many graduate students over the past 22 years, who represent the diverse cultures of North America and the world. She is grateful for their stimulating her development as a teacher and researcher.

John Thorson dedicates his contribution to his mother, Margaret C. Thorson, who had a reason for giving him Felix S. Cohen's *Handbook of Federal Indian Law.*

Sarah Britton dedicates her contribution to this book to her family and friends who have supported her throughout.

CONTENTS

ILLUSTRATIONS

ABBREVIATIONS

ADR   alternative dispute resolution
ADWR   Arizona Department of Water Resources
afa   acre-feet annually
ALP   Animas–La Plata Project
BIA   Bureau of Indian Affairs
CAP   Central Arizona Project
CAWCD   Central Arizona Water Conservation District
CERCLA   Comprehensive Environmental Response and Liability Act
CREP   Conservation Reserve Enhancement Program
cfs   cubic feet per second
CRP   Conservation Reserve Program
CUP   Central Utah Project
EPA   Environmental Protection Agency
EQIP   Environmental Quality Incentive Program
ESA   Endangered Species Act
ET   evapotranspiration
FAIR   Federal Agricultural Improvement and Reform
FHIIP   Fort Hall Indian Irrigation Project
FOIA   Freedom of Information Act
FWS   Fish and Wildlife Service
HSR   hydrographic survey report
IID   Imperial Irrigation District
IPCC   Intergovernmental Panel on Climate Change
ISPE   Institute for the Study of Planet Earth

MDNRC   Montana Department of Natural Resources and Conservation
MWD   Metropolitan Water District of Southern California
NAPI   Navajo Agricultural Products Industry
NARF   Native American Rights Fund
NEPA   National Environmental Policy Act
NGO   nongovernmental organization
NIIP   Navajo Indian Irrigation Project
ODWR   Oregon Department of Water Resources
OMB   Office of Management and Budget
PIA   practicably irrigable acreage
PVID   Palo Verde Irrigation District
RPA   reasonable and prudent alternative
SAHRA   Sustainability of semi-Arid Hydrology and Riparian Areas
SAWRSA   Southern Arizona Water Rights Settlement Act
SJCP   San Juan–Chama Project
SRP   Salt River Project
SRPMIC   Salt River Pima—Maricopa Indian Community
USDA   United States Department of Agriculture
WCWCD   Washington County Water Conservancy District
WGA   Western Governors' Association
WRC   Western Regional Council
WRP   Wetlands Reserve Program

FOREWORD

Almost everyone familiar with western water issues knows *something* about Indian water rights. What most know is that tribes have significant legal claims to water.

Westerners understand, almost intuitively, two realities about water rights: 1) *Scarcity*—All the waters in most western rivers were long ago claimed by early settlers and have been put to use; 2) *Competition*—Everyone with water rights competes with everyone else with rights on the same river system. In the inevitable dry years that plague the semi-arid region, scarcity mounts and competition for water intensifies. For all but the holders of the best—that is, the oldest—water rights, nature's uncertainties can cause anxiety and threaten economic losses. Crops may have to go unirrigated if someone with an older right demands the limited remaining flow.

Water users at least have the certainty that they will get the amount of water they need to fulfill their water rights in years when nature is kind enough to provide enough for them and for everyone with older, better rights. Water rights are usually expressed in specific numerical quantities or flows—so many acre-feet, so many cubic feet per second, or so many miner's inches. Thus, a person with water rights can figure out how much water those with superior rights are collectively entitled to take and therefore how much the river has to produce in a given year before that person can use water.

Nature's uncertainty ripples through the water rights system with the most impact being borne by those with the most junior rights. Yet almost everyone is junior to someone. Because of the anomaly that imputes to Indian reservations a priority as of the date of their creation, even the most senior claims are often junior to tribal water claims. These old Indian water rights have remained largely unused, however, allowing hundreds or thousands of junior rights to be used for the century or more since the reservations were established. So today, virtually anyone with water rights, whether upstream or downstream, even on the remotest tributary, is potentially in competition with any Indian reservation on the river system.

Not only do the tribes have old claims that could preempt later uses if water were put to use on the reservations, their claims are large. The U.S. Supreme Court, whose interpretations created and elaborated the reserved water rights doctrine, has held that tribes are entitled to as much water as they need to fulfill the purposes of their reservations. They impliedly reserved these rights when the reservations were established. The goal of federal policy for most tribes was to confine them to smaller land areas, free up land for non-Indian settlement, and enable the Indians on reservations to make a living by farming the land. The reservations, typically in arid areas, need irrigation, and so the Court approved a formula that allowed tribes on such reservations enough water to irrigate all their "practicably irrigable acreage."

This translates into huge quantities; the beautiful but desolate Wind River Reservation in Wyoming was awarded one-half million acre-feet of water from the Bighorn River based on what it would take to irrigate its lands, which is also enough water for a city of 2.5 million people. The five tiny tribes along the Colorado River were awarded rights to 900,000 acre-feet.

Most tribal water claims remain largely theoretical; only a small percentage of tribes have made legal claims, few of those claims have been resolved in court or at the bargaining table, and almost no water has actually been demanded by any tribe from other water users under reserved water rights claims. Yet states and non-Indian users find the pall of uncertainty that hangs over the water rights regime to be disturbing.

Whatever displeasure the unsettled nature of Indian water rights causes for non-Indians, the consequences for Indians are more profound. Tribes need not fret, as non-Indian water users do, that their water uses will be disrupted. Instead, they despair never having been able to make use of their theoretically formidable legal rights, and today most tribes continue to languish in poverty. Meanwhile, nearby and distant non-Indian communities are sustained on what is, on paper, Indian water.

This situation came to be such without malice by non-Indians. They were invited to move into western lands that were vacated by the Indians at the insistence of the federal government. The settlers promptly and earnestly developed water from every available source. The government heeded their call for financial help in building dams and irrigation works. Meanwhile, the tribes, lacking technical assistance, capital, and political influence, made little use of their water.

It is hard to fault even those who understood the Supreme Court's ruling in the 1908 *Winters v. United States* case—that tribes had prior and paramount water rights—for not waiting to see what the tribes would eventually do with their water.[1] They behaved rationally in the face of uncertainty, doing what was necessary to survive and thrive in a semi-arid region. As more and more non-Indians came to depend on the tribes' water, however, the non-Indians' assumption of the risk of uncertainty became, perhaps arguably, less rational and justified. The injustice to the Indians grew with each new non-Indian water use, but while one may deplore in retrospect the neglect of tribal interests, it would be overdrawn to see this as malicious.

The vindication of Indian water rights was frustrated by practical, political, and economic factors. Taking legal action to protect water rights is costly and controversial. Building facilities to divert, deliver, and use water requires funding and government support. The inertia of well-established expectations built on present non-Indian water uses now impedes the pursuit of justice for tribes seeking funding and support, wanting to raise their water claims. How can tribes muster the political and monetary support they need to challenge their more numerous non-Indian neighbors? Who will lend tribes money to build dams, canals, and irrigation facilities so that they can take back water on which entire communities depend?

Water is essential for most tribes in the arid West simply to sustain communities and cultures on their reservations, let alone for tribes to grow and prosper. Indian tribal populations are growing very fast today, and—except for the tribes near cities or highways who have been able to participate in a legalized gambling boom—almost any viable economic activity depends on a secure water supply. Thus, many are pursuing tribal farms, restored fisheries, mining, and tourism. For some reservations, the agricultural and natural resource base may never support profitable development, but the possibility of getting monetary compen-

sation for agreeing to forego using a portion of their water for a period of time would be a more acceptable option than watching water that is legally theirs being used for free by non-Indians.

The futures of tribes have long been trapped behind unclaimed, unusable water rights. In the last thirty years there have been small and fitful stirrings of change. From the time of the *Winters* case until the last quarter of the twentieth century, government attorneys only occasionally ventured into court to assert water rights for Indian reservations against non-Indian users. Interestingly, these cases typically benefited non-Indians owning land within reservations whose uses were pitted against non-Indians using water off the reservations.[2] With few exceptions, there were no major Indian water cases decided in over fifty years. Then, in 1963 the Supreme Court forcefully ruled in *Arizona v. California*, the epic interstate water battle over the Colorado River, that tribes were entitled to a major share of the river that would come out of the shares allocable to the states.[3] Even this case did not affect existing non-Indian uses.

Until the late 1970s, tribes lacked advocacy for their water rights. Before that, only the occasional efforts of a federal attorney with the temerity to rock the boat had threatened to disrupt the status quo. The most notable example was the irrepressible William Veeder, whose strident advocacy of Indian water rights inside the federal establishment is legendary. He crusaded on behalf of tribes within the Department of Justice and later within the Bureau of Indian Affairs (BIA), unrelentingly seeking to demand water rights on behalf of tribes in federal courts.[4] For his dedication—and brash tactics—he was chastised, transferred, and disciplined, but he persisted undaunted. His efforts called attention to the government's own conflict of interest in these matters, where the United States continually faltered as it purported to represent Indian interests while at the same time supporting non-Indian development of the same water the tribes might have claimed.

In the 1970s several tribes got access to lawyers willing to press their water rights claims in court against apparently insuperable odds. The most significant agent for change was the entry of poverty-program legal-services lawyers and foundation-funded attorneys, with organizations such as California Indian Legal Services and Native American Rights Fund, who began suing to force the government — legally the tribes' trustee — to take up the cudgels of claiming the water rights the tribes had long been denied. The most notable in calling attention to and advancing Indian water rights were the Pyramid Lake Paiute Tribe's claims in Nevada and the claims of several Mission Indian tribes in Southern California.

The prospect of widespread assertion of Indian water rights was threatening to established water users, and state and local opposition galvanized against tribal claims. Now these opponents found the federal government largely supportive of the Indian position. In a 1970 special message, President Richard Nixon decried the conflict of interest that existed when the government tried to represent Indians and federal interests at the same time. Moved further by a federal judge's decision in the Truckee-Carson–Pyramid Lake litigation that chastised the federal government for its conflict of interest and embarrassed by hearings on the same subject,[5] the administration set out to do a better job. The government began providing funding for tribes to hire their own lawyers in Indian water cases. The government itself also launched several cases in which it asserted Indian water rights.

This began a period of competent and robust litigation that occupied the professional careers of a generation of Indian water rights experts representing the government, tribes, and their adversaries. The professional talents and good faith efforts of these experts notwithstanding, a surprisingly small number of claims reached a conclusion in the three decades that followed.

The non-Indian water users and their state allies rigidly resisted lawsuits brought by tribal attorneys or on behalf of tribes by the government. Tribes lost a spate of jurisdictional cases that were brought in federal court. States demanded that if Indian water rights were to be asserted at all, the cases belonged in state courts not federal courts. Tribes and their federal attorneys insisted that to subject tribes to state court adjudication of water rights would be inconsistent with the essentially federal nature of tribal property rights that the United States holds in trust for Indians. Moreover, the state courts, they argued, would inevitably be biased against Indian claims. In three major cases the United States held emphatically that litigation of tribal

water rights belonged in state court. This was based on a 1950s statute called the McCarran Amendment, in which Congress consented to adjudication in state courts of water rights of which the United States "is the owner." Despite the law's obliqueness and its failure to mention Indian rights at all, the Court found that Congress had intended to hand over this kind of lawsuit to state courts.

At this point the game changed. States now saw an advantage to taking jurisdiction over Indian water rights and deciding their size and priority as part of large adjudications of all the water rights in entire river systems. This is how nearly all the legal activity resulting in water rights settlements began. Unwieldy lawsuits and administrative adjudications that implicated tens of thousands of water rights holders were started in most western states. They consumed immense amounts of time and money for lawyers and experts. Only one such lawsuit — the *Big Horn* adjudication[6] — proceeded all the way to a partial final judgment on tribal rights, and even after that, other litigation phases and collateral proceedings have continued. Many other cases were brought in state court, and several continue. As it has turned out, the fears of some that state courts would be manifestly unfair have not been realized. A much greater problem has been the complexity of the legal and factual issues. The cases simply are not well suited to complete resolution of all legal, technical, and factual issues in the courtroom.

Thus, most Indian water rights cases that began in court have evolved into negotiations. Most of the settlements of water rights claims on the nineteen reservations that are listed in table I.1 to this book began with lawsuits. Dozens of other settlement processes have been initiated to resolve key issues that were first raised in the courts, and the processes have been going on for several years.

The problems of trying to deal with sensitive issues and solve practical problems in litigation were revealed in cases like *Big Horn*, where attorney fees ran into the millions of dollars, rulings tended to favor only one party or the other, and accommodations of the multiple parties and issues became awkward within the adversarial system. As this book ably explains, settlements offer the opportunity to craft practical and just solutions to Indian water rights claims.

Practicality and justice are not easy to find where the irresistible force of absolute legal rights of tribes meets the apparently immovable object of a century of established non-Indian water uses.

Since the 1980s, settlement negotiations have been an integral part of the process used by tribes, the federal government, and states in attempting to resolve Indian water rights claims. Negotiation can fill gaps in the litigation with specific factual determinations or can take over once the parties are convened by a state's adjudication process. In some instances, such as in Montana, tribes and the state negotiate compacts or other broadly based agreements covering allocation of water and other matters. Negotiated settlements can cover many more issues than the quantification and priority dates of water rights that are usually the focus of a court ruling. New water projects can be agreed upon or water can be reallocated from existing dams. The parties can agree to use water more efficiently and to achieve environmental benefits. The rules for reservation water management — state, tribal, or other — can be determined. The parties can consent to the terms for tribal off-reservation water marketing.

All the advantages of settlements notwithstanding, the process is still long, expensive, and vulnerable to being delayed or derailed for many reasons. Probably the single greatest impediment to settlements is the unevenness of federal commitment to the process. That commitment is a combination of policy announced by the executive branch through the departments of the Interior and of Justice, and of congressional action, such as the willingness to lubricate settlements with substantial appropriations of funds for water projects, tribal economic development funds, and other expenditures. Of course, the willingness to spend can be affected by the health of the national economy. Yet in some of the nation's most prosperous times there were virtually no settlements. This likely resulted from a combination of ineffective efforts, lack of political commitment, and a division between the political parties controlling the executive branch and Congress.

With the undeniably critical significance of Indian water rights to the future of tribes and to the reliability of non-Indian water rights on nearly all the major rivers of the West, the stakes in Indian water settlements are immense indeed. The authors of this book have provided the essentials for parties to ongoing or future negotiations. Some variables that affect the success of settlement negotiations are more susceptible to being controlled by others than by the parties. This book offers the accumulated wisdom of many years of settlement negotiations, lessons that it would be well for participants to assimilate to optimize future efforts.

The declared purpose of *Negotiating Tribal Water Rights* is to inform and incite dialogue on Indian water rights, leading to their settlement. It has all the ingredients for doing this. From the historical and political background, to an understanding of the technicalities of water law, to an appreciation of why settlements can be mutually beneficial to all parties, the book is an invaluable resource. Anyone who is involved in these processes would be remiss to ignore its lessons. Those who seek the benefits that can be reaped for all sectors of modern society in the western United States — in terms of economic well-being, security, and of social justice — have much to learn from the pages that follow.

David H. Getches
Dean and Raphael J. Moses Professor
of Natural Resources Law
University of Colorado School of Law

ACKNOWLEDGMENTS

Many individuals and organizations have contributed to the creation of this book. Elizabeth Checchio, co-author with Bonnie G. Colby of a book on this subject in the early 1990s, continues to be a valued colleague and friend. The authors express heartfelt gratitude to Kathy Dolge, who shepherded the manuscript through many phases of revision and provided skillful editing and document management. Dana Smith, Trisha Grant, Dru Dunton, and Jennifer Pullen provided invaluable assistance with manuscript preparation. Nancy Bannister and Greg Fitzpatrick created most of the graphics presented.

Gary Woodard, of the SAHRA, National Science Foundation Center coordinated their provision of financial support and provided encouragement along the way. Funding for research and document production was also provided by the Hewlett Foundation's Dividing the Waters project, the Institute for Study of Planet Earth, the Water Resources Research Center and the Department of Agricultural and Resource Economics at The University of Arizona.

We very much appreciate Patti Hartmann, Melanie Mallon, and Harrison Shaffer's perseverance and support throughout the publication process with the University of Arizona Press. Several colleagues gave generously of their time and their thoughts to provide the perspectives presented in the interviews in chapter 5.

FUNDING ORGANIZATIONS

Several organizations provided financial support for research and production of this book. The National Science Foundation's Science and Technology Center for Sustainability of semi-Arid Hydrology and Riparian Areas (SAHRA) is developing an integrated, multidisciplinary understanding of the hydrology of semi-arid regions and is building partnerships with stakeholders (public agencies and private organizations) so that this understanding is effectively applied to managing water resources and to implementing public policy. SAHRA is concerned both with advancing the understanding of fundamental principles in semi-arid hydrology (through stakeholder-driven multidisciplinary research) and with developing strategies for implementing scientific understanding on a practical level (through aggressive knowledge transfer and strong education initiatives). SAHRA is located in Tucson at the University of Arizona.

The Dividing the Waters project brings together for educational purposes over one hundred state and federal trial and appellate judges (including U.S. Supreme Court special masters) who are involved in complex water rights litigation. The central purpose of Dividing the Waters has been to improve the management and outcomes of stream adjudications and other water-related litigation that directly touch western people and the environment of the region. Dividing the Waters has been financially supported by the Ford Foundation, the William and Flora Hewlett Foundation, and the General Service Foundation of Aspen, Colorado.

The University of Arizona Department of Agricultural and Resource Economics offers undergraduate and graduate degrees focusing on natural resource economics, international trade and development, econometric methods, agribusiness, and management. Faculty members have been honored on many occasions for their outstanding teaching, research, outreach, and public service. Additionally, the department's graduate students have achieved much recognition and work worldwide as professionals in water management, agriculture, advanced data analysis, natural resource economics, and international development.

The Institute for the Study of Planet Earth (ISPE) was established in 1994 at the University of Arizona to foster excellence in interdisciplinary discovery, education, and application. ISPE works to provide both disciplinary and interdisciplinary research relating to the environment of the Earth, from local to global scales, and how this environment is likely to change in coming seasons, years, and decades. ISPE encourages multidisciplinary action on and off campus, as well as with users of environmental knowledge and information. One of ISPE's main goals is to forge new paradigms in partnerships between universities and society's decision makers.

The University of Arizona's Water Resources Research Center provided a research grant to assist with background research for this book. The funding came through the U.S. Geological Survey, authorized by the Water Resources Research Act, section 104B, which provides support for small research projects on water-related issues.

INTRODUCTION

> Permanence has always been an elusive goal in American Indian policy. Throughout U.S. history the government has sought to establish a workable, long-term relationship with Indian people that would withstand the test of time. And time is no small matter; Indian policy is the oldest political issue on the continent.
>
> Daniel McCool, *Native Waters*

Negotiations and litigation over tribal water rights shape the future of Indian and non-Indian communities throughout the western United States. The rapid growth of western cities, full appropriation of dependable river flows, declining groundwater levels, and increased environmental needs for water all lead to intense competition for limited water supplies and pressure to address tribal water claims.

American Indian tribes control large amounts of land in western states, and vast entitlements to water are associated with these land reservations. In Arizona, for instance, nineteen Indian reservations account for 20 million acres (28 percent) of the state's land base (see map I.1). Reservation lands cover large areas in many other western states as well (see maps I.2 and I.3). Some observers have calculated that tribal water entitlements, many of which remain to be quantified, exceed available and currently used surface water supplies in the regions of the reservations. Control over water resources is essential for Indian tribes. Water and the wildlife and plants it supports are central to the cultural practices of many tribal people. Without access to adequate water supplies, Indian reservations in the western United States will never provide the permanent homelands promised to tribes in treaties. However, non-Indians who established and rely on water rights under state laws invested much of their lives and their money to develop farms, businesses, and cities. The federal government encouraged these investments and provided federal water projects as an incentive to settle the West. Now, non-Indian landowners confront the possibility that the water they have been using, and to which they have a legal entitlement, had, in fact, been reserved for Indian tribes.

And, tribes face the challenge of bringing old promises to fulfillment.

Although the quantities of water to which tribes are entitled vary considerably from reservation to reservation, the issues raised by these claims are widespread and significant. Uncertainty about the future availability of water raises concerns and contributes to the desire to determine the extent and scope of Indian water rights. In the 1980s, there were more settlements, court decisions, legislative actions, and budgetary appropriations related to tribal water issues than in the previous seven decades combined. The 1990s, by contrast, produced relatively few negotiated settlements ratified by Congress. However, multiple settlement negotiations were under way throughout the West. Table A.1 provides a summary of negotiated settlements of tribal water rights, and table I.1 lists the agreements and their settlement dates.

Efforts to clarify and quantify Indian water entitlements often result in protracted, costly litigation. Although litigation can foster animosity among the affected parties, it also can help settle matters of law and provide impetus for negotiated agreements. In some instances, negotiations have generated creative solutions to seemingly intractable problems, better working relations among the parties, and more integrated management of regional water resources. Many negotiated settlements (hailed as successes when ratified by Congress and the tribal, state, and local signatories) later encounter serious implementation difficulties and subsequently flounder. The choice to settle or to litigate is not an either/or decision. Over the past three decades, disputants have relied on a combination of litigation and negotiation to address the complex legal, political, cultural, and economic issues that arise in water conflicts.

Intent of Publication

We developed this book to provide information and ideas to fuel productive and well-informed dialogue among the many tribal and nontribal stakeholders

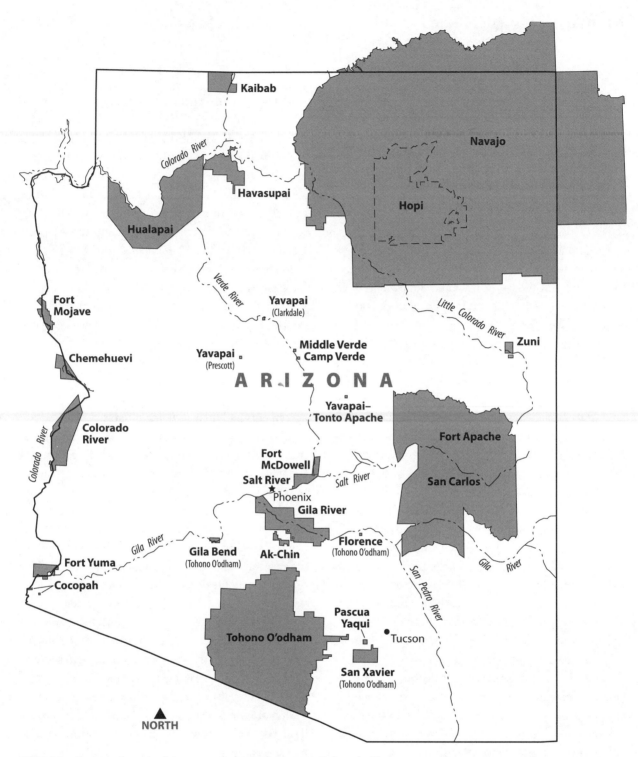

MAP I.1 Reservations in Arizona and along the Lower Colorado River

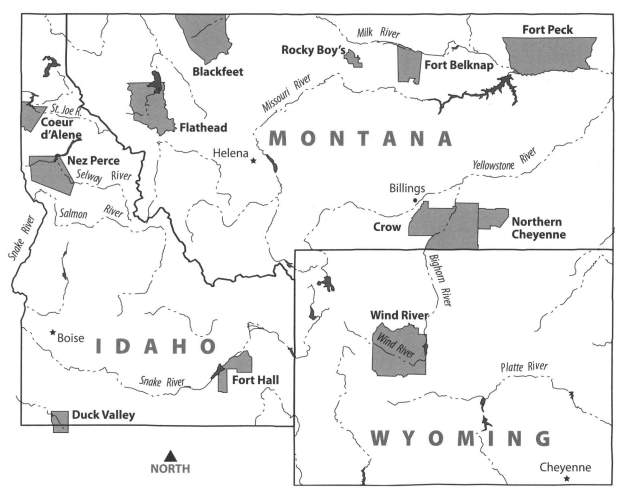

MAP I.2   Reservations in Idaho, Montana, and Wyoming

who rely upon the waters of the western United States. The book is written for those who participate in or advise water negotiations, such as tribal councils, tribal agency staff, state legislators, congressional staff, state and federal agency executives, water conservancy and irrigation district members, municipal water boards, attorneys, technical consultants, and the interested public. This book provides an overview of the many aspects of Indian water rights and the efforts to reach settlements and is designed for the generalist who desires a basic understanding of the issues.

In part 1, we describe the context in which litigation and settlement negotiations occur and alternative processes for addressing tribal water claims. In part 2, we describe the basic concerns and perspectives of the various stakeholders in the ongoing struggle over western water. This part includes interviews with some of the leaders on all sides of these issues. In part 3, we review the key stages of the settlement process from the problem of getting parties to try something other than litigation to the problems of making negotiated settlements work. Part 3 describes some of the important settlement efforts to highlight the most significant features of those negotiated and litigated settlements that have been ratified by Congress and are being implemented, and others that are currently being negotiated. Part 4 reflects on the collective experience with negotiated settlements and litigation and offers suggestions for more effective resolution of inter-jurisdictional water conflicts. We also evaluate the significance of Indian water rights settlements in the ongoing development of the American West.

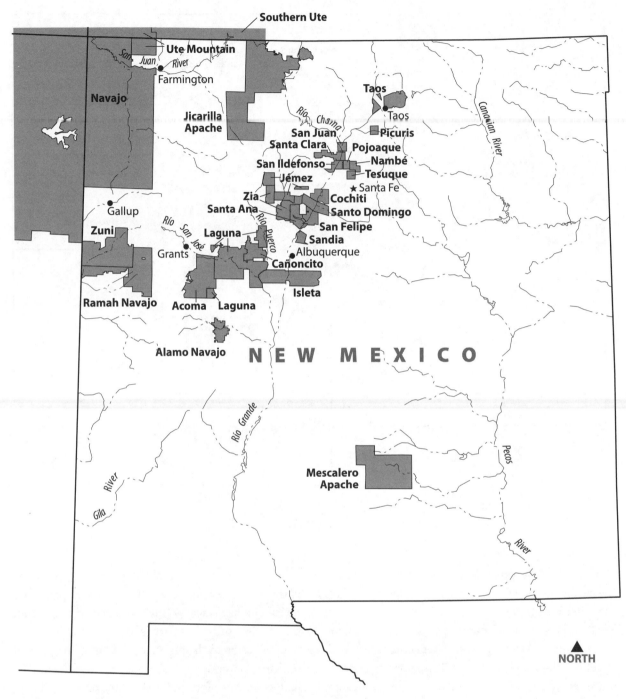

MAP I.3   Reservations in New Mexico

How Best to Use This Book

The chapters primarily provide a broad overview for readers interested in a general introduction to the topic of each chapter, with more specific information in sidebars, contributed essays on special topics written by experts on the subject, as well as interviews with key individuals active in the arena of water management and tribal water cases in the western United States. Consequently, readers not electing to read all sidebars and essays may skim through the main text for an introduction to a topic without losing continuity.

Although this book provides an overview of rele-

TABLE I.1 Negotiated settlements of tribal water rights (as of December 2004)

Settlement	State	Date of settlement
Ak-Chin	Arizona	1978, 1984, 1992, 2000
Southern Arizona (SAWRSA)	Arizona	1982, 1992, 2004
Fort Peck–Montana	Montana	1985
Salt River Pima–Maricopa	Arizona	1988
Colorado Ute	Colorado	1988
San Luis Rey	California	1988
Truckee-Carson–Pyramid Lake	Nevada	1990
Fallon Paiute-Shoshone	Nevada	1990
Fort Hall	Idaho	1990
Fort McDowell	Arizona	1990
Northern Cheyenne	Montana	1992
San Carlos	Arizona	1992
Northern Ute	Utah	1992
Jicarilla Apache	New Mexico	1992
Yavapai-Prescott	Arizona	1994
Warm Springs	Oregon	1997
Rocky Boy's Chippewa Cree	Montana	1999
Shivwits Paiute	Utah	2000
Zuni Heaven (AZ claims)	Arizona	2003
Gila River Indian Community	Arizona	2004
Nez Perce	Idaho	2004

vant issues, it is not intended as legal or technical advice; nor does it intend to provide a formula or blueprint for addressing Indian water claims. The circumstances of each case are unique, and neither negotiated settlements nor litigation can claim to be the universally superior strategy. Readers seeking in-depth discussions of specific issues or settlements can review the many legal, hydrologic, economic, and political analyses that are listed in the bibliography.

PART 1

The Context for Indian Water Settlements

Water says this, "Wherever you put me I'll be in my home. I am awfully smart. Lead me out of my springs, lead me from my rivers, but I came from the ocean and I shall go back into the ocean. You can dig a ditch and put me in it, but I go only so far and I am out of sight. I am awfully smart. When I am out of sight I am on my way home."

Wintu women, quoted in Heizer and Elsasser,
The Natural World of the California Indians

PHOTO 1.1 Bronze sculpture entitled *Water Bearers*, by Glenna Goodacre, located on New Mexico State Capitol grounds, Santa Fe. Photo: Todd Sargent

CHAPTER 1
Historical Background

And all the people were around, and they wore splendid things—beautiful buckskin and beads. The chiefs wore necklaces and their pendants shone like the sun. There were many people, and oh, it was beautiful! That was the beginning of the Sun Dance . . . it was a long time ago.

N. Scott Momaday, *The Way To Rainy Mountain*

Life changed for the Indian peoples of North America the moment strangers first walked onto western lands in the sixteenth and seventeenth centuries. These strangers were Spanish soldiers and priests who entered the region from the south, following the shallow desert rivers that would later become known as the San Pedro and the Rio Grande. Spanish, English, and Russian ships plied the coastal waters and eventually established outposts known today as San Diego, Los Angeles, San Francisco, and Seattle. Spanish explorers, along with French missionaries and trappers, traveled the Mississippi River corridor, sometimes venturing upstream on the Missouri and Platte rivers. From every direction, European exploration and settlement slowly pressed upon the many tribes and pueblos west of the Mississippi.

At the time of these first European incursions, the native people were quite numerous and diverse.[1] Resident and migrant groups in all quarters of the West had the patterns of their lives dictated by the availability of necessary resources. Some groups irrigated, while others depended on seasonal rains, to grow food and fiber. Some relied directly on the desert to provide necessities, and others hunted and raided over vast regions. Along the coasts, Indian people centered their lives on the coastal waters to provide an abundance of fish.

The native peoples lived moderately off the land with innovative and adaptive methods developed over generations. Notions of title and ownership were uncommon. Some groups, like the Plains Indians, traveled widely and asserted their presence over a vast terrain. Others, like the Puebloans, lived in a small area used more intensely.

Some of the Indian populations we find in the West today were not part of this pre-European population.

Tribes such as the Cherokee, Creeks, Choctaws, Sauk, and Fox lived in the East, and their subsequent involuntary move westward, to make way for American settlement, would mark an extremely unfortunate chapter in the nation's history.

European Incursions

The history of the West is a study of a place undergoing conquest and never fully escaping its consequences . . . conquest involving the drawing of lines on a map, the definition and allocation of ownership.

Patricia Nelson Limerick, *The Legacy of Conquest*

The first Europeans brought unknown disease, unwanted religion, and an air of superiority to their first contacts with western tribes.[2] Many of the encounters were violent, and some, such as Oñate's destruction of Acoma Pueblo in 1599, were genocidal. In some areas, the Europeans attempted to incorporate the Indians into their legal systems. Under Spanish law, most Indians were subjects of the Crown such that, although exploited unmercifully, the Indians had "a legal, recognizable place in society."[3] The official Spanish policy "was both to protect the Indians in their personal and communal land–water rights, and to convert them to the Christian religion so that they would be loyal vassals of the Crown."[4] Later, in the Treaty of Guadalupe Hidalgo (1848), Mexico insisted that land grants, including those made to Indian communities, be recognized under American law. England, at the same time, sought to assimilate Indian people through religious conversion and intermarriage. European and American Indian societies remained distinct, however, and relations came to be conducted on a sovereign-to-sovereign basis. For its part, France, probably the most successful of the European powers in its relationship with the Indians, sought to enlist their assistance in the fur trade and other commercial ventures.

When the United States assumed control of the western lands, the government viewed many of the tribes as allies of the English during the revolutionary war and therefore afforded them little respect during the post-war period. By the time the United States had acquired the land we now know as the contiguous forty-eight states and Alaska, the Indian tribes that inhabited the American West were under American dominion.

American Indian Policy

While the United States was establishing its hegemony over the western lands, it was also developing policies toward the native people that came with those lands. These policies would develop and sometimes repeat through the next two hundred years, usually to the advantage of non-Indian Americans. American Indian policy can be divided into five distinct periods.

Removal and Reservation Period

At first, the Americans sought to continue the government-to-government relationships that had been employed in the colonies by the British crown.[5] As non-Indian Americans spilled over the Appalachian range, Indian policy became dictated by the unsatiated need for settlement lands. With the Louisiana Purchase, President Thomas Jefferson considered relocating eastern tribes to the trans-Mississippi region, thereby relieving settlement pressures and allowing time for the tribes to become "civilized." Eventually, he believed, these eastern and western societies would merge into one complete society.

Since many eastern tribes allied with Great Britain during the War of 1812, Andrew Jackson, an army general involved in some of the fieriest hostilities with the Indians, had little sympathy for the tribes when he assumed the presidency in 1829. He initiated perhaps the most devastating period of American Indian policy: the relocation period. To aid American settlement of the trans-Appalachian area and reduce conflicts between non-Indians and the tribes, Jackson embarked on the vast relocation of dozens of eastern tribes to the "Indian country" beyond the Mississippi—an area centered in present-day Oklahoma. The Cherokee Trail of Tears of 1838 is the best-known story from this relocation period, although the Choctaw, Creek, Chickasaw, and other eastern tribes faced similar fates. Even eastern tribes who escaped wholesale relocation watched their tribal lands diminish.

While eastern tribes were under intense pressure to move, western tribes were negotiating a series of treaties agreeing to reductions in lands and restrictions on movement.[6] For example, in the Treaty of Fort Laramie of 1868, the Sioux and Cheyenne agreed to allow the construction of railroads and consented to fixed reservations in the Dakotas, Montana, and Wyoming in exchange for peace with the U.S. Army. In 1874, however, prospectors trespassing on the Sioux Reservation discovered gold in the Black Hills, leading to the Battle of Little Bighorn and reduction of the reservation.

While enduring the indignity of relocation and the gradual erosion of tribal land base, tribes still retained their status as sovereign nations capable of negotiating treaties with the United States. Then in 1871, Congress announced that legislation would replace treaties as the method of forming and modifying reservations.

Assimilation and Allotment Period

By the 1880s, when Indian relocation on western reservations was almost complete, the reservation system itself came under attack. Some policy makers believed that ending reservations would free Indians from their poverty and assimilate them into the broader American society and economy. Others sought to claim reservation land for growing western towns and farms, or simply for the mineral value of the land. These two sentiments combined to support passage of the General Allotment (Dawes) Act of 1887.[7] The act served as a blueprint to divide reservation lands into 160-acre (or smaller) parcels and convey them to individual Indians. Title to these allotments would remain in trust for twenty-five years, allowing the Indians time to gain agrarian skills and improve the parcels. Those lands that were not actively farmed by tribal people would be considered surplus and opened to non-Indians for homesteading or purchase.[8]

The General Allotment Act failed in its principal goal of creating thousands of independent Indian farmers. In a span of forty-five years, the allotment program passed 65 percent of reservation lands (90 million acres) to non-Indians. After obtaining title to the lands, many Indians unable to farm on small, arid parcels sold to non-Indians or lost their land due to delinquent taxes. The act fragmented Indian lands and

The Allotment Era

The Homestead Act of 1862 provided that any person who was an American citizen . . . could claim 160 acres of government land. . . . Thousands of homesteaders streamed out West to stake claims on the wild prairie. But corner stakes did not make a farm. "Free land" was not free from toil, hardship, loneliness, privation.

Walter Havighurst, "Prairie Life," in introduction to *My Antonia*, by Willa Cather

The land ownership pattern within many Indian reservations is a patchwork of tribal lands and individual parcels. Checkerboarding began under the General Allotment (Dawes) Act of 1887, under which tracts of reservation lands were allotted to individual tribal members. Subsequently, many of the allotments passed into non-Indian ownership when federal restrictions preventing alienation of the parcels were removed. The patterns of allotments and homesteading varied greatly across the western reservations. Some reservations became dominated by nontribal landowners.

The allotment of tribal lands was just one aspect of an overall effort to assimilate Indians into the larger society. During the allotment era, Indian landholdings were reduced by 65 percent, from 138 million acres in 1887 to 48 million acres in 1934.[1] The intent of allotment was to promote farming by individual Indians; notably, farming requires irrigation in most areas of the West.

Although the General Allotment Act was unclear as to water rights, the courts have held that a right to use a portion of the tribe's reserved (*Winters*) water rights passed from the tribe to the allottee when lands were allocated. Courts also found that non-Indian purchasers of allotments obtain a fair use right to reserved waters (commonly called *Walton* rights).[2] The resulting mix of Indian and non-Indian land and water ownership has generated serious controversy regarding tribal and state government regulatory powers over water use on allotment lands.[3]

tribal solidarity that presaged complex water rights issues that have yet to be resolved. (See sidebar 1.1 for further discussion of the allotment era.)

Reform Period

The failure of the allotment program and the end of the homestead era led to a significant shift in Indian policy under the leadership of federal attorney Felix Cohen. In 1934, the Indian Reorganization Act ended allotment and encouraged tribes to strengthen reservation life by adopting constitutions and bylaws approved by tribal members. Although not all tribes adopted these governmental forms, the legislation did mark a return to tribal self-government that still exists. These reforms, however, were weakened and almost derailed by developments after World War II.

Termination Period

Once again, efforts were made to assimilate tribal people completely into the mainstream of American society by terminating the federal trust responsibility for the tribes and ending the reservation system. (See chapter 2 for a discussion of federal trust responsibility.) Some critics of reservations equated them with prisoner-of-war camps, and proponents of termination argued that it would help streamline the federal government. During the 1950s, legislation was passed that ended Bureau of Indian Affairs (BIA) health services in some states, transferred civil and criminal jurisdiction on reservations to state authorities in many instances, and terminated reservations and trust status over tribes in California, Texas, Oregon, Wisconsin, Oklahoma, Utah, and Nebraska. Between 1954 and 1962, Congress ended federal services and protection for sixty-one tribes, bands, and other groups.[9]

Modern Era

These termination measures were extremely unpopular in Indian communities. With growing concern for the rights of minorities, termination ended in the 1960s and 1970s. President Richard Nixon, in a statement on Indian affairs issued in 1970, concluded that termination had failed and that legislation was needed to restore the self-sufficiency of tribes. Indeed, since the 1970s, some of the tribes that suffered termination have been restored to part of their former lands and to federal trust protection.

The last thirty years have seen an unprecedented development in tribal economies and institutions, as well as a new generation of leadership. Still, major problems remain, such as achieving viable tribal economies; addressing health and nutrition needs; funding governmental institutions like schools, police, and courts; and retaining cultural traditions. Litigation and negotiations over water rights and over access to reliable water supplies for use on reservations are central to successfully confronting the many challenges facing tribal leaders.

PHOTO 2.1   Apache woman carrying water, 1900. Photo: Arizona State Museum, University of Arizona

CHAPTER 2

Legal Background

> A great deal of Western property rights rested on this narrow margin of timing … even though the passage of years might give those property rights an aura of venerability, they nonetheless rested on a principle still in vogue in playground disputes: "It's mine; I got here first."
>
> Patricia Nelson Limerick, *The Legacy of Conquest*

By 1900, the doctrine of prior appropriation had evolved into the dominant mechanism by which most western states allocated surface waters. Prior appropriation is the concept that the first people using water should have first right to the water. The doctrine grants a water right to those who first appropriate surface waters, granting priority access as long as the water is put to "beneficial use." Later (junior) appropriators are entitled to divert only water not needed to satisfy senior rights. The priority date of an appropriative right is the date the water is first put to use and determines who receives water in times of shortage, because senior rights are satisfied before junior appropriators receive water.

The prior appropriation doctrine promoted westward expansion and development by importing diverted water to once arid land and providing secure access to water. Dependable access to water encouraged extensive public and private investment in water projects. Projects on reservations received a small fraction of overall federal investment, however, and many of these were built primarily to benefit non-Indians homesteading within reservation boundaries. In the mid 1950s, as available surface water became increasingly scarce, low-cost electricity and technological advances led to the extensive drilling of groundwater wells. By the 1960s, levels of nonrenewable groundwater supplies had declined in many western basins. Recognition of the hydrologic connection between rivers and aquifers raised concerns that groundwater pumping was depleting surface flows, thereby undermining senior surface-water rights. Many states began to regulate groundwater withdrawals and integrate groundwater into the prior appropriation system. By the early 1990s, numerous western states enacted laws that allowed some protection of instream flows, en-couraged conservation, and facilitated water transfers. Although federal policies specifically defer to state laws in matters of water rights administration, the federal government began playing an increasing role in western water management, particularly through the federal Endangered Species Act (ESA) and the Clean Water Act.[1] In addition, the federal government has strong interests in interstate disputes over shared water resources, and in negotiations and litigation involving Indian water rights.

General Stream Adjudications and the McCarran Amendment

As states attempted to improve water management and clarify existing water rights, many initiated general stream adjudications. Such adjudications are court actions to determine the type, amount, and priority date of every user's water right in a particular watershed or basin. Adjudications often involve thousands of water users and take decades to complete. The technical and legal expenses often run into the millions of dollars, and litigation frequently heightens tensions among the water users.

Since the adjudications usually involve federal reserved water rights (those rights appurtenant to tribal and federal lands), a key issue has been whether these cases should be heard in state or federal court. Many believe that tribes attain a more impartial hearing in federal court, but states argue in favor of their own court system. Under the concept of sovereign immunity, the federal government and tribes as sovereigns historically could not be taken into state court to determine their water rights. This frustrated state attempts to quantify and prioritize all water rights in general stream adjudications of basins where federal reserved water rights existed.

In 1952, Congress passed the McCarran Amendment, which waived federal sovereign immunity and allowed states to bring the federal government into state general stream adjudications.[2] Later, the U.S. Supreme Court ruled that the McCarran Amendment also applied to state adjudications of Indian reserved water rights held in trust by the United States.[3] Although the Court did not entirely eliminate the power of federal courts to determine Indian water rights, federal review is unlikely to occur in instances where state court proceedings are under way or are planned in the near future.[4] Although adjudications have been brought in both state and federal court, most suits are filed in a state forum because the cases are initiated by the states themselves. The McCarran Amendment and related court rulings do *not* mean that federal rights are quantified according to state law; the extent of the federal reserved water rights can be determined in state court only by using federal substantive law. (See appendix 2 for a summary of pending general stream adjudications in western states.)

Federal Reserved Water Rights

> If one may mark the turn of the twentieth century by the massive expropriation of Indian lands, then the turn of the twenty-first century is the era when the Indian tribes risk the same fate for their water resources.
>
> Joseph Membrino, former assistant solicitor, Branch of Water and Power, Division of Indian Affairs, Department of the Interior

In the 1800s, many Indian tribes agreed to settle on reservations that in most cases were small portions of their former lands. According to treaties and rules of reservation establishment, all tribal rights on a reservation were preserved except those expressly ceded.[5] In other words, when these lands were set aside for tribal people, the natural resources of the reservations were also reserved.

In 1908, the U.S. Supreme Court confirmed the reservation doctrine when it issued its historic *Winters v. United States* decision.[6] In *Winters*, the court held that when the reservations were established, sufficient water to fulfill the purposes of the reservations was implicitly reserved. These federal reserved water rights benefiting tribal lands are commonly known as *Winters* rights. The Court determined the priority date for these rights to be the date the reservation was established. Assigning a priority date provided a means to integrate federally reserved rights with appropriative water rights recognized under state law.[7] *Winters* rights retain their validity and seniority regardless of whether tribes have put the water to beneficial use.

By contrast, in most western states, an appropriative water right is subject to forfeiture or abandonment if not exercised on a regular basis.

Because Indian reservations were generally established before the extensive non-Indian settlement of western lands, *Winters* rights usually have senior priority dates, making them some of the most reliable and valuable rights in many western basins. For years, these senior rights had little practical value to tribes, and unclaimed *Winters* rights posed little threat to existing non-Indian water users. Substantive federal assistance is only recently available to assist tribes in asserting and developing their reserved water rights. This has placed state water rights and *Winters* rights in competition for limited water supplies.

Today, the process of settling Indian water rights claims entails the tremendous challenge of blending two sets of legal principles: the state doctrine of prior appropriation and the federal reserved water rights doctrine. Because of the typically early priority of reserved water rights, the *Winters* doctrine places a cloud of uncertainty over many water rights perfected under state law. Many current disputes involve non-Indian water users that have appropriated, under state law, water that previously may have been reserved for Indian tribes, but that was never quantified or fully used on reservations.

Standards for Quantifying *Winters* Rights

> There are two schools of thought among tribes on quantifying their water entitlements. Some tribes choose to pursue quantification through negotiated settlements so as to secure quantified rights, which they can develop before the game is over. Other tribes view quantification as a trick to limit tribal access to water. These tribes prefer to begin using water, as much as practical, to assert their rights.
>
> Kevin Gover, attorney, former assistant secretary for Indian Affairs

While clearly recognizing Indian tribes' rights to reserved waters, the *Winters* decision does not specify either the method for quantifying or any standards for administering these rights. The *Winters* decision placed no limit on the amount of water to which the tribes were entitled in the future, and merely stated

SIDEBAR 2.1
The *Winters* Decision

The *Winters* decision stemmed from a dispute between the Indian tribes and bands of the Fort Belknap Indian Reservation (see map 2.1) and upstream non-Indian irrigators over the waters of the Milk River in northern Montana. The Milk River, which borders the reservation, was the intended water source for an Indian irrigation project. This source proved insufficient, however, due to large upstream diversions by non-Indians that seriously depleted the river's flow. The non-Indian uses began after the reservation was established and were developed according to the state prior appropriation doctrine.

The United States, on behalf of the tribes, sought to prohibit the upstream diversions, while the non-Indian irrigators claimed that their earlier use of the water entitled them to its continued use under state law. This dispute eventually found its way to the U.S. Supreme Court, where the Court prohibited any uses by non-Indians that interfered with the tribes' use of their reserved water.

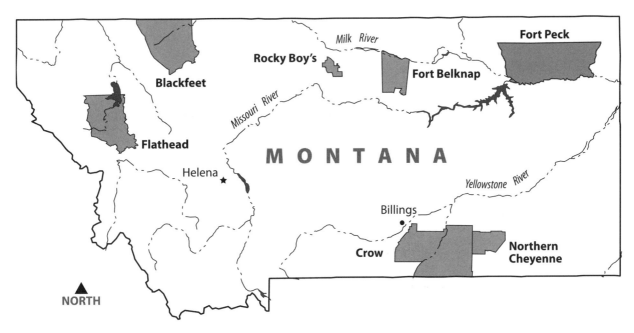

MAP 2.1   Reservations in Montana

water was reserved to fulfill the purposes for which the reservations were established. While language in treaties and other documents may describe specific purposes for a given reservation, the overall purpose for establishing Indian reservations was to create permanent tribal homelands. The intent was to set aside a land base where Indians could govern themselves and provide for their communities, as they had done before non-Indian incursions. This requires access to water and other resources that are needed for the current and future livelihood of tribes. The *Winters* decision left the magnitude of tribal water rights open ended.

Agricultural Purposes

In its 1963 decision *Arizona v. California*,[8] the U.S. Supreme Court reaffirmed the *Winters* doctrine and established the standard of practicably irrigable acreage (PIA) to quantify reserved water rights on a reservation set aside for agricultural purposes. This standard applies to all reservations, whether established by treaty, statute, or executive order.

Arizona v. California was prompted by Arizona's need to determine its share of Colorado River water in order to obtain federal appropriations for the Central Arizona Project (CAP), a canal that would deliver water from the Colorado River to the major cities and farms of the state. The United States intervened to assert, among other things, the reserved water rights of the five Indian reservations on the lower reaches of the main stem of the Colorado River.[9]

Under the PIA standard, tribes are legally entitled to the amount of water needed to irrigate all practicably irrigable acreage within their reservation boundaries. The PIA standard is intended to account for relevant costs and benefits and to reflect the actual conditions of the reservation in question. A PIA analysis typically involves

- detailed assessment of the surface and groundwater supplies of the reservation and surrounding area;
- identification of all arable land on the reservation (land that is amenable to sustained agricultural use, including currently, historically, and potentially arable lands);
- assessment of the amount of arable land that is irrigable;
- development of feasible cropping patterns for the irrigable land;
- calculation of the amount of irrigation water needed to sustain the crops;
- design of irrigation and conveyance systems capable of delivering the needed water; and
- comparison of land development and production costs with crop revenues to determine the total acreage that is economical to irrigate.[10]

Using the standards established in *Arizona v. California*, western Indian tribes have placed hundreds of thousands of acres under cultivation in the past four decades, providing employment opportunities and relieving poverty on many reservations.

Other Reservation Water Needs

Arizona v. California addressed the quantification of *Winters* rights only for agricultural purposes. Because non-agricultural uses were minimal on the reserva-

tions considered in *Arizona*, the United States did not seek to quantify them. On some reservations, however, a significant part of the tribes' reserved water rights involves other uses for the water. Such uses might include domestic use, stock watering, mineral extraction, industrial development, preservation of instream flows for fisheries, cultural or religious purposes, and recreation.

In some cases, courts have found that tribes hold reserved water rights for the preservation of fisheries or other instream uses.[11] These instream flow rights tend to be extremely controversial because they often compete with established consumptive uses. In some instances, courts have denied tribal claims to reserved water rights for instream flows.[12]

The quantification of instream flow rights is a complex process requiring detailed hydrologic studies to determine the variability of flow in a given stream, the optimal flows needed for fisheries, and a determination of the historical extent of the fisheries. Quantification also may entail determining the flows needed to preserve riparian areas to support traditional hunting and gathering on reservations. These claims are typically documented through interviews with tribal members and historical analyses to determine the extent of hunting and gathering activities.

In some instances, technical studies that determine the extent of reserved water rights may include ceded territories off the reservation (land ceded by a tribe to the United States when a reservation was established). This most often occurs in the Pacific Northwest, where many treaties guarantee the right to fish at usual and accustomed places on former tribal lands that now belong to non-Indians. In these instances, a reservation of water may be implied to support fish-harvesting activities on these ceded lands.[13] A recent ruling by the Arizona courts articulates a homeland standard for quantifying tribal reserved rights (see the discussion of the Gila River settlement in chapter 9). Although it is too early to see how this new standard will be implemented, it undoubtedly will alter the dialogue about quantification.

Pueblo Water Rights

The water rights of the Pueblo Indians constitute a special case and do not necessarily fall under the *Win-*

SIDEBAR 2.2
Concerns with the PIA Standard

The PIA (practicably irrigable acreage) standard, as a means for quantifying *Winters* rights, raises several concerns. First, the standard compels tribes and non-Indian water users to analyze the costs and benefits of new tribal irrigation development, thus detracting from a broad evaluation of many other potential uses of tribal water. The creation of skilled jobs on the reservation is a primary objective for many tribes, and modern irrigated agriculture provides relatively few year-round skilled jobs. In addition, land subjugation may disrupt wildlife habitat, archeological sites, air and water quality, and other reservation resources. By requiring tribes to document the extent to which developing new irrigated acreage has positive financial benefits, the PIA standard does not encourage tribes to explore water use alternatives that yield higher economic returns and provide better employment opportunities that are perhaps more compatible with tribal values and protection of the reservation environment. In instances where agriculture is not the intended use of tribal water, the PIA standard may award tribes either too little or too much water for other economically sound uses. The PIA standard generally results in large awards for reservations with climates and soils well suited for crop production, and limited entitlements for mountainous reservations with short growing seasons. The quantity of water awarded may be inconsistent with the intended uses for the water and the development plans for the reservation.

Further, PIA feasibility studies are still ambiguous in many respects. The use of varying, yet plausible, crop price scenarios, crop yields, production costs, and other parameters influences the resultant financial feasibility and leaves the disputing parties many details over which to disagree. Some also argue that requiring financial feasibility (as PIA does) for new Indian irrigation projects is inequitable, because feasibility tests were not rigorously applied to decades of federal water projects that primarily serve non-Indian irrigators.

Some tribal advocates argue that the PIA standard, which has been relied upon for decades, is now an established method that offers a structured and reliable approach to quantifying Indian reserved water rights. Furthermore, alternative approaches (such as a balancing of interests) sometimes suggested by western states tend to maximize the discretion of state courts that often adjudicate water rights. Some tribal advocates fear that modification or abandonment of the PIA standard will escalate uncertainty and protract litigation.

---

ters doctrine.[14] Settling Pueblo water rights is complex because determining the quantity of their rights requires a historical inquiry based on treaty rights and interpretation by three different sovereigns. Over the past six hundred years, the Pueblos were "ruled" by Spain, Mexico, and then the United States. As each sovereign ceded power to the next, the new government redefined tribal rights. In the Treaty of Guadalupe Hidalgo, the United States guaranteed it would recognize and preserve the rights formerly granted to the territory's citizens. Thus, adjudications of Pueblo water rights have revolved around the extent to which the Pueblos retain the status and rights they enjoyed under Spanish and Mexican rule.

One of the most contentious issues concerning Pueblo water is the quantity of their rights. The Pueblos argue that under aboriginal title, recognized by Spain and Mexico and perpetuated by the Treaty of Guadalupe Hidalgo, the quantity to which they are entitled is an expanding right to enable development of all the natural resources of the reservation. Non-Indians argue that if the aboriginal right is used, the quantity should be based on the uses to which the water was historically applied. Further, non-Indians argue that the Pueblos should be subject to the *Winters* doctrine like other Indian tribes.

Tribal Sovereignty

Tribal sovereignty is an ancient notion, 10,000 years old at least and perhaps far older than that. Yet, in spite of having been tested during dark and treacherous times, tribal sovereignty remains vigorous and vibrant in this modern technological society.

Charles F. Wilkinson, University of Colorado law professor

Understanding tribal sovereignty is essential in appreciating the complex framework for settling Indian water rights disputes. The governmental powers of Indian tribes generally were not granted by Congress but are inherent powers never taken away. Before non-Indians came to dominate the western United States, Indian tribes had established thriving communities with extensive trade networks and were sovereign governors of their people and natural resources. Modern courts have recognized tribal authority over tribal people and lands, and in many instances have denied state regulatory authority over Indian country, a phrase that encompasses reservations, allotments, and dependent Indian communities.[15] Although exclusive tribal authority has been eroded over the years,[16] the concept of tribal sovereignty is the basis on which tribes govern their internal affairs. The notion of tribal sovereignty has, in some respects, been strengthened since the early 1970s by successive presidential administrations that have supported self-determination in Indian country.[17]

Issues related to tribal sovereignty emerge at various stages of Indian water rights negotiations. State concerns about tribal sovereignty are strong due to the potential for tribal water policies to have significant impacts on non-Indian water users. Likewise, the impact of state water regulations on tribal sovereignty is great, given that water is inextricably linked to reservation economies and to tribal culture and tradition.[18] Although some tribes and states contend for dominant regulatory powers over water and other natural resources, many observers believe the interconnected nature of rivers, lakes, and aquifers make joint jurisdiction and management desirable.

Tribal sovereignty forms the backdrop against which attempts by other governments to limit and regulate tribal water resources must be evaluated. The courts have established that the regulatory interest of the state, if not preempted by federal law, must be weighed against the potential effect of the proposed state regulatory measure on the tribe's continued ability to make its own laws and be ruled by them. The off-reservation impact of reservation activities has come to be used by the courts as an important measure of state interest.[19]

Federal Trust Relationship

It is appropriate to educate members of Congress about the federal trust responsibility to tribes and the conflicts this trust responsibility creates in local communities. . . . We also need to educate Congress that funding settlements is an appropriate exercise of trust responsibility.

Michael Connor, former majority staff, U.S. Senate Energy and Natural Resources Committee

The federal government's relation to tribes can be viewed as a trusteeship or guardianship. At its inception, the trust doctrine reflected the Supreme Court's view of Indian tribes as domestic dependent nations and of a tribe's relationship to the United States as that of a ward to his or her guardian.[20] Although Congress enjoys broad powers over Indian affairs, these powers are subject to procedural and constitutional limitations. The trust relationship, while enhancing federal power over Indians, creates certain federal duties relating to Indian tribes.

Specifically, the trust responsibility provides federal protection for Indian resources and federal assistance in resource development and management.[21] These resources have been found to include not only land but other assets, such as timber, water, and reservation fisheries.[22] This may entitle Indian tribes to receive specific benefits not available to other citizens. The benefits that flow from the trust relationship are not based on race but derive from the government-to-government relationship between the United States and Indian tribes.[23]

Administration of most aspects of the trust responsibility was delegated by Congress to the Department of the Interior and the Department of Justice, although these obligations are not limited to those departments. The United States' trust duty to Indian tribes must be observed by any federal agency whose activities might have some effect on the tribe's trust assets.[24] The trust relationship is intended to hold all executive branch officials to strict standards in dealing with Indian trust property while allowing them the flexibility to exercise reasonable judgment. This is of particular importance in instances where the United States has a con-

Millions of Dollars

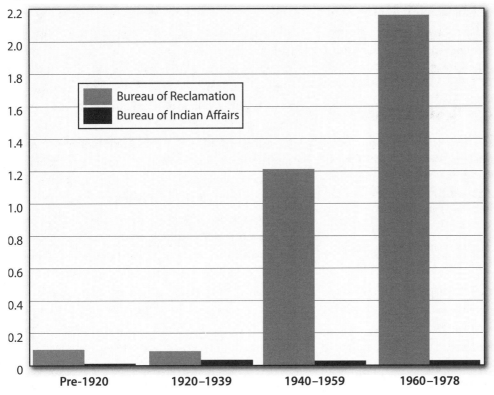

$ millions	Pre-1920	1920–1939	1940–1959	1960–1978
Bureau of Reclamation	0.0129	0.0121	1.206	2.156
Bureau of Indian Affairs	0.0015	0.0036	0.0029*	0.0037

It is not possible to identify precisely the portions of federally funded projects that serve Indian and non-Indian water users. Some Bureau of Reclamation project water may go to tribal water users, and non-Indian water users are served by BIA projects.

*The figure overstates BIA investment during this period because the Census reports the figure as an aggregate along with other expenditures by minor irrigation organizations.

SOURCE: U.S. Department of Commerce, Bureau of the Census. Census of Agriculture: Census of Irrigation Organizations. Census Years 1950, 1959, 1969, 1978.

FIGURE 2.1 Federal investments in irrigation projects

flict of interest between general public programs and the rights of Indian trust beneficiaries.

The courts have held that federal agencies cannot subordinate Indian interests to other public purposes except when clearly authorized to do so by Congress.[25] In *Nevada v. United States*,[26] the Supreme Court held that the United States could adequately represent more than one interest simultaneously and so is not subject to the same standards as a private trustee. In this case, the Court found that claims made by the United States on behalf of the Pyramid Lake Paiute Tribe (Nevada) to protect fisheries should have been asserted in prior litigation. Nevertheless, the Court found the failure of the United States to do so was not a breach of its trust obligation to the tribe, even though the United States also had protected the competing interests of non-Indian irrigators. This ruling illustrates the ambiguous and sometimes conflicting roles of the federal government in tribal water cases.

Federal Obligations to Indian Tribes

> There are four justifications for federal funding of settlements: To ensure consistency with federal trust responsibility to tribes; to avoid litigation costs to tribes, the federal government, and to local parties; to eliminate claims against the federal government; and to avoid displacing existing water users.
>
> Michael Connor, former majority staff, U.S. Senate Energy and Natural Resources Committee

Some Indian tribes receive assistance from the federal government in the course of negotiating and implementing water settlements. Assistance may include funds to defray the costs of hiring attorneys, engineers, and other experts needed to support a tribe's assertion of its water rights. Also, federal attorneys with the Department of the Interior's Solicitor's Office and the Department of Justice may represent the United States as trustee for the tribe in court. Federal monies form a substantial part of many settlement packages, often providing for economic-development programs on reservations.

A historical perspective is useful in understanding the obligations of the federal government to resolve Indian water disputes. Shortly after Congress passed the 1902 Reclamation Act,[27] the U.S. Supreme Court recognized Indian reserved water rights in its *Winters* decision. One might expect that tribes would have benefited substantially from federal reclamation efforts; however, this was not the case. As the prestigious National Water Commission observed in 1973, federal policies to establish irrigated agriculture and settle the West "were pursued with little or no regard for Indian water rights and the *Winters* doctrine." The commission concluded that "with few exceptions the projects were planned and built by the federal government without any attempt to define, let alone protect, prior rights that Indian tribes might have had in the waters used for the projects."[28] Figure 2.1 summarizes federal investment in BIA and Bureau of Reclamation irrigation projects over the 1900s.

Consequently, tribes often have been unable to put their entire water entitlement to use, and non-Indian appropriators have come to rely upon water that is reserved for tribes. As a result, Indian tribes who are today struggling to assert and develop their *Winters* rights are viewed as interlopers in the western water arena. Assistance to tribes in resolving these disputes recognizes the federal government's responsibility in these matters.

The federal government must attempt to balance the interests of non-Indians (who were often induced by federal actions and policies to rely on tribal water supplies) and the requirements of other federal agencies or laws (such as the federal ESA) against the interests of Indian tribes whose water-related needs and trust responsibilities were shortchanged during decades of federal water-development largesse. It is useful, in considering these competing interests, to recognize that although non-Indian water users have incurred substantial costs to develop water-dependent enterprises, they also have enjoyed the benefits of the disputed water resources for many years.

PHOTO 3.1 Farm worker harvests cotton near Hatch, New Mexico. Photo: Todd Sargent

CHAPTER 3
Indian Water Rights and the New West

We can require ourselves to be accountable to our grand-children . . . and to their great-grandchildren. By making the right choices now, we can promise them . . . bright streams and lasting forests . . . and rewarding employment and welcoming communities.

Charles F. Wilkinson, *The Eagle Bird*

The context of Indian water rights settlements and litigation has evolved over the decades, as have the parties' experiences and approaches to negotiations. Recent developments will strongly influence negotiation and litigation processes and outcomes in the next decade.

Demographic Changes and the New Economy

The western states continued to be one of the fastest growing areas in the country during the 1990s. There was an increase in the total U.S. population of almost 33 million persons during that time. Of that amount, almost 10.5 million (32 percent) were located in the eighteen western states (including Hawaii). Five western states topped the list of the fastest growing states in the nation (Nevada, Arizona, Colorado, Utah, and Idaho), with another state (Washington) in tenth place. Much western growth has taken place in the arid Southwest, which has numerous Indian reservations, and in the Pacific Northwest, where species of salmon are listed as threatened or endangered and tribes hold fishing rights as well as water rights claims. Continued growth will place severe pressures on the water resources of these areas.

The country's Indian, Eskimo, and Aleut population (hereafter, "American Indian population") is about 2.4 million, after an increase of 300,000 during the 1990s. Although the American Indian population remains at 0.9 percent of the total American resident population, it rose 16 percent during the decade, compared to 9.7 percent for all Americans. Six of the ten states with the largest American Indian populations are located in the West, led by California (309,000) and followed by Oklahoma (263,000), Arizona (256,000), New Mexico (163,000), Washington (103,000), and Alaska (100,000). Almost one-half of the American Indian population lives in the West, with half of them living outside metropolitan areas.

The American Indian population is young, with a median age of 27.6 years—nearly eight years younger than the median age of the country. One-third of American Indians reported incomes that placed them below the poverty line in 1997. The most daunting challenge facing many tribes is the need to provide viable reservation economies for existing residents—especially the young. An important part of those future economies will be water resources.

Agriculture plays a vital role in the future of the West as the largest consumptive user of water in every western state. In some watersheds, urban growth and industrial uses also are becoming large consumers of water. Moreover, water for habitat restoration and recreation in lakes and streams has become important in many regions. The mix of water uses is changing. In sidebar 3.1, agricultural economist George B. Frisvold examines the factors that affect irrigated acreage and agricultural water use. Frisvold observes that, because agriculture uses so much water, a small decrease in agricultural water use could provide significant amounts of water for tribal settlements and other purposes.

Water "shortages" are caused not only by drought. They also are a function of water prices and of the rules that govern who gets how much water and at what price. Between 60 and 80 percent of the water used in the West goes to agriculture, much of that at subsidized prices. If subsidies were removed and water were allocated on a market basis, some forms of agriculture would not be competitive. Considerable volumes of water could be available for tribal settlements, environmental restoration needs, urban and industrial uses, and other water needs of the changing western economy.

SIDEBAR 3.1

Agriculture, Federal Farm Programs, and Water Availability for Tribal Settlements

George B. Frisvold

Agriculture accounts for 90 percent of freshwater consumption in the seventeen western states (table 3.1). Small reductions in irrigation use, then, could provide large percentage increases in water available to other uses, including tribal uses. In regions where irrigation accounts for 92 percent of consumptive use, a 1 percent reduction of irrigation water reallocated to other uses would increase water to other uses by 12 percent.[1] A 3 percent reduction and reallocation would increase water available to other uses by 35 percent.

Because agriculture is such a dominant water user, finding water supplies to resolve tribal water disputes may require adjustments in agricultural water use. The quantity and value of water demanded by agriculture affect the cost and difficulty of settling disputes. Federal farm programs, in turn, greatly affect the quantity and value of water used in western agriculture. Commodity programs—designed to support farm income—can increase irrigated acreage and water used per acre. Conservation programs, on the other hand, provide payments to farmers to take land out of production and to invest in more efficient irrigation. American Indian farms also participate in federal farm programs. Farm programs, then, affect the costs of acquiring water to settle tribal water claims and the profitability of tribal agriculture.

Federal Commodity Programs

By providing government payments for certain irrigated crops, commodity programs create incentives to plant more irrigated acreage and increase yields by applying more water per acre. Historically, payments have been based on the difference between a government support price and the market price. Producers of corn, cotton, rice, wheat, sorghum, and barley are eligible for direct payments. The U.S. dairy program supports milk producers through direct payments, export subsidies, import con-

trols, and regional marketing orders that limit interstate milk trade. These policies stimulate alfalfa production for dairy cattle feed. Alfalfa, among the most water-intensive crops, accounts for 19 percent of irrigation water applied in western states. The government can encourage irrigated crop production, even without directly paying producers. Import restrictions maintain the U.S. sugar price at two to three times the world price. This encourages farmers to plant more sugar beets, among the most water-intensive crops grown in California and the Pacific Northwest.[2]

Until the 1996 Federal Agricultural Improvement and Reform (FAIR) Act, the USDA could require farmers to idle a percentage of their program crop acreage as a condition of receiving price support payments.[3] This was intended to control supply, raise market prices, and limit price support payments. In 1987 and 1988, nearly 20 percent of U.S. cropland was idled under federal programs.[4]

Price support programs with land idling affect total acreage decisions, substitution between crops with different water requirements, and water applied per acre to individual crops. Economists have examined these complex relationships using statistical and regional simulation models. R. Howitt estimated that large reductions in support prices would significantly reduce agricultural water use in Plains and Pacific states, but not in the Mountain states.[5] Among the latter, growers had more scope to switch to alfalfa and other water-intensive nonprogram crops. G. Horner and others found that reducing cotton prices and support payments by 20 percent would reduce California cotton acreage by 41 percent but increase acreage in water-intensive alfalfa, tree fruits, and nuts.[6] Total irrigated acreage would fall, however, as would total water use. R. Just and others found program payments increased groundwater depletion in the Ogallala Aquifer.[7] When higher payments were combined with greater acreage restrictions, depletion increased because remaining cropped acreage was irrigated more intensively. K. Konyar and K. Knapp found cotton acreage restrictions increased alfalfa acreage in California.[8] M. Moore and others found that relaxing acreage wheat restrictions reduced acreage of more water-intensive crops (rice, cotton, fruits, and vegetables).[9] By and large, these studies suggest that commodity programs encourage greater agricultural

TABLE 3.1   Irrigation consumptive use in western irrigation states

Region or state	Irrigation's consumptive use*	Irrigation's share of region or state consumptive use(%)
Pacific	**26.2**	**92**
Oregon	2.7	96
California	21.0	92
Washington	2.5	91
Mountain	**19.1**	**91**
Idaho	3.8	99
Wyoming	2.4	95
Colorado	4.4	94
Montana	1.6	93
Utah	1.7	88
New Mexico	1.5	85
Arizona	2.8	83
Nevada	0.9	79
Plains	**16.9**	**84**
Nebraska	6.0	96
Kansas	2.9	89
Texas	7.3	77
South Dakota	0.2	70
North Dakota	0.1	58
Oklahoma	0.4	56
All West	62.2	90

*Million acre-feet of water per year
Source: W.B. Solley, R.R. Pierce, and H.A. Perlman, "Estimated Use of Water in the United States in 1995," *Survey Circular 1200* (Reston, Va.: U.S. Geological Survey, Department of Interior, 1998).

water use. They also illustrate, however, that it can be difficult to predict how individual policy changes will affect water use without considering cross-policy and cross-commodity impacts.

Federal Conservation Programs

The USDA's major conservation programs are land retirement programs and technology adoption subsidies. Under the Conservation Reserve Program (CRP), farmers receive payments for idling cropland under ten-year contracts. Landowners place bids to USDA, ranked based on the land's potential for erosion control, migratory bird habitat, water pollution control, and other environmental benefits. CRP payments are based on local rental rates for nonirrigated cropland, so they are poor incentives to idle land in states with little or no dryland agriculture (California, Arizona, and Nevada). In these places, CRP payments are much lower than market cropland rental rates and CRP participation is virtually nonexistent. In the West, the vast majority of CRP acreage is in the Great Plains, Montana, and the wheat-growing areas of the Pacific Northwest. The Wetlands Reserve Program (WRP) pays farmers for thirty-year and permanent easements to restore wetlands. Restoring wetlands improves groundwater quality by filtering chemicals and increases the rate and quantity of groundwater recharge. Western WRP acreage is concentrated in the Pacific Northwest and Great Plains states.

The USDA has historically operated technical assistance and subsidy programs to promote adoption of resource-conserving technologies. These programs, often aimed at curbing water pollution, also provided subsidies to farmers to improve irrigation efficiency. One such program was the Colorado River Salinity Control Program, which provided payments to farmers who installed more efficient sprinklers and pipes and lined delivery canals. From 1984–1995, the program conserved 300,000 acre-feet of water. Salt loadings were reduced by over 190,000 tons per year at costs ranging from thirty-eight to seventy dollars per ton of salt removed. The 1996 FAIR Act terminated this and other regional programs, instituting a single Environmental Quality Incentive Program (EQIP). A third of EQIP funds have gone to improve water quality and conservation through adoption of improved irrigation technology.[10] In some states, American Indians have been able to obtain large shares of state funding (table 3.2). Indians received 47 percent of Montana's EQIP funds and 40 percent of Arizona's, and in both states, they received the largest funding levels obligated to American Indians.

Conservation Reserve Enhancement Program

The 1996 FAIR Act established the Conservation Reserve Enhancement Program (CREP). Like the regular CRP, CREP provides farmers with government payments for long-term land retirement. States must provide 20 percent matching funds, but states and tribes play a more active role in program design. The CREP state steering committees in Washington and Oregon have included participants from tribal governments along with those from federal, state, and local entities. Greater control allows states to tailor programs to local environmental problems. The Maryland program addresses water pollution affecting Chesapeake Bay and compliance with the Clean Water Act, while New York's program focuses on compliance with the Safe Drinking Water Act. Washington and Oregon's programs focus on protecting endangered species.[11]

CREP allows states to acquire conservation easements or water leases from farmers at a fraction of their cost by piggybacking on long-term federal leases. Through CREP, the USDA provides roughly the market rental rate for land for fifteen years. Timothy Searchinger notes, "the present value of a fifteen year contract will equal 75% of the cost of a permanent conservation easement. A state could then offer to pay the remaining 25% and, using a state program, obtain a permanent easement."[12]

Two innovative CREPs in Oregon and California attempt to provide adequate incentives to retire irrigated cropland missing from the regular CRP. The California program is small, targeting 12,000 acres in the North Central Valley. Farmers who idle land for wetland restoration receive payments based on the local irrigated rental rate. The large Oregon program targets 100,000 acres and is budgeted for $250 million, with $193 million from the USDA. The Oregon program seeks to restore riparian areas and to maintain instream flow for trout and salmon listed under the ESA. Farmers can receive payments based on the rental value of irrigated land if they lease water to the state of Oregon to enhance instream flow.

CREPs can provide states with substantial funds to induce farmers to voluntarily reallocate water to meet environmental objectives. Although not designed to address directly states' obligations to tribal water settlements, CREPs could be structured to protect against contamination or depletion of streams, lakes, or groundwater in and around tribal lands. This could protect native fisheries, drinking water, and water-based recreational activities and businesses.

Tribes may also directly apply for CREP funds. The Yakima Tribe in Washington has a CREP proposal pending that would provide incentives to convert irrigated cropland along the Yakima River to rangeland in order to conserve water for salmon recovery and protect wildlife habitat. The program would target 5,000 acres and obligate $1.2 million in federal funds from the USDA and $0.3 million from nonfederal sources.

Small changes in federal farm programs have large implications for the amount of water available for tribal and

TABLE 3.2 EQIP funds requested and obligated (total and to American Indians)

State	Funds requested ($ millions)	Funds obligated, total ($ millions)	Funds obligated to American Indians ($ thousands)	Share of funds obligated to American Indians (%)
Arizona	7.0	5.0	2,000	40
Nevada	Not reported	1.0	197	20
Utah	15.3	3.3	357	11
Oregon	> 6.1	3.0	320	11
Montana	9.7	4.6	2,180	47
South Dakota	Not reported	2.5	464	19
North Dakota	Not reported	3.4	697	21

Note: This table represents selected states in fiscal year 2000. Not all states provide information on funds obligated to American Indians in their annual reports.
Source: State annual EQIP summaries, USDA Natural Resource Conservation Service.

other uses in the American West. While some programs encourage greater agricultural water use, others (like the CREP and EQIP programs) can provide states and tribes with substantial funds to encourage agricultural water conservation. The 1996 FAIR Act eliminated most acreage restrictions and substituted some price supports with fixed annual payments.[13] The 2002 farm bill reintroduced some price support payments but also increased funding for USDA conservation programs, with spending projected to rise 80 percent. This includes funding for programs that could encourage water conservation. Federal farm programs can make settlement of tribal water claims more or less contentious through their effect on irrigation demand. Whether they will make settlements easier to achieve will depend on how the 2002 legislation is implemented and how future commodity and conservation programs are structured.

Climate Change and Cyclical Drought

[T]he lower the water in the river, the drier the season, the more people came to be involved in distributing the water through the valley . . . when it gets as bad as this then virtually everyone in the village becomes involved: from then on, every time someone opened or closed a ditch gate on their land, a thousand people would be watching and listening.

Stanley G. Crawford, *Mayordomo*, describing the workings of an *acequia* during a dry summer in northern New Mexico

The notion that global changes in climate are the result of increased carbon dioxide and other greenhouse gases has gained worldwide scientific acceptance. Global temperature has been increasing 0.2–0.3 degrees Celsius over the last forty years. Warming is evident in both sea surface and land-based surface air temperatures. The twentieth century's ten warmest years all occurred in the last fifteen years of the century. Of these, 1998 was the warmest year on record. Scientists expect that the average global surface temperature could rise 1–4.5 degrees Fahrenheit (0.6–2.5 degrees Celsius) in the next fifty years, and 2.2–10 degrees Fahrenheit (1.4–5.8 degrees Celsius) in the next century, with significant regional variation.[1]

Researchers for the Intergovernmental Panel on Climate Change (IPCC), which advises the United Nations, have recently compiled existing studies to try to predict the possible effects on North America (see sidebar 3.2).[2] When seasonal or multiyear climate variability is considered, the most inadequate water supplies within the United States (70 percent depletion of available supplies by off-stream uses) are likely to be in the Southwest—including the lower Colorado River basin, the southern portion of California's Central Valley, and the Great Plains river basins south of the Platte River.[3] These regions contain numerous tribal reservations, and climate variability will increase the challenge of equitably dividing and managing uncertain water supplies among tribes and other water users.

Changes in Presidential Administration

Most presidents have little direct experience with Indian issues, and a new president is frequently an unknown when it comes to Indian policy. The Clinton administration was seen in a positive light by many tribes and Indian leaders. The Clinton administration emphasized a government-to-government policy in its dealings with the tribes, but the promising prospects of the administration were not completely realized in the nuts-and-bolts of applied Indian policies. No Indian water rights settlement was enacted during Clinton's first term. It was only due to the extraordinary efforts of senior department personnel that several settlements were enacted during the second term.

The presidential administration of George W. Bush brought a new set of officials. Secretary of the Interior Gale Norton encountered tribal water issues while serving as the Colorado attorney general, which entailed many run-ins with tribes. Norton has received credit from the tribes for her support of the Animas–La Plata (ALP) settlement in southwestern Colorado.

Unfortunately, the number of members of Congress and congressional staff who understand western water issues and the importance of Indian water rights settlements has diminished in recent years. Beginning early in their discussions, negotiating parties must regularly educate and inform key members and staff so that the resulting settlement will be favorably considered when it is presented to Congress.

National and International Economic Trends

The slowdown of the American and international economies, coupled with emerging shortages of oil, natural gas, and electricity, will affect the context for Indian water rights settlements in ways that are difficult to predict. A decline in the American economy may lead to a reduction in federal surpluses and, therefore, less money for federal settlement efforts. A decline in tribal gaming revenues may also weaken the capacity of tribes to prepare for water rights settlement discussions.

Energy production invariably requires water, and the proponents of large-scale projects are unlikely to invest in these projects unless water supplies are secure. In energy-rich basins, governments and large energy development interests may need to settle outstanding Indian water rights claims so that these energy projects can be brought on-line. Also, many tribes control rich deposits of coal, oil, and natural gas. Tribes may be in a position to demand settlement of their water rights claims as the price of access to their energy resources.

Water-Management Capacity of States and Tribes

The governments and water users involved in negotiating water rights settlements have all benefited from developments in hydrology, geographic information systems, computer-based modeling, remote sensing, and communications technologies. Negotiators have an unprecedented opportunity to gather and synthesize existing water supply data. They can use and analyze information, gather missing information, present it all in colorful, revealing graphics, and transmit the information rapidly to others. Sufficient data and sound analyses often allow for creative settlements where there was an impasse before.

Hydrologic information, however, is expensive to generate. Computer models of a small geographic area commonly cost $100,000 or more. Few water users can afford to play in this league, and small users often complain that they cannot compete in areas where technical information is needed to make one's case. Tribes themselves have widely varying financial means and

SIDEBAR 3.2

Implications of Climate Variability and Water Supplies for Tribal Water Settlements

Carmen Carrion

The aridity of the western United States, combined with rapid population growth and increasing demand for water resources, makes the West highly vulnerable to climate variability and increased fluctuations in water availability. A century of investment in dams and reservoirs gives some parts of the West considerable control over water supplies. These regions are not much affected by year-to-year changes in precipitation; surface water sources are overallocated, and many aquifers are being mined. In many areas, agriculture, livestock, urban centers, tourism, and recreation face extreme pressures from limited water supplies. Climate variability exacerbates already intense competition for water, adding to the complexity of achieving stable water settlements between tribes and other water users.

Expected Changes in Climate and the Impact on Water Resources

The IPCC summarized hydrologic changes that can be expected as a result of global warming. These include changes in precipitation levels, seasonal patterns of regional precipitation, and flood frequencies. The IPCC analysis suggests that a projected increase in the average temperature will have the following effects on water supplies:

- The frequency and severity of droughts could increase in some areas as a result of a decrease in total rainfall, more frequent dry spells, and higher evaporation.
- The hydrology of arid and semi-arid areas is particularly sensitive to climate variations. Small variations in temperature and precipitation in these areas can result in large percentage changes in runoff, increasing the likelihood and severity of droughts and floods.
- Seasonal disruptions may occur in water supplies flowing from mountainous areas if more precipitation falls as rain than as snow, and if the length of the snow storage season is reduced.

Although recent studies describe possible impacts on water resources, they do not offer guidance as to the likelihood that these scenarios will occur. The important point is that climate change will occur and will shift and reshape the annual and seasonal climate patterns. For the western United States, increasing climate variability is amplified by the complex hydrology of the region. Precipitation already varies from basin to basin and within the same basin. For instance, in the upper Colorado River basin, the average winter season precipitation can vary from six to forty inches within six miles.

In the Pacific Northwest, which relies heavily on reservoir storage and snow pack to transfer water from the wet wintertime to the dry summertime, as regional temperatures increase, the amount of water stored in winter as snow will decline.[1] A greater fraction of the annual runoff may contribute to winter streamflow at the expense of summer streamflow. In the Sacramento and San Joaquin river basin of California, basin average mean annual precipitation and temperature changes are likely to cause a decline in summer streamflow and winter runoff.

Although water management has always been carried out under uncertainty, planning for climate variability will have to cope with many uncertainties that will not be fully resolved before significant impacts occur. Water users' vulnerability to climate variability could take several forms:

- Large changes in the reliability of water yields from reservoirs could result from small changes in precipitation and runoff.
- Climate changes that reduce overall water availability will reduce the productivity of hydroelectric dams, causing greater fluctuations in hydroelectric generation.
- Some river basins are so heavily developed, with complicated, overlapping management layers, that their ability to adapt to changes in climate may be compromised.
- Strategies to mitigate the adverse impacts of climate change need to be implemented before such changes occur to be effective. However, proposed changes in regional water management stir up conflict and sometimes litigation and can be slow and costly to implement.

MacArthur Fellow Peter H. Gleick identifies five indicators of a region's vulnerability to climate change:[2]

- Low storage volume relative to renewable supply. This ratio is an indicator of a region's ability to cope with prolonged drought or severe flooding.
- High consumptive use relative to available renewable supply.
- Regional dependence on hydroelectricity. In regions that depend heavily on hydroelectricity, drought will affect electricity availability and cost.
- Groundwater overdraft as a portion of total groundwater withdrawals. Regions that already pump groundwater faster than natural recharge rates are especially vulnerable to climate variability that decreases water availability.
- Streamflow variability as expressed in higher peak floods, more persistent and severe droughts, and greater uncertainty about the timing of the rainy season. Increased streamflow variability can spur costly investments in flood control, large water transfers, and storage.

Vulnerabilities to climate-related water supply variability are linked to a region's ability to respond to climatic change. A study conducted in the Columbia River basin illustrates that vulnerability to climate change depends on both system sensitivity to climate change and its ability to adapt. Adaptability to the threat of floods is high in the main stem of the Columbia, given the existence of centralized authority and adequate water storage.[3] However, another study of the basin concluded that it is already impossible to meet all current water-resources objectives.[4] With climate change, decreased spring and winter streamflows lead to decreased reliability of water supplies. The study predicts failure to provide adequate irrigation water and to achieve fishery protection target flows. New approaches in long-term water planning and management are clearly needed.

Implications for Tribal Settlements

Climate variability requires reconsideration of old approaches to tribal settlements. The negotiating parties must consider climate change as a factor in all decisions about water investments and the operation of existing facilities and systems. If parties to tribal water settlements clearly anticipate and prepare for droughts, this will be less expensive than strategies that simply attempt to mitigate damages. Climate information and forecasts should be considered as water settlements are negotiated. Monitoring and evaluation of climatic and hydrologic variables will increase the ability of negotiating parties to adapt to change. The most important implication of climate variability for tribal settlements is that settlement agreements must be very specific regarding water allocation and management in wet versus dry years. The parties need to spell out priority of deliveries in dry years and access to storage in wet years. Moreover, flexibility and mechanisms to address unanticipated problems and conflicts become even more essential in the face of climate change and increased water supply uncertainty.

often must rely on the federal government for funds or technical support. Negotiating parties would do well to consider how to avoid duplicating technical studies and how to maximize limited technical resources to ensure that all parties have the information they need to negotiate effectively.

Adaptive Watershed Management

Ecologists have recognized the interdependencies in the physical and biological aspects of a river system. Especially as certain species are listed as threatened or endangered, agencies drafting species recovery plans are turning to multidimensional efforts with an emphasis on monitoring so that management can be modified based on monitoring results—an emerging field called adaptive management. Often the recovery efforts emphasize flow augmentation or variation, pollution controls, and habitat restoration.

Many of the basic assumptions of the ESA and adaptive management are foreign to the property rights–based nature of western general stream adjudications. Increasingly, the conflicts within a watershed are multidimensional, and negotiations that address only water rights allocations are probably doomed to failure. The challenge for those involved in negotiating Indian water rights settlements is to address and resolve legitimate concerns beyond the basic water rights allocations. If these concerns are addressed, considerable goodwill and political support can be gained for the settlement. If these concerns are ignored, any proposed settlement becomes more vulnerable at crucial decision-making points. Yet, comprehensive settlements are difficult and time consuming to negotiate, and they may collapse from their own weight as multiple complex matters are added to basic questions of water rights.

Interstate Water Issues

Most Indian water rights settlements in the past have involved a tribe and other stakeholders within one state. For example, the Northern Cheyenne Compact was negotiated with the State of Montana. The Fort Hall agreement was negotiated with Idaho water users and the state of Idaho.

On some river systems, it is apparent that an Indian water rights settlement cannot be a one-state affair. For instance, the Klamath River runs into northern California, so the Oregon court conducting the Klamath basin adjudication struggles with how to assert jurisdiction over downstream users and a downstream tribe. Fortunately, negotiations can be broad enough to involve all the necessary parties on an interstate river (leaving aside, for the moment, the issue of approving such an interstate agreement). Similar interstate issues are emerging on the lower Rio Grande among interested water users in New Mexico, Texas, and Mexico. Water rights negotiators will have to develop new methods of involving water users across the state line or international boundary.

For most of the twentieth century, western water policies were a legacy of the frontier and homesteading days of the region. The characteristics of this legacy are to be found in many of the Indian water rights settlements of the 1980s and 1990s, with their emphasis on anticipated agricultural development. Future settlements will be influenced by many more external factors, some of which have been discussed in this chapter. These settlements will need to be finely crafted instruments that are responsive to the growing needs and diminishing water supplies of the West.

PART 2
Stakeholders

The value of regional diversity lies in the mutuality of our tales. Disparate voices articulating the land, remembering, discovering where the source of our power lies.

Terry Tempest Williams in *A Society to Match the Scenery*

PHOTO 4.1 Warm Springs tribal members set hoop net in place. Photo: Columbia River Intertribal Fish Commission

CHAPTER 4
Hopes and Concerns

Every watershed in the country, even those straddled by urban sprawl, has its own particular and subtle order, its own vying cultures, its own imprinted past and imagined future, waiting to be discovered.

Geoffrey O'Gara, *What You See in Clear Water*

Tribes, cities, irrigation districts, environmental advocates, and various levels of governments enter into negotiations and litigation over water for assorted reasons. Generally, they share some mutual goals and also have distinct and often conflicting objectives regarding what they hope to accomplish. Litigation tends to exaggerate the differences between these parties' objectives, but negotiation can provide an opportunity to build upon the similarities. Some of these mutual and competing goals are discussed here in an effort to articulate the hopes and concerns of the various parties who claim rights in common water sources.

Mutual Goals

Tribal and non-Indian stakeholders in the waters of the West share a number of concerns that motivate efforts to resolve conflicts over water. Tribal governments and communities, irrigation districts, cities, industrial water users, and environmental organizations are concerned with resolving water conflicts and improving water management. Some mutual goals include:

Reliable access to water. All water users, and the governments that represent them, share an interest in securing access to water of adequate quantity and quality to satisfy their present and future needs.

Effective management of water resources. Negotiated settlements can provide an opportunity to coordinate management of regional water resources across tribal, state, and federal jurisdictions. Settlements can help improve cooperation, reduce groundwater overdraft, achieve water quality standards, recover endangered fish, and meet other regional challenges.

Improved community and intergovernmental relations. Fostering improved community relations is particularly important where water conflicts negatively affect interactions among neighboring water users. Negotiations can provide an opportunity to improve communications among tribal, state, and federal agencies.

Economic development. Regional stakeholders typically share an interest in garnering federal money to support water projects and economic development in their region.

Conflict resolution. Water negotiations provide the opportunity to establish processes and protocols to deal with subsequent disagreements and to address effectively the problems that arise during implementation of negotiated agreements.

Ability to plan for the future. Stable, comprehensive, and lasting water agreements provide added certainty to water users regarding future water supplies so that they can plan for growth and new economic activities.

American Indian Tribes

Many tribes seek a decreed determination of their water entitlements to protect and assert their reserved rights. If tribal rights are to be quantified, tribes must evaluate whether this can best be done by litigating or by negotiating to achieve a settlement of tribal water claims. Litigation may result in a ruling that awards tribes entitlements to early priority water rights. However, court decrees do not provide the financial support needed to translate paper entitlements into the wet water essential to economic activities on tribal homelands. Negotiated settlements can advance important tribal goals:

Developing water resources for use on reservations. Negotiated settlements often provide tribes with the money and political support to develop their water rights. Settlement provisions can include infrastructure for water development and money for tribal economic development.

Asserting tribal sovereignty over the reservation environment. Tribes seek to exercise their sovereign authority to manage natural resources. This involves regulating how tribal water is used, as well as protecting water quality. Tribes may seek to constrain non-Indian water use when it harms tribal interests or is contrary to tribal goals for water management. Many tribes seek explicit provisions in water settlement agreements to protect reservation water quality and maintain streamflows at levels needed to protect fisheries and other instream uses.

Accommodating diverse interests within a tribe. Multiple interests exist within reservation populations, and those may be reflected in diverse goals for water management. The appropriate uses of water may be viewed differently among tribal members, with some members supporting traditional uses of water and others favoring new types of development. Likewise, owners of land allotments may have different objectives for the negotiations than tribal members who do not own land. Settlements potentially can address diverse tribal interests and a variety of potential reservation water uses.

Promoting broader recognition of tribal interests. Tribes have sometimes formed intertribal coalitions to advocate on behalf of tribal interests, for example, the Council of Energy Resource Tribes and the Colorado River Ten Tribes. These coalitions seek to promote recognition of tribal authority and interests within the larger context of federal, state, and local governments and the private sector.

Non-Indian Water Users

> Amber Spring. It was a magnificent outburst of clear amber water pouring from a dark stone-lined hole. Lassiter knelt and drank, lingered to drink again . . . Next to his horse, a rider of the sage loved a spring. And this was the most beautiful and remarkable known to the upland riders of southern Utah.
>
> Zane Grey, *Riders of the Purple Sage*

Non-Indian stakeholders include farmers, irrigation districts, cities and towns, mines, power plants, hydroelectric dam operators, and people who use water for recreational purposes. Non-Indian water users have multiple goals when negotiating and litigating over water:

Protecting current water uses. Non-Indians who have acquired rights to water under state law generally do not welcome the uncertainty created by competing tribal claims. These water users seek to protect their established uses, limit tribal rights, and develop new

sources of water as part of an overall settlement agreement.

Reducing uncertainty. Established water users desire certainty over their future access to water, and so a key element of negotiated settlements is a waiver of future tribal water claims (although even after a settlement, tribes may have the right to establish new water rights under state law in the same fashion as non-Indians).

Accommodating competing water interests. Numerous conflicts exist between non-Indians who seek to assure adequate streamflows for fish, wildlife, recreation, and aesthetic and cultural values and those who hold rights to divert water for agricultural, municipal, and industrial purposes.

Modifying laws and policies. Settlements can provide the opportunity to update state and federal policies in response to changing water-management needs. For instance, many state laws do not adequately recognize hydrologic connections between groundwater pumping and streamflow depletions. Settlements of tribal claims provide a forum to create new policies to better manage streams and aquifers on and near the reservation.

Environmental Advocates

Environmental organizations have not uniformly participated in or monitored Indian water rights settlement efforts. Many reasons contribute to this circumstance: The settlements occur in one region of the country, and many prominent environmental issues are national, coinciding with the nationwide scope of major environmental organizations. When settlements are attached to pending general stream adjudications or other water litigation, environmental groups may not have legal standing to participate directly in the talks. In settlement efforts, some tribes are seeking to restore riparian environments and fisheries. Since environmental groups share these priorities, they may defer to tribal leadership and direct their limited resources to other issues. Because water rights litigation and settlement efforts take so long, environmental groups tend to focus their attention on more pressing problems. In securing legislative approval of settlements, however, environmental organizations can be important tribal allies when the agreements include environmental protection and restoration components. When a settlement has questionable environmental impacts, environmental groups can also be vocal critics, as the ALP controversy in southwestern Colorado demonstrates.

National and regional environmental organizations may also become involved when settlements propose water-development projects, new consumptive uses of water, and inefficient uses of resources. Generally, environmental advocacy includes the following objectives:

Preventing environmental damage. Advocacy groups seek to avoid further streamflow depletions and impairment of water quality and wildlife habitat as a result of new water-development projects or changes in water management contemplated under a settlement. These groups are especially concerned about the adequacy of efforts to recover threatened and endangered species, protecting these species' habitats, and preventing the decline of other species.

Water use efficiency. To the extent settlement water will be diverted out of natural channels, environmental groups seek to ensure that the water is efficiently used and the return flow is not polluted or so elevated in temperature that aquatic species are adversely affected.

Accounting of project benefits and costs. Many early water development projects failed to account for the environmental costs of the projects. In scrutinizing the water development components of settlements, environmental groups seek a thorough and accurate accounting of the project's benefits and costs.

Preventing cumulative or growth-induced effects. Environmental groups work to educate decision makers about the importance of examining a proposal, such as a water project, in the context of other actions (completed or anticipated) to modify the environment. Similarly, many environmental groups are concerned about population growth in environmentally fragile areas that results from new water supplies.

Incorporating environmental enhancements. Settlement provisions can provide environmental assurances, such as minimum streamflows or restoration of previously degraded habitat and water quality.

Ecological management. Environmental groups are supportive of polices that promote holistic ecosystem management. Indian water rights settlements are likely to receive favorable review from these groups

to the extent the agreements advance watershed management; coordinate the efforts of federal, state, and tribal resource managers; provide for careful monitoring and research concerning critical environmental conditions; and allow management policies to adapt to new scientific information.

Addressing environmental justice concerns. Most environmental groups have a growing interest in the relationship between resource and environmental policies and social equity—the environmental justice movement.[1] For instance, even certain environmental improvement projects, such as hazardous waste clean-up facilities, should be disfavored if they are uniformly proposed for low-income, ethnic-minority neighborhoods. Indian water rights settlements can advance environmental justice concerns if they provide meaningful benefits to tribes in an environmentally sound fashion. (A more detailed discussion of the relationship between tribal water rights and environmental objectives appears in sidebar 4.1.)

Western State Governments

During my time as governor, I said to the people of Arizona: "This is not a problem, it's an opportunity.... What we have is an intergovernmental environment in which, if we could just quit thinking of Indian tribes and nations as problems and start thinking of them as peoples, communities, and governmental units, we can get on with business and make it happen."

Bruce Babbitt, former secretary of the Interior and governor of Arizona

State governments generally share some of the goals of non-Indian water interests and of tribes. States also have unique objectives.

Achieving consistency with state law. Western state governments want settlement provisions that honor the legal doctrines of state water law.

Protecting state water-management authority. State governments want to protect their authority to regulate water uses, water rights, and water quality and to enhance supply availability and reliability through new water development.

Protecting state interests in interstate waters. In some instances, states view the quantification of reserved water rights as an opportunity to bolster the state's claim to interstate water and to limit other states'

SIDEBAR 4.1

Tribes and Environmental Objectives

> Tribes need to advocate for tribes and environmental organizations for the environment. Sometimes their interests will converge and they will be advocates together for environmental protections.
>
> Tom Graff, California regional director for Environmental Defense Fund

Wetlands, rivers, lakes, and wildlife habitats have been impaired as the West was settled and water was diverted for agriculture and other uses. Tribal spokespersons often remind other water users that their uses of water have jeopardized the abundant natural resources upon which tribal communities have depended for generations. As tribes consider management of their water resources, environmental restoration sometimes emerges as a high priority.

Restoration of fisheries is a key goal of tribes in the Pacific Northwest. A number of tribes have demanded that the region's rivers be managed to promote recovery of threatened migratory salmon and steelhead populations. Dedicating water rights for instream flow purposes was an important goal of the Shoshone-Bannock tribes when negotiating the Fort Hall settlement. The Columbia River Intertribal Fish Commission, which represents the tribes of the Nez Perce, Umatilla, Yakima, and Warm Springs reservations, was established in 1977 to provide unified advocacy for the tribes in the overall management of fisheries resources and related treaty rights. In the Southwest, the 2003 Zuni Pueblo settlement includes provisions for restoring riparian habitat on the tribe's religious lands in Arizona.

The water-management objectives of the contemporary environmental movement sometimes are complementary to tribal restoration objectives. In some instances, environmental advocates seeking changes in established water allocations have formed alliances with tribes to redirect water toward fishery and wetland restoration. In the Truckee-Carson–Pyramid Lake settlement, for example, the Pyramid Lake Paiute Tribe and environmental groups came to recognize their common interests, and the tribe became a driving force behind efforts to protect fisheries in the Truckee River basin while environmental groups joined the tribe in forcing changes in river operations to address fishery needs. Likewise, when the Wind River Arapaho and Shoshone tribes elected to dedicate a large portion of their water rights to streamflow and fisheries restoration, national wildlife advocacy groups supported tribal goals through fish-stocking programs and legal efforts. In 2002, the Cabazon Band of Mission Indians joined the Sierra Club in a lawsuit over restoration of the Salton Sea ecosystem, including wetlands, fisheries, and migratory bird habitat.

Tribes have been active participants also in federal EPA programs to protect reservation resources and environments. Tribes may use certain provisions of the Safe Drinking Water Act and the Clean Water Act to assert water quality requirements against neighboring parties.[1] As part of the Reagan-era policy to expand tribal self-determination, both acts were amended to recognize qualified tribes as states under the legislation. Specifically, Congress expressed a preference for tribal regulation of its water quality to assure the achievement of the acts' goals.[2] In doing so, tribes may exercise limited regulatory power approved and enforced by the EPA. To qualify for state status, a tribe must (1) be federally recognized and have a governing body carrying out substantial powers and duties; (2) limit its exercise of regulatory power to its jurisdiction; and (3) be reasonably capable of carrying out its regulatory function in a manner consistent with the terms and purposes of the acts.[3]

Once a tribe qualifies for state status under an act, it has the power to set water quality standards for the land it controls. The U.S. Supreme Court upheld the EPA's determination that Pueblo water quality standards governed the City of Albuquerque's upstream effluent discharge, even though the tribal standards were more stringent than state or federal guidelines.[4] Under the Clean Water Act and the Safe Drinking Water Act, the EPA provides funds to develop water quality assessments, monitoring, and regulation of water resources. EPA policy allows tribes, as well as states, to assume control over EPA water quality programs under certain conditions. Tribal governments throughout the West have taken advantage of this opportunity to develop water quality–management programs and to enhance environmental regulation on reservations.

claims to the water. States also seek to protect their interests by attempting to prevent tribes from leasing or selling their water entitlements to water users located in other states.

Fulfilling multiple roles. State water administrators have played a variety of roles in negotiations and litigation involving tribal water rights. Some state engineers or departments of water resources adopt a policy of remaining neutral and assist settlements by providing technical expertise, facilitating meetings, and administering adjudication proceedings. For instance, the Arizona Department of Water Resources (ADWR) provides technical expertise to the state adjudication court, facilitates negotiations, and by law cannot equate the interests of non-Indian water rights holders with the interests of the state. Other state water agencies have aligned themselves with those parties holding water rights under state law and have actively opposed tribal assertions of water rights in negotiations and in the courtroom. The Wind River case in Wyoming evolved in a confrontational manner, leading the Wyoming state engineer to participate in decades of litigation to prevent tribal water rights from impairing water rights held under state law.

Every western state has one or more state agencies that regulate and monitor water use and water quality. Sidebar 4.2 describes the origins of these agencies and their current mandates and work.

The Federal Government's Many Hats

For decades, in repeated disputes, Congress handed responsibility for the management of natural resources over to the secretary of the interior, often with touching faith that these matters would then be safe from the pressures of politics and interest groups. By 1980, the Interior's jurisdiction was a crazy mosaic. . . . the secretary of the interior wore more hats than a head could support.

Patricia Nelson Limerick, *The Legacy of Conquest*

The federal government encourages negotiated settlement of Indian water rights claims and also supports tribes in litigation when necessary. Due to its multiple roles and often conflicting objectives, federal involvement in Indian water rights settlements is complex and includes the following specific federal goals:

Fulfilling trust responsibilities to tribes. Federal participation in Indian water settlements is driven by

federal trust responsibilities to Indian tribes. These responsibilities include protecting Indian water resources.

Protecting rights of other federal reserves. Federal participants in settlements also seek to protect the water rights of other federal reserves, such as national forests and parks and military bases.

Protecting endangered species. Federal participants desire water settlements that provide adequate protection of endangered species as required by federal legislation, principally the ESA.

Protecting water quality. The federal government also seeks to protect the nation's water quality as required by the federal Clean Water Act.

Balancing financial obligations. The federal administration seeks to balance its obligations to fund settlements with its obligations to manage taxpayer monies judiciously by requiring reasonably priced settlements that include adequate state and local contributions of money and water.

Protecting non-Indian water users. Congress and federal agencies desire settlement agreements that accommodate non-Indian agricultural, municipal, and industrial water users, especially those that depend on federal water projects. Federal reservoirs and dams often provide the infrastructure needed to store and deliver water to tribes under a settlement.

The Congress, the federal courts, and the administration play a key role in Indian water settlements. The concerns of the administration are represented primarily through the Departments of Interior and Justice and the Office of Management and Budget, although other federal agencies also can be involved in settlements.

Congress

There are many on Capitol Hill who do not understand the benefits of funding settlements, so one of the best things settlement advocates can do is to educate members of Congress, congressional staff, and the public about the importance of water settlements.

Margaret Stewart, minority staff, U.S. Senate Budget Committee

Since 1978, Congress has authorized nearly two dozen Indian water settlements, and there have been several amendments to prior settlements. Ten settlement bills

SIDEBAR 4.2
State Water Agencies

States don't like other sovereigns in their territory.

Jim Grijalva, professor of law, North Dakota University

State water-management agencies are not well understood by the public, although they have crucial responsibilities for the state's most precious natural resource. Over the last century, these agencies have evolved as western states have moved from water development to multidisciplinary water management.

These agencies were first established during the Progressive Era, commencing in the late 1880s, when reformers sought to bring increased professionalism to all aspects of government, including natural resource policy. Unsuccessful in his efforts to remove water management from the courts in Colorado, Elwood Mead (for whom Lake Mead is named) moved to Wyoming in 1888 to become that state's first state engineer. In that role, Mead worked as one member of the three-person State Board of Control to determine administratively existing water uses and permit new ones.

With passage of the Reclamation Act in 1902, the federal government urged states to improve their capacity to manage water so that planned irrigation projects could progress and succeed. North Dakota pioneered similar codes that were copied throughout the West. Morris Bien, an engineer with the Reclamation Service, prepared a model state water code, including a state engineer with responsibilities for adjudicating and permitting water rights. The state engineer position reflected the times. The incumbent was usually a civil engineer who trained in hydraulics and construction methods.

Stakeholders in many states gained influence in water management through the creation of state water commissions usually working in conjunction with the state engineer. Some of these commissions were strictly advisory; others had considerable influence over water planning and project development.

Beginning in the 1960s, many states undertook administrative reforms, including agency consolidation and gubernatorial cabinet systems. In some states, state engineers and water commissions were replaced by departments of water resources or departments of natural resources headed by a director appointed by the governor. The departments often included formerly separate agencies covering a broad range of resource issues, such as dam safety, state water projects, permitting, water planning, and adjudications.

Some states have created agencies that attempt to take an integrated ecological approach to water and other resources issues. For instance, in 1967, California created the State Water Resources Control Board, combining water quality and water rights in one agency (a separate Department of Water Resources administers state water projects and has other functions). Washington created a "super" agency called the Department of Ecology to coordinate most of the state's resource and environmental programs.

Although new types of agencies have been introduced over the last century, they have not entirely supplanted the older forms. Today, every one of these types of state agencies—state engineer (New Mexico, Wyoming, and North Dakota), state water commission or board (Oklahoma and California), department of water resources (Arizona, Oregon, Idaho, and Colorado), department of natural resources or ecology (Washington and Montana)—is represented in the West.

were enacted in just four congressional sessions during the years 1988–1992. At least a dozen more settlement negotiations currently are under way. Congress generally is interested in finding fair and cost-effective solutions to Indian water rights disputes, recognizing the federal government's responsibility in these conflicts.

Members of Congress often find Indian water settlements to be complex, controversial, and expensive. Settlement packages that are free of controversial provisions, and especially those that enjoy full state, tribal, and local support, are most likely to move swiftly through Congress. Strong leadership on behalf of the settlement from members of Congress representing the state(s) affected by the settlement, as well as support from the administration and the principal congressional committees with jurisdiction, is necessary to obtain congressional authorization of settlement legislation. The sidebars in chapter 6 on the congressional appropriations and authorizations process provide more detail about the legislative process.

Department of the Interior

The Department of the Interior, along with the Department of Justice, has the primary responsibility for exercising the federal trust relationship with Indian tribes. Trust responsibilities are carried out primarily by the BIA, which was established in 1824 (first in the War Department, then transferred to Interior in 1849) to provide services to Indian tribes.

Interior has a central role in Indian water rights settlements. The Solicitor's Office, legal counsel to Interior, works closely with the BIA and Justice to develop legal strategies for settling Indian water disputes. At the same time, Interior assists tribes with the various technical analyses needed to develop their water claims. Later, Interior provides support to implement settlements that have been authorized by Congress.

Interior has broad responsibilities to manage the use of public lands and natural resources on public lands and Indian reservations. This complicates the role of Interior in Indian water rights settlements and leads to conflicts of interest in instances where the welfare of other beneficiaries of federal land, water, timber, and mineral resources is at odds with the interests of Indian tribes. A conflict might occur, for example, if tribal water settlements involve waters delivered through federal water projects (Bureau of Reclamation) or endangered fish and federal wildlife refuges (Fish and Wildlife Service, FWS). Such is the case in the Colorado Ute settlement, when the FWS opposed construction of the ALP, a key component of the settlement, due to concerns about the endangered pikeminnow.

Department of Justice

> To many people, the issue of Indian water rights is a matter of justice; the United States is duty-bound to honor the treaties it signed with Indian nations. But for others, it is simply a matter of money; prolonged litigation generates costs for all parties.
>
> Daniel McCool, *Native Waters*

The Department of Justice represents the United States in litigation and has participated in many cases on behalf of tribes. In litigation over Indian water rights, Justice represents Interior, which in turn represents the Indian tribe as federal trustee. Many tribes also hire their own counsel to represent them. Justice must balance the multiple and sometimes conflicting interests of the United States in water settlements. Attorneys in Justice's Indian Resources Section represent tribal interests, and attorneys in the General Litigation Section represent all other federal interests. As a practical matter, attorneys from the Indian Resources Section may be the only ones involved in the early stages of settlements. Conflicts that emerge between Justice's Indian Resources attorneys and General Litigation attorneys must be addressed by high-ranking Justice and Interior officials.

Justice stays closely involved with Indian water rights negotiations because it must be prepared to litigate on behalf of Interior and tribes if negotiations break down and litigation is activated. Justice works to ensure that technical studies done in preparation for negotiations also provide sound documentation that may be needed for litigation.

Office of Management and Budget

The Office of Management and Budget (OMB) presents financial assessments of proposed water settlements to Congress and to the president. OMB, with watchdog responsibilities for federal monies, strives to ensure that executive agencies adhere to the administration's budget. OMB is concerned with the cumulative financial consequences of settlements and their overall implications for the federal budget. OMB's position on settlements is that federal and non-Indian contributions to settlements should be proportional to the benefits each party receives under a proposed settlement, with benefits estimated by comparing them to the likely outcome for each party if the dispute were settled in court.

During the 1990s, the administration began requiring more local cost sharing than in earlier settlements. Based on OMB's fiscal concerns, the administration has opposed many of the Indian water settlements that have gone before Congress.

Other Federal Interests

In addition to the specific federal actors discussed here, other federal agencies may become important participants in the settlement process when their specific mandates are relevant. For instance, the Environmental Protection Agency (EPA) becomes involved when water quality is a key issue. Likewise, the U.S. Department of Agriculture (USDA) may participate in negotiations when a proposed settlement affects local irrigators, the National Wild and Scenic Rivers System, wildlife, national forests, or grazing lands under Forest Service (USDA) jurisdiction. USDA programs also play a crucial role in determining how much water is used to irrigate crops.

Concerns with Federal Participation

Some parties to Indian water rights negotiations feel that the federal government represents too many con-

flicting interests, creating great difficulty for settlement efforts. Concerns voiced by seasoned negotiators include difficulty knowing which interests a federal negotiator is representing in the negotiations, lack of confidence that a federal negotiator has the authority to deliver on a promise (in particular, that Justice, Interior, and OMB will support the settlement as it moves through Congress), and lack of consistency in federal representation during the course of negotiations.

In 1989, a special task force on Indian water settlements was created within Interior. In 1990, the secretary of the Interior took steps to provide uniformity of federal participation in the settlement process by adopting federal negotiating guidelines.[2] These guidelines continue to provide a framework for federal settlement teams and are designed to assist federal participants in developing a unified and consistent position. Interior appoints interagency federal teams for several stages of the settlement process: assessment of a case and the potential to negotiate a settlement, active settlement negotiations, and implementation of negotiated settlements.

The development of Indian water rights settlements is perhaps the most unusual experience in American federalism. All types of governments are involved: federal, tribal, state, and local. All branches of government are involved: executive, legislative, and judicial. If well negotiated, the resulting agreement is an organic document through which the many participants can continue to work toward realizing their distinct and shared hopes and concerns.

PHOTO 5.1   Three men in fishing boat. Photo: Columbia River Intertribal Fish Commission

CHAPTER 5

Perspectives

The bottom line is we are trying to save our homes, our land, and our culture.

Curtis Cesspooch, vice chair, Northern Ute Tribe

The hopes and concerns of the major stakeholders in addressing the water rights claims of western Indian tribes are best understood in the words of the stakeholders themselves. In this chapter, we present interviews with four active participants in the litigation and negotiation of Indian water rights.

Few people have worked in this field longer than John Echohawk, executive director of the Native American Rights Fund (NARF), and the chapter appropriately begins with an interview with him. We continue with interviews with Nelson J. Cordova, former governor of Taos Pueblo, and George Britton, former Phoenix deputy city manager. We conclude this chapter on perspectives with the observations of David J. Hayes, who worked on Indian land and water settlements throughout the United States as deputy secretary of the Department of the Interior during the Clinton administration.

Tribal Perspective: Interview with John Echohawk

We were met by John Echohawk in the conference room of NARF's comfortable headquarters in Boulder, Colorado. John commented that the purchase of this Spanish-style house close to the University of Colorado campus was the best real estate decision he had ever made. A Pawnee, John was the first graduate of the University of New Mexico's special program to train Indian lawyers and was a founding member of the American Indian Law Students Association while in law school. John has been with NARF since its inception in 1970 and has served continuously as executive director since 1977. He has been recognized as one of the one hundred most influential lawyers in America by the *National Law Journal*. He shared with us the organization's pivotal role in the Indian water rights settlement movement.

Q: How did NARF become involved in Indian water right issues?

ECHOHAWK: Indian water rights became an important program emphasis for NARF soon after its founding in 1970 as a Ford Foundation–funded offshoot of the California Indian Legal Services program. One of its initial priorities was to influence federal administration policies. Two of its attorneys, Reid Chambers and Tom Fredericks, were appointed as associate solicitors working on Indian law issues with the Department of Interior. Much of the litigation in the late 1970s involved a rush to the courthouse by states seeking to file water adjudications in state courts and by federal and tribal parties seeking to lodge these cases in what they believed were more independent federal courts. That effort became more difficult after the U.S. Supreme Court's decision in *Arizona v. San Carlos Apache Tribe* [1983],[1] recognizing state court jurisdiction over general stream adjudications even in states that had previously disclaimed jurisdiction over tribal lands.

Q: What were some of the pressures on tribes at the time?

ECHOHAWK: During the late 1970s and early 1980s, energy development was at its peak throughout the West. As large energy companies sought water for their developments, they first encountered the federal reserved water rights doctrine and the large, senior, and unquantified claims of tribes. The Western Regional Council [WRC], a regional organization of energy companies, transportation companies, and utilities, began to pressure Congress to bring more certainty to western water supplies through an administrative commission's quantification of tribal claims. Tribal organizations reacted vehemently to this effort to strip them of judicial safeguards.

Some energy development was occurring on reservations, such as on Black Mesa in Arizona, and WRC and its members had established a working relationship on those issues with the umbrella organization for those tribes, the Council of Energy Resource Tribes [CERT]. WRC wanted to discuss water issues with tribes in an effort to reduce the outrage over WRC's commission proposal, and CERT put them in contact with NARF, and the three groups began discussions.

Q: Some of the early settlement efforts occurred during the Reagan administration. How did that come about?

ECHOHAWK: President Ronald Reagan had vetoed the Tohono O'odham settlement in 1982 because he believed the federal government had not been sufficiently involved in the talks and was obligated to pay too much money. The veto became a test of WRC's good intentions as NARF and CERT asked the industry organization to help in securing approval of the settlement, which they were able to do quickly. This success led to more substantive discussions among the groups (later joined by the National Congress of American Indians and the Western Governors' Association), and the effort ultimately evolved into the Ad Hoc Group on Indian Water Rights. We soon approached Reagan's controversial secretary of the Interior, James Watt, who was flabbergasted at the cooperation among these former adversaries. Gradually, the Interior Department got on board about the importance of these settlement efforts.

Q: Did you have difficulty convincing tribes to negotiate rather than litigate?

ECHOHAWK: At first, it was hard for tribes to rely more on negotiations and less on litigation, and this view was shared by Justice Department attorneys who had spent whole careers litigating Indian law issues. In 1989, the U.S. Supreme Court sent up a big red flag warning to tribes in *Wyoming v. United States*.[2] Oral arguments before the Court had focused on the use of the PIA [practicably irrigable acreage] standard to quantify tribal claims, with Wyoming and other states arguing for an alternative, reasonable needs test. The Court affirmed the lower courts' decisions, based on PIA, but did so by an equally divided court (4-4), with Justice O'Connor abstaining. Tribal leaders and attorneys realized they were one vote away from losing the PIA standard, and Justice O'Connor might exercise that vote in a future case.

The emphasis shifted to settlements, and these efforts received the support of the first Bush administration. Settlement efforts were elevated to the secretarial level at the Interior Department with the estab-

lishment of an office of Indian water rights. Procedures and criteria to guide the federal government's negotiating efforts were drafted—although we were concerned that this guidance could be used as much to stall settlements as to craft them.

Q: Did you feel enough was accomplished during the Clinton administration?

ECHOHAWK: Tribes were optimistic when Bruce Babbitt became President Clinton's secretary of the Interior in 1993. We didn't think we had to go see *this* secretary! Babbitt was familiar with water and Indian law issues from his years as Arizona's attorney general and governor. Babbitt had been an energetic force as the Western Governors' representative to the Ad Hoc Group on Indian Water Rights. But Babbitt was soon distracted on controversial issues such as mining and grazing reforms. The shift in Congress to Republican control in 1994 compounded budgetary politics. Tribes became whipsawed as settlement funding became framed as a competition between tribes and environmental advocates for scarce dollars.

The situation began to improve as a result of the work of the Western Water Policy Review Advisory Commission, commissioned by Congress in 1992 to recommend improvements for the federal role in western water issues. Babbitt appointed me to the commission. We invited Babbitt to attend a commission meeting on Indian water rights in 1997. The meeting turned into a candid appraisal of the administration's settlement efforts. Babbitt promised improvements. They were forthcoming through an easing of financial restraints and in the appointment of David Hayes, a Washington, D.C., attorney, to chair the secretary's Working Group on Indian Water Rights Settlements. Hayes, who was later elevated to deputy secretary of the department, energetically organized and prioritized the department's settlement initiatives. Still, only a few settlements were finally approved during the Clinton administration.

Q: In which settlements has NARF been involved?

ECHOHAWK: Over the years, we've been involved in settlement efforts involving the Tohono O'odham and Fort McDowell Indian Community settlements in Arizona (Rick Dauphinais and Arlinda Locklear, lead attorneys), the Northern Cheyenne settlement in Montana (Jeanne Whiteing, lead attorney), the Pyramid

Lake settlement in Nevada (Bob Pelcyger, lead attorney), Utah Ute (Dan Israel, lead attorney), and the Animas–La Plata settlement in Colorado (Scott McElroy and Dan Israel, lead attorneys).

At present, NARF is working on settlements for the Rocky Boy's Reservation in Montana (Chippewa Cree), the Nez Perce in Idaho, and the Tule River Reservation in California. NARF has also been involved in discussions involving the Klamath Tribe in Oregon.

Q: What is the climate now for settlements?

ECHOHAWK: The downturn in the economy starting in 2000 and rigidity in the federal budget process all contribute to the problem of finding money for future settlements. The federal budget cap on new expenditures has meant that money for new settlements has come from other parts of the Interior budget or the Bureau of Indian Affairs budget. In addition to funding water settlements, money is needed for the federal negotiating teams, assistance to tribes, technical work, settlement implementation, and some Indian land settlements. The Ad Hoc Group on Indian Water Rights has worked with members of Congress to find additional funds for settlement. Senator Pete Domenici has a proposal to exempt $200 million from the budget cap that would be used for settlements. Additionally, the Ad Hoc Group is attempting to make sure ranking Office of Management and Budget officials are familiar with the settlement program.

Q: Is the federal government's reluctance to approve tribal water codes slowing tribes' efforts to manage their water?

ECHOHAWK: Many of these controversial water-management issues are being addressed in the context of specific settlements rather than in separate tribal water codes. Off-reservation leasing of Indian water rights is now being handled on a case-by-case basis rather than as a generic West-wide issue. The settlements in Arizona are good examples on how leasing issues can be resolved. However, state officials still resist out-of-state leasing.

Q: From a tribal perspective, what are the prospects for future settlements?

ECHOHAWK: Tribes still have a lot of enthusiasm for settlements. The situation will probably get worse for Indian law cases in the courts, especially before the U.S. Supreme Court. NARF has had good cooperation with the second Bush administration, aided by the fact that both Secretary Gale Norton and her assistant secretary for Water and Science are from Colorado. As state attorney general, Norton gained experience and knowledge about settlement processes through her involvement in the Animas–La Plata efforts.

The tension between tribes and some environmental advocates over the water development features of some settlements remains unresolved. Tribes see the protection and utilization of their reserved rights as an environmental justice issue that should resonate more strongly in the environmental community. Tribes need to remain diligent concerning their water rights. Things are always changing; we can never give up!

Pueblo Perspective: Interview with Nelson J. Cordova

Nelson Cordova's professional background is in education and tribal administration. He has a bachelor of arts degree in government and a master's degree in educational administration. Cordova began working for the BIA at Taos Pueblo as an elementary school teacher. When he left the classroom, he was hired as a tribal planner and worked several years in that position. He later served as tribal administrator, three terms as a tribal secretary, one term as warchief, and one term as governor of Taos Pueblo. Cordova is now a member of the tribal council, a lifetime position. Cordova was interviewed by his son, Jeffrey Cordova, a University of Arizona student, in Tucson.

Q: Of those many tribal positions you mentioned, which one did you find the most challenging?

CORDOVA: Governor was probably the most challenging one, because the duties and responsibilities of that position far outweigh the other positions that I've held. However, the position of tribal administrator is pretty demanding in itself.

Q: What type of training or education would you recommend for tribal youth planning on working on tribal water issues?

CORDOVA: For a young person planning on working on tribal issues, the kind of training needed would depend on the tribe itself, the location of the tribe, the history, the culture, and most importantly, the relationship between that tribe and the local non-Indian community and also with the state. So, in terms of what kind of training is required to work in water resources, it takes an education that is wide in scope and includes a formal western education and training and understanding of tribal culture, traditions, and values. It should cover the fields of history, archeology, and anthropology, as well as the hard sciences. Certainly math is an important requirement, because tribal hydrologists have to deal in mathematics. Also, there are certain requirements that touch on economics. So it would seem to me that a person that wants to work with water resources certainly has to have some background in fields that deal with water, for example, the related fields of history, let's say, mathematics, economics, and those kinds of things. It's a subject that touches on a lot of disciplines, so a person has to be flexible.

Q: What are the challenges today that Taos Pueblo is facing in managing its water resources?

CORDOVA: Right now, one of the challenges that we are facing is drought. We do not have enough water. Streams are drying up. Springs have dried up, and there is no telling how long this drought is going to last. So we need to find alternative sources of water, and right now that seems to be pointing to development of our groundwater resources and also the improvement of our watershed. There are many who say that the improvement of our watershed is the key to providing additional water resources. Tribal members, especially the youth, need to realize that the key to protecting and managing tribal water resources is education and involvement in the political process.

Q: Do you have any suggestions on how tribal leaders can protect tribal sovereignty over their water supplies?

CORDOVA: Again, it depends on the setting of the tribe. We have always contended that as a sovereign, we do have certain responsibilities, and being a sovereign means that you have to act in a fair and responsible manner. You not only have to look out for the welfare of your tribe, but you have to think about the water needs of the local non-Indian communities. If you can demonstrate fairness, along with being firm, in terms of allocating water resources, then the respect that the

non-Indians have towards the Indian community increases. That is very important in terms of negotiating settlements and also in terms of going into future agreements. If you do not have the respect of the non-Indian community and respect within the tribe, it's going to be very hard to manage water resources in the future.

Q: How did you come to be interested in water issues?

CORDOVA: It did not happen by design. I became involved in tribal water issues because when I started working as a planner and also as a tribal administrator for Taos Pueblo, we had already been involved in a water adjudication suit with the state of New Mexico. During that time (in the early 1980s), even though we were working on preparing for litigation, there was no one in the tribe that was responsible for working in this area. As a result, when the tribal attorneys and the federal attorneys and federal technical folks came in to do studies or provided information to the tribe regarding the adjudication, there was nobody to tend to these issues. As a result, reports from the attorneys, technical studies from the consultants and other experts ended up in a box that was stowed away in the corner of one of the tribal buildings. I started going through some of those materials and found that some of the information that was contained in those reports and letters needed to be responded to. So I started doing that, and I just kept track of all the correspondence that came from our attorneys and also from the federal government. That's how I became involved. I became involved because nobody else was doing it.

Q: As far as technical capacity is concerned, what do the tribes need to do to manage their water resources in an efficient manner?

CORDOVA: That's a very important question. First of all, I feel that in order to manage tribal water resources, you need individuals that are trained in some of the areas I alluded to earlier. Also, there needs to be a commitment by the tribe to allocate tribal resources to this cause. If you depend on federal resources, the resources sometimes are just not there. Also, we all know that the federal government, even though it has a trust responsibility to the tribe — sometimes that trust responsibility is just not there. So those are some of the things that we need to do in terms of building up our capacity.

It would seem to me that one of the things that the tribe has to do is to encourage and motivate students about the importance of water as a resource. Also, we need to impress upon our students the need for them to go into professions that are required to deal with water resources. Right now, we have a problem with students not being motivated, students saying there is no relevancy in their education. Water is certainly one area where it can be demonstrated that some of the skills that a student learns can be used to manage water.

So we need human resources, we need financial resources, we need a commitment from the tribe not only in terms of providing the two resources I named but also having a commitment to protect its water resources in the future. Without the technical capacity to manage our water, this is not going to happen. We need to develop a capacity within the tribe to manage this water because water has certain cultural connotations that only a tribal member can understand well. Maybe a nontribal person can come in and assist in a technical capacity, but as far as understanding the importance of water to the tribe, that's going to require a tribal person.

Q: Can you briefly elaborate on the Taos Pueblo view of water and if it makes an impact on the negotiation process?

CORDOVA: Certainly. The Pueblo view of water is that without water, nothing can survive. Water is the basis for all life. The protection of this water resource has been given to us, and we revere water as a part of our environment. One of the most important things about our Pueblo regarding water is that we are fortunate to be located at the headwaters of our two streams: the Rio Pueblo and the Rio Lucero. These two streams originate in our mountains, the Blue Lake Watershed, and produce approximately 40 percent of the water in the Taos Valley. Being at the headwaters gives us a sense of protection and a sense of comfort. We know of tribes that are at the tail end of their streams, and sometimes the water does not reach them. In terms, again, of the importance of water to the tribe or for our cultural survival, it is imperative that we retain rights to water in our streams, in our springs, and in our

lakes. As you know, the Blue Lake is a mountain lake that is revered by our people. So water plays a very important part in our daily lives, in our traditional activities, and also is a very important asset for our future.

Q: Which parties are involved in the water adjudication in Taos?

CORDOVA: The parties that are involved in *New Mexico v. Abeyta*[3] include the following, and all the individual water rights claimants in the Taos Valley: the State of New Mexico, the Taos Pueblo, the acequia associations, the sanitation districts, and then there's another one I can't remember now, and certainly the federal government is involved in this because it involves the trust asset, water.

Q: Why has the Taos Pueblo selected negotiation as a means to settle the water adjudication instead of litigation?

CORDOVA: Well, the *Abeyta* case was filed in 1969. It was dormant in the 1970s, pending the outcome of the *Aamodt* case[4] [pending northwest of Santa Fe]; activity picked up around 1985. Around 1989, our non-Indian neighbors, the Taos Valley Acequia Association, approached the tribal council with a proposal, and their proposal was to negotiate as neighbors rather than facing each other as adversaries in court. After looking at the relative advantages of litigation versus negotiation, we felt that we needed to give negotiation a try. Also, in the early 1990s there was a policy in the federal government which supported negotiations. They felt that by negotiating, some of these water cases could be completed much sooner and at a lesser cost.

Now, this remains to be seen. Negotiation certainly takes a heck of a lot more time. The important advantage that we felt negotiation has over litigation is the fact that the parties that are involved in the negotiations have the ability to craft an agreement whereby they can allocate the water that is available. Also, they have the ability to put that water to use, especially at the tribal level. On the litigation side, basically the judge decides the allocation of water. Also, I feel in a litigation setting, the judge sets out the priority date and the quantity of water that one is entitled to. In some cases you don't have or you do not obtain the resources or the money that are required to put this water to use. In a tribal setting, one of the biggest problems that we've had is that we have not had the monies to get our irrigation systems in shape. As a result, we have not been able to use the water that we were entitled to.

Under a negotiation setting, we have what is called a homeland plan, whereby we are planning at least a hundred years into the future what our water needs are going to be and how we are going to address the infrastructure needs to allocate and use this water. We don't know how the negotiation process is going to work out. We are in the process of negotiating with the parties that I named, but in some cases it is very difficult to address some of the critical issues.

Key issues include, How much water does each party get? What is the priority date? We feel that negotiations have definite advantages over a litigated outcome, but it remains to be seen whether we come out with a settlement. It is possible that if there is no settlement, if the parties cannot agree on certain issues, then it might end up in court, where it appears that both the tribes and the non-Indian parties may stand to lose a lot.

Q: You mentioned the drought that Taos Pueblo has been facing. How has the drought impacted you and other people from Taos Pueblo?

CORDOVA: Well, the drought has been a humbling experience. It has certainly been an eye opener. It has probably had some psychological impact on a lot of people in our community. I myself have never seen the Rio Pueblo [the stream that runs right through the village of Taos Pueblo] run dry. This summer was the first time that I saw that happen, and it was a tremendous shock. I had always seen that water or the stream flowing, and one morning when I went out, it was dry. I am certain that I was not the only one that was affected. There were a lot of people that began to question themselves, and certainly tribal leaders, religious leaders, and everybody else started questioning why these things are happening. So it's had a tremendous impact.

Another impact has been that we have not been able to irrigate our crops. Some of the crops that people had planted for religious purposes just dried up or the seeds did not even germinate. So it has had a tremendous effect in that way. One of the things that we have had to do is haul water to our animals. This is something that we have never done. Now you see tribal members with their pickups carrying all sorts of water tanks, cans of water, trash cans filled with water to their animals because the ditches have run dry. Also, in the pasture area where we keep our animals, the forage is very bad. There is not only a human impact, but also impact on the livestock, and certainly there's an impact on the plants in the area and also on the forest. We are beginning to see juniper dry up. There are huge patches of juniper trees that are turning brown.

The impact of the drought, even in this year, is beginning to affect people. The hard part is we don't how long the drought is going to last. We are in the process of developing a drought contingency plan to hopefully mitigate some of the impacts next year and the coming years. We're hoping that we have a good winter and we have some spring rains so that we will have some water. Right now, there is a big deficit that needs to be made up, and it probably is going to take many years for this deficit to be overcome.

In view of all the water issues that we have on the table right now, including the adjudication, we've had to deal with this drought, too. Who knows about the water data we have been using over the past? In terms of available resources, we're not sure if we can rely on this information in the future because, if the drought persists, we are still not going to see the quantities of water that we've seen in the past.

Q: The Pueblo has a unique history in that the area was under Spanish rule for some time, and then it came under the jurisdiction of the United States. How has that affected any of the parties involved in the water negotiation?

CORDOVA: Well, certainly that is one of the most important things we are dealing with in our adjudication. The history regarding the parties goes way back. The Pueblo itself has been in its present location since time immemorial. The non-Indians moved into the area around 1540 and started to colonize the area in the early 1600s, so they have a long history too.

How that translates into what is happening today is that the non-Indians, or the Spanish irrigators, in the area claim priority dates that are very old and have an impact on the tribe's priority dates itself. Now, in terms of an adjudication, the state of New Mexico became a state in 1912. I understand the state has no control over water rights that were established prior to 1907, but it does have authority over those that were established after 1907. That creates a problem. The non-Indians claim that they have certain customs and traditions regarding the sharing of water, which is true. They do have those customs, but if the non-Indians continue to use a system that is separate and different than the state's prior appropriation doctrine, then it makes it very difficult for them to enforce and also to manage water.

This is one of the problems that the state engineer is facing: How does it get the non-Indians to conform to its rules and practices? In the long run, it's going to make it very difficult to engage in meaningful water rights management practices in the Taos Valley if you have systems that are not compatible. So that's one of the things that we need to address.

Urban Perspective: Interview with George Britton

George Britton was deputy city manager of Phoenix, Arizona, from 1986 to 2001, where he was responsible for both water- and wastewater-management activities for the city. Formerly executive assistant for Arizona governor Bruce Babbitt, Britton was responsible for the governor's natural resources policies and activities from 1980 to 1986. Presently deputy city manager in Modesto, California, Britton oversees economic development and resource infrastructure for this rapidly growing area, located in California's agricultural heartland. Britton was interviewed by his daughter, Sarah Britton, who graduated from the University of Arizona School of Law in 2003, in Tucson.

Q: When did you first become interested in the politics of water?

BRITTON: In the 1970s, when the Central Arizona Project [CAP] was being debated, I was the assistant to the city manager in Scottsdale and was responsible for the lobbying activities. CAP was increasingly viewed, because of the 1980 Groundwater Management Act,[5] as an essential part of the water future of the communities of the Phoenix metropolitan area. I also got involved in Native American water issues regarding the Salt River Pima–Maricopa Community, and later with the Fort McDowell Indian Community.

Q: Why do municipalities contribute money to water settlement arrangements?

BRITTON: There are a number of reasons that cities contribute money. Cities on the whole, particularly large metropolitan areas, really want to settle Indian claims. Uncertainty, when you're a water provider at the domestic level, is one of the highest risks you can have. Your people expect water, so the supply is what is important over a long period. Agriculture has traditionally owned water rights in Arizona and wants to retain them. So when Indian settlements provide opportunities to acquire water, it's in the interests of the cities to get as long a term of access to those water supplies as possible. Since we as cities are not historically senior surface-water rights holders (though Phoenix has some 1888 rights), we did not have surface-water access and were almost fully dependent on groundwater. Of course, as groundwater overdraft became a problem with the adjoining Native American communities, the cities got caught up in the whole issue. Long and short, it is important for cities to have secure water contracts, and the best way to secure such water contracts is to purchase them. Money is the best way to purchase such rights, because the cities also have the money that flows from being a domestic water supplier.

Q: How willing were tribal parties to previous settlement negotiations to receive money in exchange for their water rights?

BRITTON: You can't truly sever a tribal reserved right, so the agreement was a lease. Typically, the lease operates for ninety-nine to one hundred years, so you meet the assured water supply requirements of the Groundwater Act. The Indian communities know they don't have any short-term use for the water. The other thing that occurs is that the cities, particularly the sophisticated cities, understand that if they are at the table, they can frame the settlement, and that virtually no congressional member is going to support a settlement that is going to do damage to the existing domestic water supply. The iron fist in the velvet glove of the cities is that if we're not taken care of, if we feel we do not receive a fair settlement, we will simply make it publicly known that this damages long-term domestic water resources, causing tremendous political agitation. It's certainly not an empty threat. It is a reality, because the cities need this water supply. The domestic sector is the fastest growing sector other than Indian agriculture water use in Arizona. The cities have a legitimate place at the table. As long as it is a fair and equitable settlement, then the cities have the right to be able to lease water. I don't think that bills would get through Congress if the cities did not support them.

Q: How is the monetary contribution amount reached between the parties of the settlement? How is the water valued?

BRITTON: There is not an active water market per se in Arizona, so it's generally valued at its replacement value, or its derivative value. As an example, most of it is CAP water. You capitalize it over the period of the lease, and then look at it in relation to other available water supplies or options. That is generally how the $1000 to $1500 per acre-foot number has been arrived at. The pricing in the Salt River Pima–Maricopa settlement came out of an analysis of replacement CAP water. That kind of set the standard. The price has moved around that number, but it's not really moved off that number. One of the important elements of Indian water is that it does not have a capital repayment obligation. So you only pay OM&R on it. [OM&R is the abbreviation for operations, maintenance, and repairs. Obligations to repay capital costs to the federal government are not charged to tribes receiving a CAP allocation.] Thus, you can pay a slight premium for that water because there's not a capital charge. In each of the Arizona settlement acts while the leases are in place, you'll notice a provision that says the water retains its nature as Indian water. This protects the Indians at the end of the lease agreement because the water is nonseverable, and it is also important to the local people who buy the water. We are able to pay a premium for that water because there isn't a capital obligation of $50 to $60 per acre-foot annually.

Q: You've had quite a number of years of experience in water law, which is an evolving and relatively complex area of law. How do you educate others, like council members or general politicians?

BRITTON: It's not something you can dabble in and not be dangerous. To educate elected officials at a policy level, you generally address the shorter term issues. As an example, if I were to explain water law in Arizona to

someone, I would have to explain the prior appropriation concept—fundamental to Arizona water law—then the *Winters* doctrine, and then *Arizona v. California* and practicably irrigable acreage, and finally the Arizona Groundwater Act. Those are the four pillars of Arizona water law. If somebody can understand those concepts, then you can talk about the shorter term policy questions, like contracting for water, delivering water, the groundwater situation, and putting a water budget together where you consider how each element of the budget affects the others.

Q: How willing was the Phoenix City Council to go along with the major water changes that happened in the last couple of decades?

BRITTON: In a sense, they were only one actor in a large process. The primary actors in water law change in Arizona have been the Arizona Department of Water Resources in the last two decades, as well as the agricultural community, the Native American community, and then the two major metro areas. Phoenix, with the Arizona Metropolitan Water Users Group, has been really in the trench forces that have developed. Increasingly, the Central Arizona Water Conservation District [CAWCD] is becoming more than just a member agency and a delivery agency, and is getting into water policy. A lot of that comes out of the litigation over their repayment obligations on the CAP that affected Indian settlements, capital forgiveness, essentially all the issues that came back to the city council. Generally, city councils recognize the complexity of this area, and, if you're a large community, hire water advisors, who act on behalf of the council.

The smaller communities have been at a disadvantage. The City of Phoenix position has traditionally been, "We will buy any water that will provide a one hundred–year supply." Like the axiom "you can never have enough money," in Arizona, you can never have enough water. We had a proactive policy that we would acquire any appropriate water supply. We were always at the table.

Q: The city has acquired water from tribes under long-term leases. What happens at the end, or towards the end, of the lease?

BRITTON: Your grandchildren will have employment opportunities. Actually, there are reopeners in the agreements, but it's ninety-nine years away—though in some of the early leases, the time remaining is shorter. Frankly, there are just some issues that can't be solved in perpetuity. Also, who knew ninety-nine years ago that there would be the *Winters* doctrine and *Arizona v. California*? So, you try to introduce as much certainty over as long a period as possible. You also need to understand that the legal system is inherently uncertain.

Q: One of the aspects of the proposed Gila River settlement is payment to the Gila River Indian Community for damage to the land caused by subsidence from surrounding groundwater pumping. Is any of this money going to come from municipalities that may have used the groundwater underneath the reservation?

BRITTON: The Arizona Water Company serves Casa Grande and is currently being exposed to subsidence claims. That was one of the most difficult issues. Tucson, because of the Avra Valley pumping, was very concerned about subsidence claims. One of the issues essential to Tucson, and probably the Pinal County pumpers, is quantification of subsidence claims. You don't want open-ended damage claims—for property or other kinds of claims. One of the big unknowns is the natural resource damage under federal law. If you look at things like CERCLA [Comprehensive Environmental Response and Liability Act, commonly known as Superfund][6], it's an exploding area, so the goal was to quantify the subsidence damage and preclude litigation. In other words, grant as much certainty as possible to the settlement.

Q: Are cities exploited as deep pockets?

BRITTON: Are we willing victims? I think some cities would like to characterize themselves as victims. If you have a long-term water resource plan as a city, and if you are willing to capitalize that plan—i.e., pay now for future needs—I think you sit at the table not as a victim, but as a participant. If you don't have a long-term water resources plan, and if you are in denial over your effect upon your neighbor, like the Native American community, or if for some reason you believe the Native American community should not receive settlements, you would characterize yourself as a victim. I would suggest that Tucson and Phoenix really view themselves as partners, because we are committed to settlement of the Indian claims. Some communities probably view themselves as victims either because they do not share the goal of settling Indian claims, in other words, "we've had the water, we've enjoyed it; the Indians have not had the water, and not enjoyed it, and the longer we keep it, the better off we are," or because the cities have not developed a long-term water policy and water plan which recognizes Indian settlement as part of their water budget.

Q: Are the cities supportive of the after-acquired trust land portion of the proposed Gila River settlement? [The issue of whether Indian reserved water rights attach to lands subsequently acquired by a tribe; see chapter 9 for discussion of the proposed Gila River settlement.]

BRITTON: I think the cities on the whole view the trust land issue as a problem, but not a problem related to the water settlement. The issue of after-acquired trust land potential incompatibility with neighbors, kind of a good neighbor thing more than anything, is an issue that any urban area is concerned about. We've seen some examples where after-acquired lands have been disruptive to the surrounding community. The issue was raised relatively late in the discussion and negotiations surrounding the Gila River settlement, and the question of its nexus to a water settlement troubled the cities. That's why we tried to work with the congressional delegation on language that wasn't our issue in the settlement.

Q: I understand that Senator John McCain [R-AZ] has come out and said that a water bill is not the proper vehicle for this after-acquired trust land legislation. Would the cities like to see a separate bill as well?

BRITTON: The cities would like to see more certainty and more involvement of the local communities, and less noblesse oblige on the part of the federal government in the determination of after-acquired trust lands. There are some cities that would like to see it as part of this water bill. But you see, the language of this bill wouldn't bind all communities. One of the troubling issues, that at least Phoenix and Tucson struggled with, is why should this language only apply to two Indian communities. If after-acquired trust lands really are an issue, then it should apply to the Zunis and the Navajos. In this case, the settlement only has two Indian communities involved, then you have only two groups who will be bound by this legislation. I think the language is an unusual complication to an already complicated bill.

Q: If the problem is not water allocation, or use of natural resources, in regard to after-acquired trust lands, what do the cities see as a problem in regard to these lands?

BRITTON: There are three issues: One is urban compatibility, incompatible uses. The second is a revenue issue. These lands, when they're acquired, require services. And yet they're tax-exempt. That raises some very significant concerns about its burden on the community if they contribute little or no revenue back to the community. The third issue has to do with local control. Essentially, you take a city or a town that controls the area, and you simply impose another country in the middle of it. That has some fairness and community implications. I think the absolute power of the secretary of the Interior to declare after-acquired trust lands needs to be restrained. It's unreasonable to leave the secretary to decide without a more inclusive process. Should the process require congressional approval as is being suggested? Most things do, and there's nothing wrong with congressional approval. If the power and sovereignty in the Native American community flow primarily from federal and congressional authority, then perhaps after-acquired trust lands ought to flow from congressional authority.

Q: So you think municipalities support Secretary of the Interior Gale Norton's withdrawal of the regulations approved during the Clinton administration in regard to the process of approving after-acquired trust lands?

BRITTON: Yes, I think the municipalities believe the former regulations did not go far enough in providing an open and equitable opportunity for the communities to be involved in after-acquired trust lands.

Q: Do you have any concluding thoughts?

BRITTON: Yes. Municipalities aren't all the same. There are different interests in each city, and different levels of sophistication and concern, depending on where they are geographically located, proximity to Indian communities, and their historical relationships with those Indian communities.

Q: What advice would you give first-time municipality participants in a tribal water settlement?

BRITTON: Have a plan, understand the law, and stay at the table.

Federal Perspective: Interview with David J. Hayes

David J. Hayes is a partner in the Washington, D.C., office of the national law firm of Latham and Watkins. From 1997–1999, he served as counselor to secretary of the Interior Bruce Babbitt. In 1999, President Clinton nominated Hayes as deputy secretary of the department. The Senate confirmed Hayes's nomination, and he remained in the post until January 2001, when he returned to private practice. Throughout his tenure at Interior, Hayes was chair of the department's Working Group on Indian Water Rights Settlements. Hayes was born in Rochester, New York, and received his bachelor of arts degree from Notre Dame in 1975, summa cum laude, and his juris doctor degree from Stanford Law School in 1978. Before entering federal service, he practiced law for nearly twenty years in the environmental and natural resources field. Hayes was interviewed by John E. Thorson.

Q: How did you find the Indian water right settlement process when you arrived at Interior in 1997?

HAYES: There was a high level of frustration in Indian country over the lack of settlements during the Clinton administration's first term. Several factors accounted for the settlement slowdown. Interior was spending an enormous amount of energy on a few very difficult negotiations, such as the Little Colorado settlement [northeastern Arizona]. Also, budgets were tight and, in 1994, the Republicans took over the Congress and were hostile to administration initiatives.

Q: What was your strategy when you arrived?

HAYES: We had about thirty to thirty-five federal negotiating teams in the field, and I worked to improve the communications between the teams and headquarters. We took stock of the progress in each of these matters and prioritized our attention on settlements that looked like they might benefit from high-level attention. By way of example, the settlement between the Warm Springs tribes, the State of Oregon, and the United States had been languishing, and we made direct contact with Governor John Kitzhaber to help kick-start discussions. The Rocky Boy's settlement in Montana and the Shivwits settlement in Utah became priorities. We also worked to save some settlements—partially completed agreements that were encountering implementation problems. We refereed a major dispute between the San Carlos Apache Tribe [Arizona] and Phelps Dodge Corporation that was disrupting implementation of the San Carlos Apache settlement. And we embarked on a plan to help implement the long-delayed San Luis Rey [California] settlement. We also began to take a fresh look at the stalled Animas–La Plata [Colorado] settlement which, as originally enacted by Congress, could not be implemented. We also sought to raise the awareness level of the importance of Indian water rights settlements in the administration and Congress, through briefings at OMB and on Capitol Hill.

Q: How did you seek to work with the tribes?
HAYES: I was always governed by the department's role as trustee for the tribes. When I first took over the responsibility for Indian water settlements, we held regional, government-to-government consultations with a large number of tribal leaders. These consultations helped us identify priorities, improve communications with tribes, and understand the frustration level in Indian country.

In connection with specific settlement negotiations, we consulted frequently with the tribes. We jointly strategized with tribes and worked closely with them. As trustee, it was our responsibility to do so.

Q: What are your observations about the roles of other participants in the Indian water rights settlement process? Office of Management and Budget?
HAYES: Some OMB personnel are very knowledgeable about the Indian water rights settlement process. OMB has an institutional resistance, however, to some settlements because they involve nonprogrammatic expenditures.

Q: Congress generally?
HAYES: Successful settlements need champions, and we are lacking some of the congressional giants of the past who provided leadership on western land and water issues. Congressional staff turnover also diminishes congressional understanding and support. We have to grow a new generation of leaders who appreciate these issues. Until this happens, leadership needs to come from states and tribes. There are encouraging signs in this regard, including the increasingly influential congressional tribal caucus.

There is an East-West tension in Congress over many of these settlements. If eastern members sense that a proposed settlement is really nothing more than an expensive and environmentally damaging water project "wrapped in an Indian blanket," they will resist it. If you strip away water development unrelated to tribal needs or convincingly demonstrate water development is really necessary for tribal purposes, however, these issues tend to go away.

Q: States' congressional delegations?
HAYES: Settlements must emerge as bipartisan efforts supported by the state's delegation. State, tribal, and federal parties must continually work to keep their delegation members informed about the importance of, and need for, specific settlements.

Q: U.S. Department of Justice?
HAYES: The Department of Justice [DOJ] lawyers involved in Indian water rights settlements are excellent lawyers. In my experience, they have a keen sense of responsibility pursuant to the federal government's trust obligation to the tribes. DOJ lawyers have an important role to play in the process; they must review and approve settlement language. Because they have many conflicting responsibilities, it is important that Interior officials obtain the attention of Justice's political leadership, so that settlements can be prioritized and moved through the DOJ bureaucracy.

Q: Tribes?
HAYES: Many tribes have become very sophisticated about water rights issues and are undertaking very effective advocacy on their nations' behalf. Others, however, have not prioritized water rights issues, or they are suffering from limited institutional capability. Budget cuts in BIA programmatic funds to support the pursuit of tribal water rights have had a significant, negative effect on many tribes' ability to push forward with water rights claims.

Q: Lawyers?

HAYES: Lawyers play an absolutely critical role, for good and bad, in the settlement process. Some attorneys are problem solvers. Others are not. Some lawyers lack experience in making settlements work; others are excellent. In any event, however, the role of lawyers is critical to the success or failure of Indian water rights settlements. I often could successfully predict how negotiations would progress based on whether the lawyers involved in the process were skilled in problem solving.

Q: Environmental groups?

HAYES: Environmental groups have had relatively little presence in the Indian water rights settlement landscape. Instream water rights adjudications typically have not been on their radar screens. Environmental groups tend to get involved on ESA [Endangered Species Act] issues, where they can be allied closely with tribal interests, as in the case of the Pacific Northwest, where tribes have strong instream interests. Or they can oppose the tribes, such as in the arid Southwest, where tribes often are proposing water storage and development.

Q: What is your assessment of the "Principles and Guidelines"?

HAYES: It's useful to have something on the books to provide general guidelines. They set forth a basic settlement philosophy. In the end, the "Principles and Guidelines" that are published in the *Federal Register* are not going to drive a bad settlement or defeat a good one.

Q: What about PIA? Does it remain a useful standard?

HAYES: I think that the practicably irrigable acreage [PIA] concept has been useful as a rule of thumb, to help parties evaluate the scope of a tribal water claim, but it shouldn't be slavishly followed. The recent Arizona Supreme Court decision [rejecting PIA as the exclusive standard for quantifying Indian water rights] is quite helpful because it firmly recognizes the homeland purpose for these reservations and allows flexibility in quantifying the water rights.[7]

Q: What are the appropriate obligations of the various governments and parties involved in these settlements?

HAYES: Working with tribes, the federal government is in the best position to show leadership on these issues. With the exception of Montana, most states come to the table in a reactive mode, being quite passive at the beginning. It's helpful when a state and its water users have thought out in advance their interests and needs. In some cases, settlements have become a one-way street of benefits, with states getting certainty, tribes getting economic and water development, and the federal government paying the bill. States could contribute more to some settlements, but each case needs to be evaluated on its individual merits. You don't want to have too high of an expectation for a state's contribution, because you may lose political momentum when you need it the most.

Q: Is there a necessary dance between litigation and negotiation?

HAYES: Often, a credible litigation threat is necessary in order to prompt reluctant parties toward a settlement. Litigation risk can be a prime motivator for settlements. Arguably the number of settlements has declined in recent years because there has been less litigation activity in the Indian water rights arena. Litigation pressure works on the parties who have the most to lose—the non-Indian users of Indian water. Litigation pressure also is a galvanizing force requiring the tribe and federal government to evaluate and prepare their claim and obtain technical information.

Q: Some settlements have been criticized as a Christmas tree of benefits for multiple parties. How much can you add to a settlement in order for it to be approved and work?

HAYES: The basic settlement concept needs to be kept simple. The lawyers and parties involved in one case often have difficulty seeing across the western landscape to see what has or has not worked in another drainage. Tribes and other parties often want to resolve land claim and tax issues, but at the end of the day, there need to be water settlements. This is an area where leadership from Congress and the administration can be helpful: reining in expectations.

Q: What things work or don't work in settlement processes?

HAYES: There are thousands of reasons that settlements can fail. The parties need to be committed to finding a solution. Too often, the parties think Interior has all the responsibility for finding a solution. In fact, settlements will not succeed without the personal commitment of the leadership within tribal and state governments and the water user community.

Q: What is the utility of a mediator or settlement judge?

HAYES: Mediators or settlement judges can play a helpful role, but scoping a potential mediator's role is important. A mediator can't solve the whole problem, and sometimes parties use a mediator as an excuse not to make progress. Mediation works best when the mediator's role is shaped to some extent by the progress already made by the parties. For example, in the Gila River Indian Community's settlement in Arizona, the parties agreed on a water budget and other key terms without the involvement of a mediator, but they called in a mediator to help with a discrete set of issues (in that case, water rights in the upper Gila River valley). The parties have to be serious about trying to reach an agreement for mediation to work.

Q: In your experience, where have mediators been used in Indian water settlement discussions?

HAYES: I'm aware of Judge [Michael] Nelson's role as a settlement judge in the Gila and Little Colorado River adjudications. Colorado governor Ray Romer and his lieutenant governor facilitated some sessions among the parties in the Animas–La Plata discussions. [Law professor] Francis McGovern has been working on the Nez Perce claims in the Snake River adjudication. Oregon has used mediation to help resolve long-standing water rights disputes as part of the Klamath adjudication.

Q: Why aren't third-party neutrals used more often in Indian water right settlement discussions?

HAYES: It is difficult to generalize why mediators are not used more frequently in water rights matters. Some lawyers may be reluctant to cede control of the process. Also, the federal government is sometimes concerned about bringing in third parties who might be seen as making decisions. Most of the time, the parties simply do not think about bringing in a third party because they are making some progress, and additional expense and uncertain benefits may be involved. From a personal perspective, I am more concerned about engaging high-level managers or officials in the settlement process. If you have the right people engaged, you don't need a mediator. The right federal officials have their hands on the tools and levers necessary to deliver money and services.

Q: Where are some of the future hot spots?

HAYES: It often takes a crisis to make a settlement. You need galvanizing events to make people realize they need to forge a solution. The recent difficulties in the Klamath basin in southern Oregon illustrate the point. Out of that crisis is likely to come some clarification of the fishing rights of the Klamath Tribe and several downstream tribes (including the Hoopa Nation). Likewise, the current drought in the Southwest may trigger renewed attention on water rights settlements, particularly in New Mexico.

Q: What is your assessment for the future of the settlement process generally?

HAYES: You can't *will* these settlements into happening. For some negotiations, their time may not have yet come. For these, it may take years of technical and political preparation.

Q: What has been your most important contribution to this process?

HAYES: I am proud of my work on the emerging settlement for the Gila River Indian Community in Arizona. In addition to resolving issues on the Gila River, it also addresses many disputes over the CAP. When done, it will be the largest water rights settlement in history. I also enjoyed helping to bring "home" settlements for the Warm Springs tribes in Oregon, the Rocky Boy Tribe in Montana, the Shivwits Paiute Tribe in Utah, the San Carlos Apaches, the San Luis Rey tribes, the Southern Ute and Ute Mountain Ute tribes, and many others. Helping tribes realize their water rights was extraordinarily rewarding work.

Q: Other observations?

HAYES: It takes lots of courage by lawyers, tribes, governors, and others to cut a water rights deal. Critics are around every corner. By definition, parties who agree to a settlement will never know how well they might have done if they had not settled. As a result, all parties need thoughtful, far-sighted leadership if they are to strike a settlement, and see it all the way through to execution, congressional authorization, and imple-mentation. For my money, however, settlements represent the most effective way for tribes to confirm their water rights and to obtain the programmatic benefits of developing those rights into meaningful wet water assets for future generations.

PART 3

Making Settlements

My advice for those participating in settlement processes:

- Respect all parties involved.
- Obtain public buy-in.
- Work hard to promote federal partnership.
- Be patient.

Susan Cottingham, program manager, Montana
Reserved Water Rights Compact Commission

PHOTO 6.1 Windmill, symbol of water in the West. Photo: University of Arizona Agricultural Communications

CHAPTER 6

Settlement Processes

If the pie is going to be carved up, it's better that we do it ourselves than let the court do it for us.

John Bushman, former special assistant to the assistant secretary for Indian Affairs

Resolving water rights disputes through negotiated settlements is generally lengthy and complex. Negotiations can take several years and in some cases a decade or longer. Some settlements unfold systematically, but many proceed by fits-and-starts, accentuated by changes in leadership, episodes of litigation, one or more attempts to secure congressional authorization and funding, disagreements after congressional approval has been gained, and ongoing efforts to ensure that the terms of the settlement are implemented. In lengthy negotiations, the process is handed down like an inheritance from one generation of representatives to another. Along the way, the political, legal, economic, and environmental context has changed. By the time the settlement has been secured, the cast of negotiators may be very different from the ones who began the process years before; and the goals and methods of the settlement may have changed as well.

Each agreement has a unique evolution, but the settlement process typically involves specific key stages, although they may not always occur in the same order. These stages are discussed in this chapter.

Preparing for Negotiations

A strong incentive to settle is a prerequisite for good faith negotiations. Serious negotiation efforts generally have been motivated by litigation or an impending administrative decision that threatens the parties' access to water or federal resources. Concerns about water availability, costs, and uncertainties can prompt local water users and tribes to craft their own water allocation agreement, rather than to have one dictated to them by the courts.

The timetable for reaching a settlement is of particular concern when there are pressing needs for certainty or immediate threats to the resource itself. In the Truckee-Carson–Pyramid Lake settlement, for ex-

ample, the rapid decline of endangered fish populations made the negotiating timetable of prime importance. As one tribal leader put it, "If we wait too long, there won't be a resource left to negotiate."

Who Comes to the Table?

Deal in all the right stakeholders or you won't get a solution. Any one stakeholder can kill a deal. Federal involvement is only productive when all appropriate federal agencies are involved in the proceedings.

David Hayes, former deputy secretary of the Interior

Often the first step in negotiations involves identifying which parties will be represented in the settlement process. (See sidebar 6.1 for tips on initiating and negotiating a settlement.) Although it is important to include all the major parties, too large a group may prove unwieldy. One experienced negotiator recommends including only the most important parties and only those with the authority to bind legally those whom they represent. Others suggest a more inclusive process, noting that a settlement will endure only to the extent that affected parties have meaningful participation in the process. For example, in instances where settlements must be approved by a court, parties that have been excluded from the negotiation process may object to the proposed settlement when it comes before the court. Negotiations also may need to involve tribal allottees in the process and clearly identify who will represent them. In the water settlement involving reserved rights of the San Xavier and Schuk Toak districts of the Tohono O'odham Nation, for example, the allottees were not effectively included in the negotiating process and have objected to filing the dismissal of their claims, leaving the entire settlement in question. In contrast, the Fort Hall settlement process was open to anyone with an opinion on the issues.

The question of who should be involved becomes even more difficult in the case of groups or agencies that do not have water rights but, nevertheless, have an interest in the water source. These interests may include persons who receive water under contract from

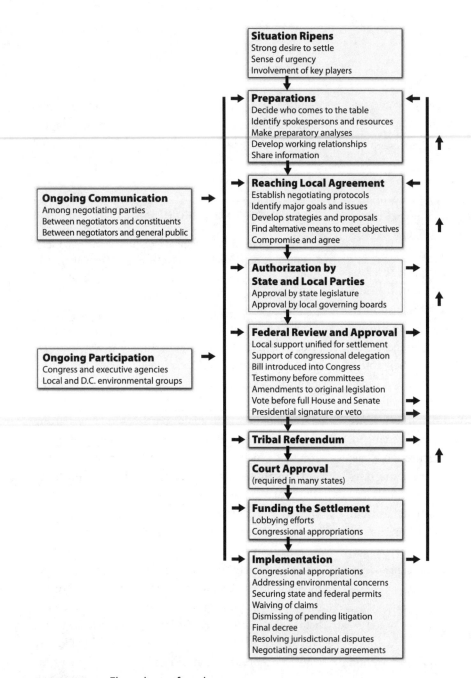

Situation Ripens
Strong desire to settle
Sense of urgency
Involvement of key players

Preparations
Decide who comes to the table
Identify spokespersons and resources
Make preparatory analyses
Develop working relationships
Share information

Ongoing Communication
Among negotiating parties
Between negotiators and constituents
Between negotiators and general public

Reaching Local Agreement
Establish negotiating protocols
Identify major goals and issues
Develop strategies and proposals
Find alternative means to meet objectives
Compromise and agree

Authorization by State and Local Parties
Approval by state legislature
Approval by local governing boards

Ongoing Participation
Congress and executive agencies
Local and D.C. environmental groups

Federal Review and Approval
Local support unified for settlement
Support of congressional delegation
Bill introduced into Congress
Testimony before committees
Amendments to original legislation
Vote before full House and Senate
Presidential signature or veto

Tribal Referendum

Court Approval
(required in many states)

Funding the Settlement
Lobbying efforts
Congressional appropriations

Implementation
Congressional appropriations
Addressing environmental concerns
Securing state and federal permits
Waiving of claims
Dismissing of pending litigation
Final decree
Resolving jurisdictional disputes
Negotiating secondary agreements

FIGURE 6.1   Flow chart of settlement process

other water rights holders, groups that use water as a recreational resource, agencies that have responsibility for fish and other aquatic species, environmental organizations, and water quality agencies. In some cases, these groups neither have the interest nor the resources to participate actively in the negotiations. They want only to know of major developments and to have an opportunity to be heard on the issues that concern them. The concerns of other interests, such as

those of fish and wildlife agencies, can be addressed in consultation processes that run parallel to the main negotiations.

Identifying Spokespersons and Resources

Once the various parties are identified, they select those who will speak for them in negotiations and in court and define their objectives in asserting and pro-

SIDEBAR 6.1
Experienced Negotiators' Tips for the Settlement Process

Who Comes to the Table?

- Ideally, include everyone and everything in the settlement process.
- Include people who can make or break a deal.
- Don't underestimate the ability of any group, albeit minor, to scuttle the process.
- Include people who will be there from beginning to end.

Building Good Working Relationships

- Reconciliation and relationship building are the keys. Settlements are not one-time events. They have consequences for generations.

- Establish good working relations with everyone, especially when you disagree.
- Recognize that each individual has equal dignity.
- Explore the other side's thinking. Assume that you need to learn more.
- If representing tribal interests, invite the other parties to attend tribal social functions to become acquainted with reservation communities and resources.
- Get the technical staff (ditch masters, biologists, and soil scientists) working together on practical problems. Build trust and good communication on the ground.
- The parties each must have sound technical expertise so that they can negotiate based on information that has been confirmed by their own experts.
- Appoint tribal representatives to state boards and commissions. Ask non-Indians to serve on appropriate tribal committees (e.g., state judges are often invited to serve on tribal courts). Get familiar with each other's governance systems.

tecting their water rights. Another essential first step is to identify available financial resources and in-house expertise to help with what likely will be a lengthy and expensive process.

Many considerations go into deciding who should be actively involved in negotiations. Political leaders are especially adept at expressing the interests of their constituents and making things happen but have many other demands on their time. Technical specialists are necessary to help develop and evaluate alternatives. Lawyers help the parties understand the legal context in which the negotiations occur, evaluating the benefits of a proposed settlement against the risks of litigation, and drafting the many necessary documents.

Most parties form a multimember negotiating team that builds in all these roles: political officials for leadership, senior employees for continuity, and technical specialists. The team leader must have strong organizational skills. The lead negotiator, who may be different from the team leader, must have excellent communication skills—both as a listener and as a speaker.

Role of the State Administration

Depending on the state, the governor may have a formal institutional role, an informal leadership role, or an ancillary role in Indian water rights settlement processes. In states like Oregon, Indian water rights settlements have been a priority of the Department of Water Resources director, with more general support from the governor. In Montana, the governor makes a number of the appointments to the Reserved Water Rights Compact Commission but is sometimes called upon the engage in high-level, sovereign-to-sovereign discussions with tribal officials. In other settings, negotiations have gone on so long that they are part of the daily operations of the state and are handled by the state engineer or legal and technical experts. In some states, the settlements develop locally, with less visible involvement by the governor. Whenever a settlement requires state money, however, the governor and his or her budget staff will have a say.

As an influential regional organization, the Western Governors' Association (WGA) has been a leader in Indian water rights settlement issues for over two decades. WGA's recommendations have influenced how the Department of the Interior and Congress view this issue.

Federal Participation and Support

The federal government becomes involved in a variety of ways. If litigation such as a general stream adjudication is already pending, Department of Justice attorneys may already be involved. When settlement discussions begin, these attorneys may defer to Department of the Interior officials. The Interior has taken the lead in establishing federal negotiating guidelines and interagency federal teams to set settlement priorities and marshal and assign scarce resources. In the late 1980s and early 1990s, this coordinating role was undertaken by a working group of the various assistant secretaries for Indian Affairs, Water and Science, and Policy Management and Budget; and heads of the agencies of the BIA, Bureau of Reclamation, FWS, the National Park Service, and sometimes the Office of Surface Mining. Getting all these people together was difficult. In recent years, such coordination has been under the leadership of a senior Interior official.

There are also federal parties not in the working group that have significant interests. These include the Department of Justice, which is concerned with whether the litigation risks are appropriate for the proposed federal expenditure, and the OMB, which might argue that the litigation risk is not high enough to mandate expenditures.

The federal negotiating guidelines, adopted in 1990 by Interior, were created to guide federal participants. They establish criteria for evaluating proposed settlements of Indian water claims and procedures for federal participation in negotiations. The guidelines set forth a standard method of measuring the costs and benefits of settlements by establishing the following criteria:

- Total federal cost of a settlement should not exceed the value of existing claims against the United States.
- Federal contributions should not exceed the sum of federal legal exposure (the cost of litigation and judgment obligations if the court were to find the

federal government liable) and additional costs related to federal trust responsibilities.
- Nonfederal cost share should be proportional to benefits received by nonfederal parties.
- Settlement should resolve all outstanding water claims and achieve finality.
- Settlement should promote economic efficiency on reservations and tribal self-sufficiency.
- Settlement should foster long-term harmony and cooperation among all parties through respect for the sovereignty of the states and tribes in their respective jurisdictions.

The criteria emphasize that litigation risk is the way to determine necessary federal expenditures. A criticism of this approach is that a successful settlement addresses far more than litigation risk, for example, sound management of the ecosystem and collaboration to produce a meaningful water resource plan.

If Interior decides that the federal government should take part in a negotiated settlement, the guidelines require that a federal negotiating team be appointed to coordinate the participation of the various federal parties. All communications with other negotiating parties are to be made through the team chair. Negotiating teams consist of key federal players and typically include representatives of the BIA, the Department of the Interior Solicitor's Office, the Department of Justice, the Bureau of Reclamation, and the FWS. Other federal parties may participate, depending on the particular issues raised by a settlement. Twenty federal negotiation teams and one assessment team were active in 2002. Table 6.1 lists current active federal assessment, negotiation, and implementation teams. The presence of teams for the early (assessment), middle (negotiation), and post-settlement (implementation) stages illustrates the recognition that settlements are lengthy undertakings progressing over many phases.

The guidelines also outline the procedures that federal participants are to follow to coordinate among Interior, Justice, and the OMB. Procedures include a fact-finding period, during which background information is compiled, settlement options are evaluated, and recommendations are made for settling claims. The settlement options are to be assessed based primarily on economic factors. The federal negotiating team presents Interior, Justice, and the OMB with a written summary of this information, and any negotiating position is to be approved by the secretary of the Interior, with input from the OMB and Justice, before it is presented to nonfederal parties. If disagreement occurs between the secretary and the OMB, the issue should be resolved prior to being made public. The guidelines then call for negotiations to proceed with periodic updates to Interior and the OMB. Federal negotiating teams also may provide briefings to the congressional delegations and committees.

Some parties perceive the settlement guidelines as inflexible and unduly narrow, in terms of both the procedures to be followed by federal participants and the criteria used to establish negotiating positions and evaluate proposed settlements. In addition, most parties want the OMB's participation to be better integrated to reduce last-minute opposition to settlement packages before Congress.

These guidelines apply only to federal agencies and not to tribes, the Congress, or local and state interests. They are intended, however, to put settlement parties on notice about how the federal teams will conduct themselves and what types of criteria the administration will use in evaluating settlements.

Over in Congress, local settlement proponents typically enlist the support of their senators and representatives and congressional staff. These members initiate communications with relevant federal departments and agencies to identify potential issues of concern.

Public Participation in Mediation and Negotiations

> The lengthy Little Colorado River negotiations have been made more difficult because the public on reservations and off reservations don't understand how settlements work. It is hard to devote time and resources to public involvement.
>
> Susan Williams, attorney representing Indian tribes

The negotiators will sooner or later have to review the fruits of their efforts in the public spotlight. Indian water rights negotiations have been characterized by two distinct approaches to public participation in settlement discussions. In most negotiations, there is less public participation than in other pub-

lic policy settings, such as the preparation of environmental impact statements under the National Environmental Policy Act (NEPA) or similar state statutes.[1] Some of Indian water rights discussions remind one of the closed-door approaches that characterized water policy decisions in the past, with several notable exceptions. For one, the tribes are now inside the door. For another, the usual group of participants represents a large array of state, local, specific district, federal, tribal, and water user interests. Many would say that public members are fortunate they don't have to spend years on such complex and tedious work.

One example of significant public involvement in tribal water settlement negotiations is in Montana. Because of its constitutional sunlight provisions, Montana's compact commission has taken a distinctively different approach to public access to these discussions. The negotiations are structured as government-to-government talks, so noncommission members are not formally involved in the talks. Yet, the negotiation sessions are open, and the public has frequent opportunities to comment. Between meetings, commission members and staff meet with members of the public and interested organizations about issues that are in discussion. This openness does deter the discussion of sensitive issues that should be addressed among the tribe, federal government, and state. The participants have found ways around this problem, however, such as raising these issues in technical meetings or through staff contacts.

Sometimes agreements cannot be reached if they must be negotiated in public. Sometimes good public policy cannot be developed in private. The challenge is to move these discussions more into the public's view while still preserving the occasional need for confidential communications on critical issues.

Coordinating Litigation with Negotiations

In addition to their importance to tribes and water users, settlement efforts are significant to courts since successful agreements can resolve large parts of a pending general stream adjudication or other complex water law case. Courts, however, are faced with the dilemma of moving litigation forward while encour-

TABLE 6.1   Federal assessment, negotiation, and implementation teams (June 2002)

Assessment	Negotiation	Implementation
Tohono O'odham, Arizona (lower Colorado region)	Aamodt (pueblos of Nambé, Pojoaque Valley, San Ildefonso, Tesuque), New Mexico (upper Colorado region)	Fallon, Nevada (Mid-Pacific region)
		Fort Hall, Idaho (Pacific Northwest region)
		Fort McDowell, Arizona (lower Colorado region)
	Abousleman (pueblos of Jemez, Zia, Santa Ana), New Mexico (upper Colorado region)	Jicarilla Apaches, New Mexico (upper Colorado region)
	Blackfeet, Montana (Great Plains region)	Las Vegas Paiutes, Nevada (lower Colorado region)
	Crow, Montana (Great Plains region)	
	Duck Valley, Idaho and Nevada (Pacific Northwest region)	Northern Cheyenne, Montana (Great Plains region)
	Flathead, Montana (Pacific Northwest region)	Pyramid Lake, Nevada (Mid-Pacific region)
	Fort Belknap, Montana (Great Plains region)	Rocky Boys, Montana (Great Plains region)
	Gila River Indian Community, Arizona (lower Colorado region)	San Carlos Apaches, Arizona (lower Colorado region)
	Kerr McGee (pueblos of Acoma and Laguna), New Mexico (upper Colorado region)	San Luis Rey, California (lower Colorado region)
	Klamath, Oregon (Mid-Pacific region)	Shivwits Paiute, Utah (lower Colorado region)
	Little Colorado (Navajos, Hopis, San Juan Southern Paiutes, Zuni Pueblo), Arizona and New Mexico (lower Colorado region)	Southern Arizona Water Rights Settlement Act, Arizona (lower Colorado Region)
	Lummi Nation, Washington (Pacific Northwest region)	Southern Utes and Ute Mountain Utes, (Colorado Ute Indian Truckee-Carson tribes), Colorado (upper Colorado region)
	Navajo-San Juan, New Mexico (Upper Colorado Region)	Uintah and Ouray Utes, Utah (upper Colorado region)
	Nez Perce, Idaho (Pacific Northwest region)	Warm Springs, Oregon (Pacific Northwest region)
	Zuni Ramah Navajo Pueblo, New Mexico (lower Colorado region)	Wind River, Wyoming (Great Plains region)
	Soboba, California (lower Colorado region)	Yavapai-Prescott, Arizona (lower Colorado region)
	Taos, New Mexico (upper Colorado region)	
	Tule River, California (Mid-Pacific Region)	
	Upper Gila, Arizona (lower Colorado region)	
	Walker River, Nevada (Mid-Pacific region)	

Source: U.S. Bureau of Reclamation

aging and allowing sufficient opportunities for settlement to occur. If a court too aggressively pushes a case toward trial, the parties may not have the time or inclination to talk settlement. The emphasis is on legal positions—not underlying cultural, social, and economic interests. If a court is too hands off concerning negotiations, other priorities frequently take over, and the negotiators may lack the necessary pressure or incentives to reach agreement. Even when a court pursues a balanced emphasis on litigation and settlement, the results may be that the parties incur double technical costs and attorney fees.

Many of the factors that promote settlement are beyond a court's ability or propriety to influence. The best a court can do is to have a well announced plan about how settlement efforts may proceed within the context of pending litigation and, at the appropriate time, apply lots of pressure on the parties. Thus, a court should consider such steps as

- setting an overall litigation and negotiation schedule
- if the parties have not used a mediator, requiring the parties to establish criteria for determining when a third person should be brought in
- appointing a neutral, such as a settlement judge or mediator, at the appropriate time or ensuring the parties arrive at a choice themselves
- requiring regular reports to the court (not on the merits but of the efforts being made)
- identifying and promptly litigating specific issues that may resolve roadblocks in the discussions
- applying constant, credible pressure of litigation

Ultimately, the court needs to be constant and firm in these situations. The court's role is to resolve disputes that cannot be resolved otherwise. A court's decision may be less optimal than a settlement, but it is a decision.

Developing Information and Positions

Tribes, states, cities, irrigators, and other parties generally conduct detailed technical, legal, economic, and political analyses to establish their position regarding the strength and magnitude of their claims relative to other parties. This preparation, which typically involves hiring attorneys, engineers, and other experts, can be costly. Careful compilation and assessment of information is essential to developing viable strategies and positions for negotiations and a defensible case for litigation. If involved early in the negotiations, the federal government can make available substantial legal and technical resources to the tribe and other parties. Federal efforts, however, are prioritized nationally, and the current budget may not include money for a particular negotiation. The tribe and other parties may need to lobby federal officials to move their case higher in the priorities.

Information Gathering

Indian water rights negotiations tend to be information and data intensive. The negotiators need information on hydrology, soils, environmental conditions, and population. They need engineering, cost, and feasibility data for storage projects, irrigation projects, and environmental restoration projects. They require economic data concerning the regional economy, the benefit-cost ratio of storage or irrigation projects, and, if off-reservation leasing is anticipated, the regional value of water in different uses. As an example, in preparing for negotiations, the staff of the Montana Reserved Water Rights Compact Commission prepares an in-house assessment of the land and water resources of the particular reservation in order to reach an early understanding of the magnitude of the reserved water rights claims.

The parties often face an enormous and costly task of gathering existing information and developing information that does not exist. The parties themselves may have some of this information. In other cases, consultants may need to be hired. Occasionally, the negotiating parties create technical committees to cooperate in gathering the needed information.

Information Sharing and Confidentiality

During these early stages, the parties attempt to decide on confidentiality limits and the extent of information sharing. Although concerns about potential litigation may make the parties reluctant to share some information, mutual access to the best technical data avail-

SIDEBAR 6.2
Freedom of Information Act

> Freedom of Information requests can be very disruptive. There is great hesitation now to communicate on legal theories, data, case preparation and analysis of a case's strengths and weaknesses.
>
> Pam Williams, Office of the Solicitor, Department of the Interior

Congress passed the Freedom of Information Act (FOIA)[1] in 1966, after a decade of campaigning for increased media access to government records, incited by the U.S. government's denial of information resulting from nuclear bomb tests in the South Pacific. FOIA procedures allow the general public to obtain records from federal agencies with the policy of government openness and accountability in the pursuit of the democratic ideal. FOIA procedures direct government agencies to disclose certain records and describe the manner in which disclosure must occur.

There are limits to what a FOIA request must yield. First, FOIA applies only to federal agencies. Second, parties subject to the requirements of FOIA are only the agencies, offices, and departments of the executive branch, not municipal corporations, Congress, or the courts. Third, the information requested by FOIA must be a "record." A record may be written material or other "information-bearing" material (such as photographs). Further, an agency is required to disclose such a record under a FOIA request if the record already exists and the agency has both posses-

sion and control over the record at the time of the request. Thus, an agency is not required to prepare a record in response to a request. Finally, the contents of the requested record must not fall within one of the nine FOIA exemptions that allow federal agencies to withhold disclosure of material exempted from the public. Most FOIA litigation concerns the scope of the nine exemptions, which include factors such as law enforcement investigations and national security.

FOIA became a litigated topic in the Klamath adjudication when a local water users association petitioned under FOIA for the release of documents submitted to the Department of the Interior and the BIA by the Klamath Tribe in preparation for the adjudication.[2] The governmental entities objected to the release of the documents based on one of the exemptions to FOIA disclosure that protects interagency or intra-agency memorandums or letters that would not be available by law to a party other than an agency in litigation with the agency. Courts have held this exemption to mean inter- or intra-agency documents that would not be available via civil discovery mechanisms to an adverse party in litigation with the governmental agency are exempt from FOIA. In the Klamath case, the court said that the tribal communication to the BIA and Interior was not inter- or intra-agency memoranda and was not protected by the particular FOIA exemption asserted. The ramifications of FOIA on future settlements is uncertain, and sensitive information between tribes and their governmental trustees may be subject to further FOIA requests.

able helps to inform the negotiation process. To this end, the parties should analyze existing data and decide whether they are useful.

Confidentiality issues appear in two ways in negotiations. First, each party must identify documents that must be closely held by its negotiating team. Private parties will have more leeway to keep information in confidence than do public agencies that may be subject to public records requests. For example, a recent U.S. Supreme Court decision, *Department of the*

Interior v. Klamath Water Users Protective Association,[2] held that certain documents provided by the tribe to the Department of the Interior during the course of litigation over water in the Klamath River basin were not exempt from release under the federal Freedom of Information Act, or FOIA. (See sidebar 6.2 for a summary of FOIA). Second, the parties may provide information to one another that they do not want disseminated any further. In these cases, the negotiators need a memorandum of understanding about how this confidential information will be exchanged and protected (see "Establishing Protocols" later in this chapter).

Reaching Agreement

> The tribe has established true "partnership" relations with the State of Montana. The collaborative process benefited all those involved by enabling continuity of scientific and legal expertise. Without shared access to appropriate and consistent scientific and legal expertise, collaborative efforts would have faltered.
>
> Jim Morsette, water resources director, Chippewa Cree Tribe of Rocky Boy's

Local commitment to the settlement agreement must be enduring to overcome the many hurdles it is certain to face in Washington, D.C. In order for local parties to have long-standing and unified commitment, both the process and the final outcome of settlement negotiations must be satisfactory to participants.

Development of Working Relationships

During the preparatory stages, working relationships evolve among the various parties as they gather factual information about regional water resources and attempt to reach agreement about technical definitions and assumptions. The tone set among the parties early on may be adversarial or cooperative and can critically influence the course of settlement efforts. Ideally, the early stages of negotiations provide a time for building trust and discovering each others' histories, positions, and needs. These negotiations are especially difficult because they involve different cultures. (Sidebar 6.3 provides thoughtful suggestions for working with tribes.)

Establishing Protocols

Negotiating parties must decide on the protocols to be followed during the settlement process. These may involve issues such as voting procedures, breaks for caucusing, setting and meeting deadlines, information exchange, and talking to the press. The parties may choose to retain a neutral facilitator to mediate the

negotiating sessions. In any case, it is important to clearly define the role of each party and its appropriate level of participation.

Identifying Major Goals and Issues

Once the negotiating protocols have been defined, the parties identify the major goals to be accomplished through the settlement. Equally important is deciding which issues will be addressed in the process and which will not. The parties then assess the various issues to identify which can be readily agreed upon and which will be more difficult. Often, negotiators choose to address the easier issues first, providing the opportunity to build trust among the parties. In addition, this provides momentum, increasing the likelihood of successfully resolving more difficult issues later. Reaching a settlement agreement may require leaving some ultimate jurisdictional and sovereignty issues to be resolved in another forum.

Developing and Exchanging Proposals

Knowing what the likely outcome would be in court is essential in formulating negotiating strategies and settlement proposals. Generally there is more room for candor in settlement negotiations than in litigation, making it possible to start closer to each party's bottom line. Reaching an agreement may entail a commitment to protect existing water uses; otherwise, the settlement may never enjoy the local support needed for congressional approval. Throughout the settlement process, negotiators should have continuous contact with the groups they represent to explore concerns and get recommendations and authorization for new approaches.

In reaching an agreement, creativity is essential to find the water supplies, capital, and other resources needed to satisfy tribal entitlements. A successful settlement identifies the specific means for accomplishing its major goals. The Truckee-Carson–Pyramid Lake settlement, for instance, included a water rights acquisition program to ensure that the wet water promised under the settlement would be available to the tribes. Although exploring alternative means to meet the key objectives is essential, the parties still may have

SIDEBAR 6.3
Thoughts on Working with Tribes

Lucy Moore

I hesitate to issue a set of recommendations about how to interact with tribal entities in collaborative or negotiation settings. On one hand, these representatives need and deserve the same respect and accommodation accorded to any participant. Many tribes would say, "Give us the same respect you afford others, and we will be better off than we are now." Certainly, there are non-Indian participants who would agree that tribes should have equal treatment and nothing more. On the other hand, history and culture have combined to create challenges in tribal-nontribal interactions, which I believe deserve special attention. Thanks to the patience and good humor of many American Indians with whom I have worked, I have gained some insights that I think are useful to anyone—Indian or non-Indian—who is considering negotiations or collaborative efforts that cross jurisdictional and cultural lines.

- Visit the tribal community, government, or representatives as early as possible in the process, preferably before the process has begun. Find out what it will take for a tribe to participate comfortably and organize your process accordingly. This may require certain times and places for meetings, separate funds for technical expertise, or certain written acknowledgments of tribal sovereignty or other concerns essential to the tribe.
- Approach the tribe with genuine respect and without prejudging the result of the visit. Each tribe is different, so each encounter will be different. Make no assumptions about one community based on your relationship with another.
- Understand that tribal governments may have different operating principles and structures than local or state governments, or federal agencies. You will need to understand the nature of the government, and its accountability to its members, in order to work together successfully. Understand the stress on modern tribal leaders. They are pulled in many directions at once. Listen very carefully to what is said. As with any

exchange, the message may be clear, or it may not. If you are confused or don't understand, say so. Make sure you leave with an understanding of what the tribe needs, and that they understand what you need. Depending on those needs, you may want to discuss ways to adjust the working relationship or make changes in the process that will accommodate tribal needs.
- Be prepared to make—and admit—mistakes. The relationship is inevitably difficult. There may be a painful history that is still alive for many. There may be cultural differences and conflicting views of the world. There may be decision-making processes on both sides that appear illogical to the other and result in frustration. All this means that it is easy to make errors, to offend, or to confuse. Don't overreact to the mistake of another, or to your own mistake. Name it, learn from it, ask how to do better, and move on. If you are willing to learn from your mistakes, chances are you will be readily forgiven.
- Be patient, and hope for patience from the other side!

Why Are Tribes Reluctant to Participate?

Any party that considers participating in a collaborative or negotiation process should be wary. Potential participants should carefully scrutinize the process's origins, ground rules, and goals. For tribes, there are additional reasons for caution.

The Risk of Compromising Power

A tribe's closely guarded sovereignty may be jeopardized if they agree to take a seat at a table created by a lesser authority, particularly if they have had no role in the development of that process. Tribal entities are reluctant to participate officially (or even unofficially) in a process that is created or sanctioned by the state or other governmental entity that has no authority over the tribe, particularly if the other jurisdiction offers no understanding of tribal sovereignty. The offense can be compounded by the assumption on the part of non-Indian organizers that the tribe can be treated as another interest group or subset of the public.

A Painful History and Cultural Sensitivity

Besides their status as sovereigns, most tribes have a history of broken promises and treaties with the United States. It is inevitable that these experiences, even if all participants in those events are long gone, will affect the incentive of the tribal community to participate and their response to an invitation to collaborate or negotiate.

In addition, a tribal community may view natural resources differently from other participants. Land, water, rocks, plants, and wildlife may have cultural or religious significance that is not apparent to an outsider. It is also possible that tribal members may not be free to identify or discuss this significance in the interest of protecting the resource and the cultural knowledge surrounding it.

Concerns about Consensus

Tribal representatives are understandably concerned that they may find themselves subject to an agreement that compromises sovereignty or is contrary to tribal interests. The concept of consensus can be problematic for a tribe. Often, invitations to participate do not address what is meant by consensus, how the process will work, and what the result will be if it fails. I find that tribes have felt betrayed—and rightfully so—by processes that were advertised as "consensus-based" but that turned out to be "majority rules."

A true consensus process allows any single voice to prevent consensus and therefore be reckoned with by the group. This provides equal power to all participants. A representative of a minority view need not fear being out-voted by the majority on the other side. If, however, the consensus process devolves into a voting process, in order to save time or to resolve stalemates, that minority view may be disregarded. The group can choose to present its decision, recommendations, or product as consensus, implying that all participants are supportive. For a tribe, this scenario is troubling. The implication is that the tribe supports the outcome because they participated in the consensus-building process.

Suggestions for Workable Interjurisdictional Processes

Involve the tribal community or government as early as possible in the planning for the negotiation or collaborative process. Clarify (and negotiate, if necessary) the purpose, the participants, and the expected outcome. Find out about preferred dates, times, and places. Adjust the process to accommodate tribal needs.

All participants must agree (and negotiate, if necessary) on the decision-making process of the group. How a group handles a failure to reach consensus must be part of these agreements before negotiations over water issues begin. At the earliest possible moment, raise the following issues with all participants:

- authority of the group
- purpose of the group
- roles within the group (Who is convening, who is staffing, who is spokesperson, who is recording, who is facilitating, and related matters.)
- decision-making processes (Consensus? Voting? Other? How will deadlocks be broken?)
- outcome, product (How will the settlement be presented? To whom? By whom? If there are minority views, how will they be represented?)

Informal Participation

There are a number of reasons why tribal governments may choose not to join formally with non-Indian entities in a collaborative process. In these cases, it is important for others to respect that choice and, if possible, remain open to tribal participation at a later time.

Before giving up on tribal participation, make every effort to adjust the process to accommodate tribal needs. If tribal representatives cannot join as an official party, the group must weigh what is more important—having each participant be a formal member of the process, or the presence of the tribal voice. I have seen some creative solutions that have enabled tribal participation without tribal membership in the process.

In an effort to plan for future water supplies, a region in New Mexico created a water-planning process led by a regional council. The expectation was that the council would include representatives of government and key interests in the region—agriculture, business, environment, recreation, public interests, and others. The tribal government within the region, with significant jurisdiction over land and water resources, declined to sign the memorandum of understanding to join the council. They did so for many of the reasons described above, and to avoid revealing information about water resources that might be used against the tribe in a future adjudication. The council set aside the issue of membership and the memorandum, which in the beginning had seemed essential, and invited the tribe to attend council meetings and participate as they felt comfortable.

Over a two-year period, tribal representatives attended meetings, reviewed all documents, offered perspectives and advice, took information back to the tribe, and in general kept in touch with the planning process. Each time a tribal representative spoke, he first reminded the group of the importance of sovereignty and of the fact that his tribe was not a member of the council. Each time, the council expressed appreciation for the presence and the contribution of the tribal voice. The council helped the tribe secure a planning grant to support water

planning within the tribe with no strings attached. The council's hope was that eventually the two parallel planning efforts would merge, or at least inform each other, but it was understood that the tribe had complete authority over those funds and their processes. There may be some future merger of plans or there may not. The important thing is that there is communication and some exchange of information and a mutual respect for choices made.

With the regional water plan nearing completion, everyone agreed that one of the most valuable products of the planning process was the open working relationship between the tribe and the council. The participants are concerned that relations will not remain as smooth when difficult choices have to be made about quantities, uses, and management of the water resources. When the tough times do come, participants hope there will be a degree of trust that will see them through.

In closing, I want to emphasize that (as with any unfamiliar group) the best way to understand tribal concerns, values, and needs is to speak with, listen to, and learn directly from tribal representatives themselves. I urge you to take every opportunity for that kind of learning.

---

to compromise on how completely their goals are satisfied.

Federal Review and Approval

> Be aware, not in awe, of D.C. and the settlement process. Be tough, confident, and prepared.
>
> Patricia Nelson, former chair, Pala Band of Luiseño Indians

Proposed Indian water settlements must undergo a complex series of federal review and approval procedures. When the local parties, with the support and participation of the federal negotiators, arrive at an acceptable agreement, they typically work together to obtain congressional approval for the settlement. Broad-based support for the agreement and a united effort among the parties is necessary to shepherd the settlement package through the federal maze (see sidebar 6.4).

The various interest groups engaged in the water settlement process frequently engage the services of professional lobbyists to help represent their particular concerns with federal and state policy makers. State governments typically retain lobbyists to assist in articulating state interests in Washington, D.C., and similarly with tribal governments, large municipalities, water districts, and environmental nongovernmental organizations (NGOs). Casinos and energy-development revenues have increasingly provided tribal governments with the financial resources to hire lobbyists to promote their interest in water matters.

Once a local settlement agreement is drafted into legislation, the proposed bill usually is introduced to Congress by the state's congressional delegation. The views of the delegation often fade into the background as the legislation is referred into the principal congressional committees with jurisdiction over Indian water settlements. These committees include the Senate Select Committee on Indian Affairs, the Senate Energy and Natural Resources Committee, and the House Committee on Natural Resources (formerly the Interior and Insular Affairs Committee). Other congressional committees may be involved as well, depending on the nature of the issues raised by a particular settlement. The committees then hold hearings on the bill, at which time local proponents of the settlement, as well as parties with concerns about the proposed bill, may testify.

Working with the congressional committees and their staff before going to Washington will help the committees become familiar with the details of a settlement prior to its introduction to Congress. This preparation is invaluable when there is an urgent need to move a bill through Congress. This might occur, for example, if local parties reach a settlement agreement near the end of the congressional session with insufficient time for the bill to move through the proper committees. Some suggest enlisting the services of an experienced lobbyist based in Washington, D.C., who is well versed in the congressional process.

Meanwhile, the OMB, Interior, Justice, and the USDA develop their positions on the proposed legislation in order to make formal recommendations. The secretary of the Interior then presents the administration's views to the congressional committees. Frequently, congressional committees hear testimony before the executive agencies have time to make formal recommendations, and instead, the agencies must testify directly before the committees. Some experienced settlement participants recommend involving federal agencies early in the negotiation process to avoid surprises and disappointments before the Congress. Others suggest bringing them in only when absolutely necessary, finding the federal bureaucracy a hindrance to the settlement process.

Congressional committees typically amend settlement bills based on testimony presented at hearings. This usually results in different versions of the original legislation moving through the House and Senate. Ideally, if enacted by either or both chambers, staff members from the House and Senate or a conference committee work together to reconcile differences before returning the bill to the full House and Senate for final approval. Rarely does the process work so smoothly, however, especially as rules are suspended toward the end of the congressional session, when the most controversial bills, including Indian water settlements, usually are enacted.

Members of Congress have a host of issues that are important to them and their constituents, and they tend to evaluate Indian water settlements in the context of these priorities. Congress is also aware that the Supreme Court regularly refers to congressional documents and deliberations to interpret congressional intent when making important decisions, and so Congress is concerned with setting controversial precedents. This means that congressional concerns about a proposed settlement go far beyond the particular bill under consideration. Settlement proponents may experience frustration in dealing with the Congress, feeling that their specific needs get lost in the bigger picture.

If the bill passes the House and Senate, it is sent to the president and is either signed into law or vetoed. If the proposed legislation fails to win congressional approval, or if it is later vetoed by the president, the settlement parties must renew their efforts and devise alternate strategies. If Congress changes substantive features of the proposed legislation, parties to the settlement may have to renegotiate some issues.

Funding Settlements

One of the major challenges in satisfying Indian water entitlements is securing the funds to implement settlement agreements. Although the United States generally recognizes its responsibility to help resolve these disputes, federal budget constraints raise concerns that congressional funding for settlements will not be forthcoming. Part of the difficulty is that settlements in the 1980s were more numerous and costly than expected. Due to the ad hoc nature of the settlement-funding process, Congress never knows for sure how many new settlements to anticipate. This makes it nearly impossible to predict the cumulative costs to the federal government to satisfy Indian water entitlements. By late 1992, the federal government had spent over $600 million on Indian water settlements, and the settlements under negotiation at that time were anticipated to cost even more.[3]

Although the United States paid the entire cost of the early Ak-Chin settlement, the federal government

SIDEBAR 6.4

Experienced Negotiators' Tips for Moving a Bill through the Federal Maze

- Have a champion in Washington, D.C., who will go to bat for the settlement over and over again.
- Do your consensus–building homework at home. A small group of disenfranchised people can create big problems in Washington.
- Involve congressional members and committee staff, the local congressional delegation, and relevant executive agencies early on.
- Communicate regularly with the OMB and any other federal agencies likely to have jurisdiction over the settlement package to address their concerns and avoid last-minute confrontations.
- Identify one person from the staff of each congressional committee through whom to funnel all settlement-related information.
- Work with the environmental community early on, so that major controversies can be resolved prior to congressional consideration.
- Invite congressional delegates and staff to tour the reservation and nearby communities. Allow them to become personally acquainted with the people and resources at stake.
- Avoid controversies, present complete solutions, and strive for unified local support. In general, Congress is more receptive to settlement packages that have these characteristics.
- Agree in advance that all parties must approve any modifications of the settlement to avoid the divide-and-conquer pitfalls often encountered in Washington.
- Be vigilant. Keep the pressure on through phone calls and visits. Otherwise, you may simply be forgotten.

has insisted on contributions from local parties to all later settlements, with the exception of the Northern Ute settlement, passed in 1992.[4] The original Southern Arizona Water Rights Settlement Act (SAWRSA), for example, was vetoed by the president and received federal approval only when the local parties agreed to contribute to the settlement. Even though the local cost share was relatively small in SAWRSA, it signaled a change in federal policy regarding settlement funding. More recently, federal policy on settlements requires the local cost share to be proportional to the benefits received by local parties.

Early settlements (Ak-Chin and SAWRSA) included provisions that held the federal government liable for damages if it failed to deliver the tribes' water entitlements in a timely manner. Since then, the administration (the OMB, in particular) has strenuously opposed such damage payments, and consequently, no recent settlements have provided for federal damage liability of this type. Without strong damage provisions, tribes fear that they will not have the legal leverage to ensure that the United States will deliver on the promises that it makes to tribes in water settle-ments. Typically, the only recourse left to tribes is to sue the federal government. In other instances, settlements rely on conditional decrees that do not become fully finalized until all pledged resources are delivered and federal funding is received.

The costs of Indian water settlements are absorbed out of the BIA's budget, which means that settlement-related expenditures must be offset by reductions to services available to other Indian tribes. Because of the annual limit on the portion of the Interior Department's budget that can be used for Indian water rights settlements, funding has proved inadequate. Interior views satisfaction of Indian water entitlements as a general obligation of the United States and is hopeful that a separate Indian water settlement fund will be established. OMB, on the other hand, believes that funding Indian water settlements is an Interior obligation.

Several approaches to inadequate funding have been identified. One response has been to fund settlements incrementally over a period of years. Spreading the funding out over several years implies that each successive Congress will need to be convinced of the importance of the settlement and the continuing need to fund it. Another approach is to identify contributions to settlements that do not require going through the federal appropriations process each year. In the Fort Hall settlement, for example, a portion of the United States' contribution was to provide non-Indians with previously unallocated federal storage water to mitigate the impact of the agreement. In addition, the OMB endorses the concept of off-reservation water marketing as a means to generate money for settlements. Some observers argue that this merely makes tribes finance their own settlements through asset leases.

The Appropriations Process

> Take the time to understand the federal budget process. . . . One of the key reasons for no settlements over the years 1994–1999 was the Clinton administration's commitment to avert enactment of a balanced budget amendment.
>
> Steve McHugh, minority deputy chief counsel, U.S. Senate Committee on Indian Affairs

The initial congressional enactment of a settlement merely authorizes the settlement and does not ensure its funding. Settlements that involve new water supply development, irrigation projects, and money for tribal economic-development funds typically are funded in stages through the annual congressional appropriations process, often over a period of years. The availability of funds depends on many factors, and lobbying efforts by tribal, state, and local parties normally are needed to secure the necessary appropriations from each successive Congress to fully implement the settlement. See Sidebars 6.5 and 6.6 for an overview of the authorization and appropriations processes.

Some settlements have included damage provisions that hold the federal government financially liable for failure to deliver tribal entitlements within a particular time frame. Such provisions, though highly unpopular with the OMB, can help guarantee federal cooperation in implementing key settlement features. Comparing the subsequent histories of the Ak-Chin settlement with that of the Fallon Paiute-Shoshone (Nevada) illustrates this point.[5] In 1978, Congress passed a law requiring the secretary of the Interior

to make it his or her first priority to develop irrigation on the Fallon Indian Reservation to provide water owed to the tribe since 1906. The same Congress passed the Ak-Chin settlement to develop a water supply to satisfy the Arizona tribe's reserved water entitlement. When the intended water supplies for both reservations proved infeasible, the Ak-Chin settlement, which included specific deadlines for water delivery and provisions for damage payments, quickly was amended. In contrast, the Fallon statute had no deadlines or damage provisions, and Congress did not adopt an alternate solution until twelve years later.

Recent settlements have included various measures to ensure funding. The Fort Hall agreement, for example, allows the tribes to obtain judgment in the Court of Claims against the United States if Congress fails to appropriate settlement funds in subsequent years. Under the San Luis Rey settlement, interest on the trust fund accrues from the date of enactment of the legislation. The Truckee-Carson–Pyramid Lake settlement provides strong incentives for all parties, including and especially the federal government, to ensure appropriations. For instance, the tribes' dismissal of claims for water and past damages are contingent upon full appropriations by Congress, and interest accrues on any fund installment not appropriated by a specified date.

The Domenici Bill

> Tribes and their collaborators continue to stress the need to separate Indian water rights settlement appropriations from Interior appropriations. Western Governors should continue to support the Domenici Bill in order to achieve that end in the near term.
>
> John Echohawk, executive director, Native American Rights Fund

In July 2001, Senator Pete Domenici (R-NM) introduced the Fiscal Integrity of Indian Settlements Protection Act of 2001.[6] This act proposes to amend the Budget Enforcement Act of 1990[7] to provide for an annual adjustment to specific budget caps when appropriations are to be made under the adjusted cap for the purpose of "fulfilling the Federal Government's aggregate commitments in any fiscal year to the settlement of Indian water rights and land claims" authorized and enacted by congressional legislation and signed

SIDEBAR 6.5
Congressional Authorization Process

Bills Introduced in the House

1. The sponsor (a House representative) introduces the tribal water bill.
2. The bill is read into record at the full House floor.
3. The bill is referred to the House Resources Committee, which has jurisdiction over Interior water resources issues and Indian issues (except Indian education).
4. The bill is referred to the Water and Power Subcommittee.
5. The bill is scheduled for hearing before the subcommittee, with testimony from opponents, proponents, experts, administration officials, and environmentalists.
6. The subcommittee revises, or "marks up," the bill.
7. A majority vote releases the bill back to the House Resources Committee.
8. The House Resources Committee marks up the bill.
9. A majority vote releases the bill to the House floor.
10. The full House considers and votes on the bill.
11. A majority vote passes the bill to the Senate for consideration, or to the president for approval (if the Senate has already approved identical legislation).

12. The president approves the bill.
13. Authorizing legislation is completed.

Bills Introduced in the Senate

1. The sponsor (a senator) introduces the tribal water bill.
2. The bill is read into record at the full Senate floor.
3. The bill is referred to either the Committee on Indian Affairs or the Committee on Energy and Natural Resources (which has jurisdiction over the Bureau of Reclamation).
4. Both committees claim jurisdiction on issues of tribal water.
5. Each committee lobbies the majority leader of the Senate to receive the referral.
6. Committees may work out joint referral, where each considers and marks up the bill for a specific amount of time.
7. Committees hold hearings and solicit testimony.
8. One committee amends the bill.
9. A majority vote releases the bill to the full Senate (or to the other committee).
10. The full Senate considers and votes on the bill.
11. A majority vote releases the bill to the House or to the president for approval (if the House has already approved identical legislation).
12. The president approves the bill.
13. Authorizing legislation is completed.

into law by the president. Currently, appropriations made to fulfill the federal government's responsibilities in water rights settlements or land claims are lumped together under the Function 302 cap with spending for all other Indian and Department of the Interior programs. Since 1978, Congress has appropriated more than $3.5 billion to settlements of Indian water rights and land claims.[8] Most of these appropriations were included within the annual budget of the BIA, and to a lesser extent, the Bureau of Reclamation under the Department of the Interior. Thus, comparatively large appropriations for Indian water settlements or land claims effectively displace fund-

ing for other Indian and Interior programs under the Function 302 budget cap rule, and may appear to be imbalanced increases in programmatic funding for individual tribal programs. Parties advocating the Domenici Amendment argue that the "number and size of pending settlements makes imperative the need to ensure that the Federal Government's share of the cost of settlement of its own legal and trust liabilities to individual tribes is not paid at the expense of programs serving all tribes."[9]

About a dozen land claims remain in negotiation with possible settlement on the horizon. Likewise, more than twenty negotiations of tribal water rights

SIDEBAR 6.6
The Appropriations Process in Indian Water Rights Settlements

The public most often interacts with the authorizing committees of Congress, not the appropriations committees. Authorizing committees draft bills intended to set policies, establish programs, and recommend certain budget levels. All authorization does is permit the possible appropriation of money in an amount up to the amount authorized. If federal funding is required to implement the legislation, however, the program authorized in the new law cannot proceed until an appropriation is approved by one of the appropriations committees.

The U.S. Constitution mandates that "no money shall be drawn from the Treasury, but in Consequence of Appropriations made by Law."[1] Some authorizing legislation itself creates budget authority. Such laws are referred to as direct, or mandatory, spending programs. This type of spending is not subject to discretionary changes in the annual levels of spending amounts. The authorizing legislation of direct spending programs is a binding legal obligation by the federal government to provide funding for an individual program or activity. For example, most major entitlement programs like Social Security, Medicare, and veterans' assistance are direct spending.

Most authorized programs or activities are subject to annual funding decisions. These expenses are considered to be discretionary spending. Annual discretionary spending currently totals only about one-third of all federal expenditures. Authorizing legislation for discretionary spending provides guidance to the president and Congress as to what level of funding is appropriate for the program or activity. Such authorizations may be limited to cover only specific fiscal years or may be permanent and remain in effect until altered by Congress. Billions of dollars of authorized programs "on the books" are unfunded. When Congress passes appropriations bills to fund authorized programs, it is enacting the legal authority for the agency or governmental entity to expend a certain dollar amount.

The budget process restricts congressional funding and appropriation acts. The congressional budget process is set out in the Budget Act and requires Congress to establish annually its level of spending and to allocate total spending among the twenty major functions of government. The first Budget Act was enacted in 1974 as a way to restrict presidential authority to impound money already appropriated by Congress. Further, the act introduced a means to develop an overall budget plan for the government and established a permanent congressional committee devoted exclusively to the national budget. In 1985 and in 1987, Congress passed the Balanced Budget Act, also known as the Gramm-Rudman-Hollings Act, that established maximum deficit amounts.[2] Despite the Balanced Budget Act procedures, the deficit continued to increase, and Congress passed the Budget Enforcement Act of 1990. This act set budgetary levels for upcoming fiscal years.

The Budget Enforcement Act of 1990 requires an agreement through conference by both sides of Congress called the Budget Resolution. This resolution must be approved by both sides of Congress and allocates specific levels of budget authority. The Budget Enforcement Act also requires the appropriations committees of both the House and the Senate to subdivide their allocations among their thirteen subcommittees. These allocations are limits on spending, or a spending cap, to each subcommittee and to the executive agencies in the subcommittee's jurisdiction. If any part of the House or Senate wants to spend beyond the limits set by the Budget Resolution, any legislator can require the proposed appropriations legislation be approved by a super-majority vote (three-fifths), rather than the usual majority. This point of order created by the Budget Enforcement Act puts procedural obstacles to congressional overspending and is used to enforce established spending limits.

Each year, the OMB reviews and compiles requests from executive agencies for funding. Most often, these agency requests are accompanied by the pertinent authorizing legislation. After the OMB compiles all the budget requests, it submits the information to the president. The president then officially drafts and submits his annual budget request to the Budget Committee of Congress. This committee reviews national budget functions and sets spending priority levels for each function for the year. The Budget Committee then submits this information in the annual Budget Resolution. Once the House and the Senate both pass the Budget Resolution, the spending levels are sent to each appropriations committee.

The appropriations committees are the congressional bodies that draft legislation to allocate federal funds to government agencies, organizations, and departments. The Constitution has been interpreted to mean appropriations bills should originate in the House of Representatives, though the Senate Appropriations Committee often preemptively hears testimony on a measure anticipated to begin in the House. Consisting of twenty-nine members, the Senate Appropriations Committee is the largest committee in the Senate. The House Appropriations Committee has sixty-five members. The full House and Senate appropriations committees are split into thirteen subcommittees that have identical jurisdiction on both sides of Congress. These subcommittees are allocated an annual spending limit through the budget resolution process. The subcommittees consider how to divide the total available annual allowance between the executive agencies and their authorized requests. In doing so, the subcommittees review the presidential budget request (submitted by the first Monday in February) and authorizing legislation, request and hear oral testimony from relevant governmental entities, and draft a bill of spending plans for the upcoming fiscal year. Once the appropriations bill is passed in subcommittee by a majority vote, it goes to the full appropriations committee for a majority vote. If passed, the bill then goes to the full House or Senate for a vote. If approved by the majority, the bill is then passed to the other house of Congress, and goes through the same process. If the other house of Congress makes changes to the bill, the houses set up a Conference Committee to hammer out the differences. From the Conference Committee, the bill is referred to the floor of both the House and the Senate, usually with a proviso that the bill is not amendable. If the bill passes both houses by a majority vote, the bill goes to the president for his approval or veto. Once the bill is signed into law, the executive agencies have passed the constitutional hurdle to receive funds from the U.S. Treasury for its authorized function.

Congressional Appropriations Process

1. Executive agency with authorized function submits a request for funding to the OMB.
2. The OMB reviews and compiles all executive agency requests.
3. The OMB submits this compilation to the president with recommendations.
4. The president submits an annual budget proposal to the Budget Committee.
5. The Budget Committee reviews the presidential proposal, considers the national priorities of twenty budget functions, and sets spending limits in a Budget Resolution.
6. The Budget Resolution is approved by both houses of Congress (majority vote required).
7. The appropriations committees of both House and Senate pass spending limits on to each of thirteen subcommittees (each appropriations subcommittee has identical jurisdiction in both House and Senate). Note: spending limits passed to each subcommittee may not be identical in both House and Senate because House funding issues tend to focus on small constituency projects, and Senate issues focus on more national projects.
8. Most tribal water appropriations bills are referred to the Energy and Water Development Subcommittee and Interior and Related Agencies Subcommittee.
9. The subcommittee considers the appropriations bill. The bill passes to the full Appropriations Committee by majority vote.
10. The Appropriations Committee passes the bill to the full House or Senate for their vote.
11. The bill is sent to the other house of Congress for the same process.
12. If the bill is passed by the second house of Congress with different language from first house (as is typical), then a Conference Committee is established, and committee members from both houses meet to hammer out differences.
13. The conference bill is released to the House and Senate floors by majority vote, usually with provision that the bill cannot be amended further.

14. The bill passes the House and Senate majority votes.
15. The bill goes to the president for approval.

16. The appropriations bill authorizes an executive agency to receive money for authorized activities from the U.S. Treasury.

claims are in progress. Another ten to twenty Indian water rights cases may be negotiated and settled over the next two decades. One estimate foretells that the aggregate of these claims is likely to cost between $2 and $5 billion.[10] For fiscal year 2002 alone, the budget request contained approximately $60 million in the BIA for land and water settlements, and approximately $30 million in the Bureau of Reclamation for water settlements.[11] Further, of the $60 million requested through the BIA, about $24 million is for implementation of already enacted land and water settlements.[12] Finally, the five most active Indian water settlement cases that are prime candidates to be brought before Congress in 2002 or later are projected to cost between $500 million and $1 billion.[13]

At such high costs, the Domenici Amendment may be a critical solution to the already difficult obstacle of funding tribal settlements without adverse consequences to Indian programs. In addition, unless the limited resources available under statutory discretionary spending caps are altered, the conclusions to years of negotiations of tribal water and land claims may be delayed while the parties question whether sufficient funds will be made available for the federal government to meet its commitments under the settlement agreements. For example, President Bush has stated that he will place a high priority on funding Indian schools in the BIA budget.[14] Such a statement may raise significant concerns as to the emphasis that Congress will place on making money available for water settlements out of the BIA budget cap.

Finally, though the Domenici Amendment would adjust annual Function 302 caps for discretionary spending to fund tribal water and land settlements, the amendment limits the amount by which the budget cap could be increased in any fiscal year to $200 million.[15] Any amounts authorized for appropriation over the amount of the increased budget cap would be subject to spending limit enforcements. Likewise, the

total dollar amounts of the federal government's obligation in settlements would continue to be scrutinized through the authorization process.

Authorization by States and Tribes

In some instances, state legislatures must formally approve Indian water settlement agreements. This generally is the case if the settlement entails state funding, or if the state compromises its legal position as part of the agreement. In addition, because municipal governments, counties, and irrigation districts may incur financial and legal obligations, settlements usually must be approved by their governing boards.

Tribal governments generally follow a formal public process to obtain tribal members' approval of a proposed settlement. This often entails a referendum or convening of a general council at which all tribal members may participate. Tribal ratification of settlements sometimes is conducted before congressional authorization and sometimes afterwards, when there is a final document to consider. If state or federal funds will support construction activities, an environmental assessment or impact report may be required.

Court Approval

Court actions may be needed to confirm some aspects of settlement agreements. Some of the earliest settlements, such as the Southern Arizona Water Rights Settlement, were negotiated in the context of relatively few issues, such as interference with tribal water rights, and involved relatively few parties. In these cases, the settlement might be approved by a court (usually a federal district court), using a good faith standard, or the case might simply be dismissed by the parties without court review. Some issues may be settled as part of a reopening of old decrees, such as Arizona's Globe Equity Decree on the Gila River or Nevada's Orr Ditch Decree on the Truckee River, and the fruits of settlement and the litigation of certain issues may be added as amendments to the original decree. In some instances (such as the agreement resulting in the Navajo Indian Irrigation Project), a settlement may not require court approval, or the settlement may ultimately be incorporated in a general stream adjudication decree many years in the future. Most of the settlements discussed in this book occurred against the backdrop of an active general stream adjudication pending in state court.

Relatively few Indian water rights settlements have been submitted to general stream adjudication courts for approval, but more will be in the future as settlements are completed and adjudications progress. The first settlement ever successfully approved and incorporated into a general stream adjudication was the Salt River Pima–Maricopa Indian Community Water Rights Settlement, approved by Arizona's Gila River adjudication court in 1991.

Court approval may be necessary because the determination of tribal water rights in the agreement may affect other water users on the river system. For instance, a settlement recognizing 100,000 acre-feet per year for irrigated agriculture on a particular reservation could mean that a downstream non-Indian water user may see his or her water supply diminish in the future. The downstream user may not have legal injury, however, because the tribe would likely prove up that amount of water, with a senior priority date, if forced to trial. As a practical matter, the downstream user may see no actual harm because the settlements have been especially creative in protecting existing non-Indian water uses.

In many cases, court approval has been required by Congress as one of the conditions necessary to finalize all aspects of the agreement and release any funds appropriated by law. Specific congressional deadlines for securing final court approval have been a powerful motivator for the settling parties to work out any remaining differences. Congress probably has the authority to approve a settlement quantifying Indian water rights without state court approval (so long as other users who might be harmed have recourse). Congress' court approval requirement acknowledges the long-standing primacy of western states over water.

Some courts have adopted special procedures in anticipation of being asked to approve settlements. Other courts rely on existing rules of civil procedure. Still other courts have used a mix of both. Usually, only the water right features of the settlement are submitted to the court for approval, perhaps in the form of a relatively concise stipulation. Notice of the proposed settlement is provided to other claimants in the adjudication who might conceivably be harmed. In long pending adjudications, with stale names and addresses, notice can be cumbersome and expensive. In the late 1990s, the San Carlos Apache Tribe reportedly spent $80,000 in mailed and published notice of a proposed settlement to Gila River adjudication claimants.

Usually, only those claimants who assert water rights in the same river system or source have standing to object. Surprisingly, relatively few do. This may be a combination of factors: settlement provisions that safeguard non-Indian users, successful efforts to keep water users informed as the settlement progresses, and realization that settlement is better than years of protracted litigation. When objections have been filed, many are withdrawn as objectors better understand the features of the agreement. They may also begin to appreciate the legal and political resources of the state, federal, tribal, and major water user parties who are aligned together in their determination to secure settlement approval.

A peculiar incident concerning the governor's role arose when the Gila River adjudication court considered the San Carlos Apache Tribe settlement in 1999. Although the settlement had been submitted for approval, important differences remained among some of the parties, and Governor Jane Hull was concerned about protections for neighboring nontribal communities. Her attempt to file an objection to the settlement—not as a water user but as the representative of statewide public interest—was rejected by the special master, but the remaining issues were resolved and the settlement approved before the governor's standing was finally determined by the court.

Different courts have experimented with the criteria against which to evaluate proposed settlements. The criteria must be sufficient to protect the lawful interests of other water users in the case. When the Arizona Supreme Court first promulgated a special procedure for the Gila River adjudication court's evaluation of proposed settlements, the criteria included a showing that the tribal water rights be no greater than what the tribe would likely be able to prove at trial. Courts in other states (and later, the Arizona Supreme Court in rules for the Little Colorado River adjudication) have emphasized the overall good faith and reasonableness of the settlement. Other water users are still afforded an opportunity to demonstrate specific injury, but for the reasons discussed earlier, few can. Frequently, final court approval comes on a pretrial motion for summary approval of the settlement, with the settling parties arguing that neither the facts nor law remain in dispute.

Implementation

> It's only 50 percent over when the President signs the settlement. Turning paper water into wet water is a difficult task.
>
> Joe Ely, former chair, Pyramid Lake Paiute Tribe

Carrying out all the provisions of Indian water settlements can take decades, and most settlements passed by Congress have not yet been fully implemented. This is particularly true when settlements involve major new construction projects. Local parties must lobby Congress to appropriate the funds needed for incremental stages of project construction and also may need to address environmental or other concerns that emerge when construction is planned. Often, state and federal permits are required to develop the water supplies provided for in the settlement.

In some instances, settlement implementation may require addressing issues that were avoided deliberately during the settlement process in order to reach agreement. Unresolved issues can threaten the integrity of the settlement and may require that the parties negotiate subsequent agreements. Such issues frequently involve jurisdictional disputes between tribal governments and state and federal agencies—all of whom have some jurisdiction over various aspects of water rights, water management, and water quality.

Interior Department officials recognize the many obstacles to full implementation of settlements and have begun to assign implementation teams to assist local and tribal parties. In 2002, seventeen federal implementation teams were active. Generally these teams include some members of the original federal teams that participated in negotiating the settlement agreement. See Table 6.1 for a listing of recent federal implementation teams.

Negotiators of Indian water rights settlements sign up for the long haul. They address problems that originated with the settlement of the American West. They attempt to fashion solutions that will allow different cultures to coexist peacefully and prosperously in the future of the American West. Along the way, they will encounter almost every major institution and process of the American federal system: local, state, tribal, and federal governments; public participation, legislation, appropriations, implementation, and litigation; advocacy, coercion, accommodation, and cooperation. Rarely are the solutions to public policy problems so complex and the challenges to leaders so daunting.

PHOTO 7.1 Jigsaw pattern of dried desert lands. Photo: University of Arizona Agricultural Communications

CHAPTER 7

Settlement Components

We are at a crossroads in our efforts to manage water in the West. . . . Some of the most intractable disputes continue . . . some of our most challenging negotiations remain: the immensely difficult conflicts between endangered species, the traditional uses of water, and the often as yet to be quantified water needs of the tribes. And of course, the continuing dynamic between the need for new and innovative ways of managing water for a burgeoning population and decades of established water law and practice.

Susan Cottingham, program manager, Montana Reserved Water Rights Compact Commission

In much of the West, rivers and groundwater already are overallocated. Indian reserved rights claims typically are senior in priority to many water rights held by non-Indians. The recognition, quantification, and development of reserved rights threaten to devalue and, in some cases, effectively eliminate non-Indian uses that would be bumped down in priority. This threat has the potential to disrupt significant social relations and economic activities in many western communities.

This stark possibility has provided the primary impetus for negotiating the settlements of Indian water rights claims. The completed settlements have usually been successful in providing water to satisfy Indian claims while avoiding or mitigating any harm to existing non-Indian users. Although some settlements recognize very large and senior tribal water priorities, these agreements are usually found in water-abundant basins or where excess storage can be made available. These agreements still may contain subordination clauses protecting certain non-Indian users (Fort Peck). In more arid regions, a tribe may exchange a contractual guarantee of water for its reserved right and senior priority (Yavapai-Prescott). Negotiations that languish often do so because the negotiators have been unable to fashion a water budget that provides water to a tribe while holding non-Indians harmless.

Although the settlements may protect many existing users, they are not necessarily painless agreements. Many settlements are premised on the pledges of water made by major non-Indian water users. Several Arizona settlements (such as Fort McDowell and the Salt River Pima–Maricopa Indian Community) are based on the transfers of previously decreed water rights or on Bureau of Reclamation contract water (including CAP allocations) from non-Indian users to a tribe or Indian community.

This section sets the stage for a series of case studies presented in chapter 9. Those case studies illustrate how the water-acquisition strategies described here have been applied to provide water to satisfy tribal water claims, usually in the context of a settlement.

The amount of water quantified in settlements varies greatly, usually in relation to the abundance of water in the area. Entitlements of 500,000 acre-feet annually or more have been recognized for the Fort Peck (at 1,050,472 acre-feet per year, the highest quantity recognized in a settlement), Crow, and Fort Belknap reservations in Montana; the Northern Ute Reservation in Utah (dependent on water development that may never be completed); Pyramid Lake Reservation in Nevada; and the Fort Hall Reservation in Idaho. The Seminole agreement in Florida has no explicit quantification limit.

Most of the remaining settlements—all located in the more arid Southwest—quantify the tribal water right at less than 100,000 acre-feet annually (although it is difficult to estimate how much groundwater some tribes will be able to pump from beneath their reservations because many settlements do not set specific quantity limits on groundwater use). These amounts are representative: Ak-Chin, 85,000 acre-feet per year; San Carlos Apache (partial settlement on Salt River portion of reservation), 77,435 acre-feet per year; Tohono O'odham (partial settlement), 66,000 acre-feet per year; Colorado Ute, 92,000 acre-feet per year; Southern Ute, 39,900 acre-feet per year; and Jicarilla Apache, 40,000 acre-feet per year. Some settlements involve very small amounts of water, although they may include important water- and economic-development funds: Yavapai-Prescott, 1,550 acre-feet per year, and Shivwits, 4,000 acre-feet per year. Water quality is rarely addressed in settlement agreements; however, tribes may apply for status and qualify under the Clean

Water Act to regulate surface water as if they were states, and so they have another venue in which to protect surface-water quality.

Sources of Water

The northern settlements are principally based on surface-water sources, with the groundwater beneath the reservation included as a bonus, a secondary source for reservation needs. The surface-water award may be very large if no storage or water-development project is available, but the surface-water entitlement may be substantially discounted when firm proposals are made for water storage and delivery. For instance, compare Fort Peck's award of 1 million acre-feet per year but no water-development component with both the Northern Cheyenne's 91,000 acre-feet annual quantification, premised on enlargement and use of the Tongue River Dam, and the Rocky Boy's expectation of 10,000 acre-feet from Tiber Reservoir. Specific storage arrangements can make a smaller entitlement more firm and reliable during dry years, providing greater security during drought for tribal water users.

The southern settlements rely on a much more complex mix of water sources. When surface water is provided, it is usually made available through some existing water-development project. For most of the Arizona settlements, this is water from CAP. Arizona has been fortunate to have underused CAP water to apply to settlements or otherwise to place limits on tribal groundwater use. The Yavapai-Prescott Indian Tribe receives its settlement water from the City of Prescott's municipal system and a local irrigation district. The Jicarilla Apache Reservation in New Mexico agreed to accept surface water from Navajo Reservoir and the San Juan–Chama Diversion Project (or San Juan–Chama Project, SJCP). Although groundwater is usually a component of these settlements, the use may be more explicitly limited than in the northern settlements. For example, groundwater use in the Jicarilla settlement is limited to nontributary sources. Several Arizona settlements require the Indian community to develop groundwater-management plans similar to the state's own requirements or to place other limits on tribal groundwater use.

Strategies to Obtain Water for Tribal Settlements

Specific methods used to obtain water include building new water projects; reallocating water storage and altering dam operations; saving water through conservation, salvage, and improved water conveyance; reusing effluent; creating groundwater allocation and management agreements; creating interjurisdictional water service agreements; and making use of existing state water rights held by tribes.

Build New Water Projects

In the past, the response to growing water needs was to build new dams. Now, new large-scale water projects are difficult to build due to scarce federal funds and opposition to environmental and economic costs. Nevertheless, pressures to settle Indian water claims have paved the way for federal investments in new water projects. Several recent and proposed settlements include such projects. The Colorado Ute settlement, for instance, relies on the ALP to supply a portion of the water needed. The federal government shares a large portion of the ongoing costs of operating CAP (the last large-scale project completed in the western United States), because several hundred thousand acre-feet per year of project water go to various tribal settlement obligations.

Reallocate Existing Federal Water Project Supplies

Sometimes unallocated supplies from federal water projects (when projects have not been completely built) are available for resolving Indian water claims. This was the case in the Fort Hall settlement, where unallocated federal supplies mitigated the impact of the settlement on non-Indian irrigators. In the 1980s, the secretary of the Interior allocated a small amount of CAP water for use by Arizona Indian tribes, and this amount has now swelled to several hundred thousand acre-feet per year as irrigation districts have relinquished their CAP subcontracts. Much of this water has been used in recent settlements or is dedicated to settlements still being finalized.

The Fallon Paiute-Shoshone settlement in Nevada also relies on water deliveries to the tribe from a federal project, as do the Rocky Boy's settlement and the Northern Cheyenne settlement in Montana. Similarly, settlement negotiations of water claims for Pueblos involved in the *Aamodt* adjudication, in north-central New Mexico, envision pueblo rights to water stored behind Nambé Falls Dam as a key component. The dam was constructed between 1974 and 1976 on Nambé Pueblo lands as part of the SJCP.

Reallocate Water Storage and Alter Dam Operations

In the arid West, streamflows are highly variable, and adequate storage facilities are essential to assure reliable supplies across wet and dry seasons and years. Lack of access to reservoir storage or lack of control over timing of releases can create a problem for tribes. The Shoshone and Arapaho tribes in Wyoming, for example, have extensive senior rights to the Wind River but have no recognized storage rights and so have difficulty coordinating releases from upstream reservoirs as needed for tribal programs. In contrast, new storage arrangements provide important components of the Salt River and Fort McDowell settlements in Arizona by enabling the Indian communities to use fully their existing entitlements to natural flows of the Salt and Verde rivers.

Tribes may need access to storage to facilitate tribal water-leasing programs. Effective leasing arrangements require the authority to release water as needed by lessees. Management of storage water is an essential component of the Fort Hall agreement, which authorizes a tribal water bank to allow portions of the tribes' entitlement to be leased off reservation. Likewise, in the Truckee-Carson–Pyramid Lake settlement, the rules for delivering water to the cities of Reno and Sparks and to a federal irrigation project have been modified to assure releases for fishery restoration, a key objective of the Pyramid Lake Paiute Tribe. The Northern Cheyenne settlement includes water made available for the tribe by enlarging the Tongue River Dam.

Water Conservation, Water Salvage, and Increased Efficiencies

Water saved through conservation, salvage, and improved conveyance presents another potential source of water for Indian water settlements and is discussed in detail in chapter 8.

Effluent reuse. Effluent (treated municipal wastewater) has been used to satisfy tribal entitlements. Under SAWRSA, the Arizona agreement involving the Tohono O'odham Nation, the City of Tucson must provide the secretary of the Interior with effluent for use in satisfying a portion of the nation's entitlement. Similarly, the Salt River Pima–Maricopa settlement, also in Arizona, specifies a three-way exchange involving the transfer of municipal effluent to local irrigation districts and is designed to match each user's need with the appropriate type of water. The districts will in turn provide groundwater to the Salt River Project (SRP), a large federal irrigation project, enabling the SRP to deliver additional surface water to both the city and the Indian community.

Groundwater allocation and management agreements. A number of settlements have included agreements regarding groundwater pumping from aquifers that underlie reservation and non-Indian lands. These agreements do not actually produce new water not otherwise available in the region, but they provide security regarding the future availability of groundwater by limiting groundwater overdraft. Most of the Arizona settlements have included provisions that define the amount of groundwater that can be used on and off the reservation. The Yavapai-Prescott settlement, for instance, allows the tribe to pump water for on-reservation use, but the withdrawals must be pursuant to a tribal groundwater plan that is compatible with the Arizona Groundwater Management Act. The Las Vegas Paiute and Northern Cheyenne settlements also address groundwater pumping. Proposals to settle the Lummi Nation's water rights in the State of Washington include finding an alternative renewable supply for non-Indians pumping groundwater on the reservation so that the groundwater underneath reservation lands becomes available solely for tribal uses, including support of instream flows for fisheries.

Interjurisdictional water service agreements. Settlements may rely on direct contract deliveries to a tribe from an established urban water provider. The 1994 settlement of the Yavapai-Prescott Tribe requires the City of Prescott to continue to provide water service, up to 500 acre-feet per year, to the reservation in perpetuity. The agreement contemplates that this source will be accessed when there are shortages in other settlement sources. State groundwater-pumping permits held by the city serve as security for performance. Many other settlements provide contractual arrangements for water to be delivered to tribes from federal water projects.

State water rights held by tribes. An obvious place to look for water to meet a settlement's water budget is in any existing tribal water right established under state law. Under provisions for the Las Vegas Paiute settlement, for instance, the tribe continues to hold water use permits issued by the State of Nevada and subject to the same restrictions as other state permit holders. The 1987 settlement of Seminole Tribe claims in Florida places tribal groundwater and surface-water use under the state water-management framework, with the important exception that the tribal water rights are perpetual in nature and not subject to renewal or revocation by state authorities. As a variation of this method, the proposed Lummi Nation settlement in Washington State contemplates that the tribe would acquire non-Indian lands located on the reservation and retire the state water rights associated with those lands.

Water Markets, Transfers, and Exchanges

In meeting a settlement water budget, negotiators may have to acquire water rights from existing users and transfer them to tribal use. Water markets, voluntary water transfers, and exchanges (where rights in one source are exchanged for rights in another) are essential elements in acquiring water in this fashion. Growing urban water demands were responsible for the development of the earliest western water markets. Over the past two decades, water transfers have become a valuable tool also for environmental protection and restoration.

Transfers and Exchanges in Settlements

Water transfers may serve various purposes in helping to achieve settlements. In some cases, water transfers may provide water to meet a tribe's on-reservation water needs. In other instances, water transfers to off-reservation users provide a source of money to meet the monetary component of the settlement.

Difficulties with building new water projects often prompt negotiators to arrange transfers and exchanges of existing supplies to meet a settlement's water budget. In the Fort McDowell settlement in Arizona, for instance, a portion of the water supply for the Fort McDowell Indian Community comes from the transfer of the Wellton-Mohawk Irrigation and Drainage District's CAP entitlement. Settlements sometimes provide for the water transferred to the tribe to then be leased to non-Indian water users. In-state leasing arrangements are prevalent in several Arizona settlements in which complex agreements allocate CAP water, surface water, groundwater, and treated effluent among Indian and non-Indian water users.

The recent settlement of the claims of the Zuni Pueblo in the Little Colorado River basin contemplates tribal purchase and retirement of surface-water rights held under state law in order to restore streams and habitat on lands held by the tribe. The tribe already had acquired some state water rights associated with its previous land purchases. Concerns were raised regarding the nature of the water rights once transferred to the tribe. Would the rights become tribal reserved rights, not subject to forfeiture and abandonment, or continue to be governed by state law? This was answered by the Zuni Indian Tribe Water Rights Settlement Act of 2003 that declared lands taken into trust by the secretary of the Interior for the benefit of the Zuni Tribe shall not have federal reserved rights to surface or groundwater.[1]

Exchanges among water sources can provide improved water supply reliability and a better match of water quality with water user needs. The Northern Cheyenne settlement involves exchanges among native surface flows and water stored in federal reservoirs to provide a reliable supply for the tribe. The water supply arrangements associated with the Navajo Indian Irrigation Project (NIIP), negotiated many decades ago, provide upstream surface-water storage for reservation and other nearby water uses in the Colorado River basin. These arrangements laid the framework for the SJCP, a transbasin diversion that is a vital water supply for cities, for agriculture, and potentially for other tribal settlements in the Rio Grande basin of New Mexico.

Water-Marketing Policies

Western states and the federal government have a long legacy of policy making regarding water transfers.[2] Water-marketing policies have vacillated between opening up water markets and encouraging transactions on the one hand, and imposing new restrictions and procedural requirements on changes in water use on the other hand. This is not surprising as state agencies and elected officials struggle to balance the water desires of the New West (lushly landscaped and rapidly growing cities, abundant water-based recreation, and restoration of species and their habitats) with agricultural and rural consternation over the fading of the Old West and its customary water use patterns. Law professor David Getches observes that most state policy changes of the 1990s restricted water transfers, and few changes were promulgated to open up and broaden water market activity.[3]

The agricultural sector is party to most water transactions. Agriculture is the primary consumptive use of water in most of the West and represents a source of water others look to in order to acquire water. In addition, there is enormous diversity in western agriculture. Farmers in many regions grow irrigated pasture using water that costs them only five dollars per acre-foot. Southern California avocado growers earn profits even while paying six hundred dollars per acre-foot for water. Differences in the economic value of water across different types of crops, particularly during dry years, lead to frequent water transfers between irrigated farms throughout the West.

Another force behind water markets is the growing recognition that the ability to transfer water generates regional economic benefits by making water available for higher value uses. Water transfers are also more cost effective than developing new water supplies and are generally more environmentally acceptable than new water development.

Concerns about Transferring Water

Agriculturally linked rural communities and local governments (such as irrigation districts and counties) often respond to proposed water transfers out of agriculture with suspicion and alarm. They are concerned that movement of water away from local agricultural uses will undermine the local economy by reducing business activity and property values. The specter of the dewatering of California's Owens Valley to favor Los Angeles persists over the decades.

Due to the wide variation in the local economic consequences of water transfers out of agriculture, each case must be examined on its own merits. A number of economic studies have examined actual transfers and have modeled the effects of proposed transactions. Studies of transfers out of agriculture find that local economic impacts are small relative to the amount of irrigated land that is fallowed, even when the water is moved to a new use away from the area of origin.[4] The consistent findings of relatively small impacts are due to several factors. Farmers fallow their lowest value crops and their least productive acreage. A portion of water payments received by farmers is generally spent in the county from which the water is exported. Income from crop sales is a small portion of county income in nearly every rural county in the West. Rural county households rely more on income coming from off-farm employment and government payments than on income from crop sales. Water transfers stimulate off-farm jobs and income.

Even though water transfer impacts are generally small, they may be more significant if concentrated in certain businesses or specific agricultural communities.[5] Several approaches can be used to address these concerns. The parties most affected by proposed transfers generally are not those who have water to sell. Farmers and irrigation districts holding transferable water rights will look after their own interests when negotiating a water transfer; but no forum may exist for rural residents, local governments, and affected local businesses to have a voice in the process. Some states have enacted legislation to give local governments a role in reviewing and approving proposed transfers of water out of their jurisdiction.

Market transactions can be designed in ways to help minimize negative third-party effects and maintain agricultural activity in rural areas. Making transfers contingent on drought conditions is one approach to preserving an agricultural base, because farming will occur as usual in normal years, and farmers can be adequately compensated in dry years to allow them to remain in farming. Other approaches include paying for farm water-conservation practices and transferring only the water conserved, and rotating acreage fallowed (and water lease payments) among landowners to maintain the baseline agricultural economy. Partial buyouts of the water used in farming can preserve property values and a rural lifestyle by leaving adequate water rights with the farmland to support gardens and horse pasture. In general, economic impacts of changes in water use in the area of origin can be addressed through structuring water transfers to minimize impacts. Beneath concerns over local economic impacts, however, lie more fundamental and well-founded concerns that the water transfer movement signals a change in society's priorities and values for how water is used.

Water Management and State-Tribal Jurisdiction

Often the most difficult issues to confront in implementing tribal water settlements involve defining the jurisdiction of tribal and state governments in managing and regulating shared water resources. For tribes, jurisdiction over water is a critical aspect of tribal sovereignty and their ability to govern tribal resources and to plan for the future. States also have a strong interest in jurisdictional issues because of their role as managers and regulators of state water resources. The courts have not yet fully clarified the jurisdictional boundaries between states and tribes, and this challenges the parties to forge their own working agreements. Conflicts over jurisdiction are particularly pronounced on the many checkerboard reservations where non-Indians own and irrigate fee lands within the reservation boundaries. Non-Indian landowners commonly prefer to be regulated by the state, but tribal governments often desire to regulate all water use on the reservation. Jurisdictional disputes also concern the allowable uses of the tribal water right, including the possibility of off-reservation leasing.

Factual Context

In addition to the unsettled body of law concerning state-tribal jurisdictional conflicts, these disputes are defined by their specific factual context. Several factual issues affect the nature of these jurisdictional concerns:

What is the physical and legal character of the water resource involved? Surface water contained within reservation boundaries presents different challenges than a groundwater aquifer that underlies both reservation and non-Indian lands, for instance. In addition, reserved rights raise different jurisdictional concerns than does federal contract water.

To what extent and under what legal structure are non-Indians using water on the reservation? On many checkerboard reservations, state water permits were granted to non-Indian landowners, and these water users are accustomed to being under state, not tribal, jurisdiction.

Are federal facilities and federal water contracts relevant? On some reservations there are Bureau of Reclamation projects that provide water under long-term contract to non-Indian water users. The operation of federal reservoirs and conveyance systems has played a crucial role in a number of settlements, including the Truckee-Carson–Pyramid Lake settlement, the Colorado Ute settlement, and the many Arizona settlements that involve CAP.

What are the potential impacts of water regulations proposed by a state or tribe on water users under the jurisdiction of the other party? The issue of regulatory impacts is particularly crucial where there are specific water quality concerns. For instance, the Pueblo of Isleta, located downstream on the Rio Grande from the City of Albuquerque, is enacting strict water quality standards for the river as it passes through the Pueblo. Compliance with these standards requires substantial additional investment in wastewater treatment by the city. Water quality issues have arisen also in the Truckee River basin, where the Pyramid Lake Reservation lies downstream from the Reno-Sparks metropolitan area and Pyramid Lake is the receiving body for discharges from the urban area.[6]

Although there is no blueprint for resolving these jurisdictional questions, an essential component of any solution is the mutual recognition of the sovereign nature of tribal and state governments and appreciation of their respective concerns as sovereigns.

Financial Components of Settlements

Although litigation might ultimately award a tribe a larger water right, the decree would likely be a paper water right, with no money to develop or make use of the water. In pursuing settlements, tribes may compromise their claims to water in exchange for an overall settlement package that includes money to develop both water and the reservation economy. The interplay between water and money, however, is often controversial and economically difficult to fashion, as is explored in sidebar 7.1.

Federal Contributions

The size of the federal contribution to settlements appears to correlate directly with aridity and the complexity of the water budget necessary to forge a settlement. The Fort Peck–Montana Compact, although quantifying the largest tribal water right, has no financial component. The financial package for Fort Belknap will be finalized when Congress approves the agreement. In Montana, the most complex financial package was arranged for the Northern Cheyenne Reservation, involving the enlargement of the Tongue River Dam, and will probably require between $57 million and $72 million in federal appropriations.

The Arizona settlements include very large federal-funding obligations: Ak-Chin, $29.2 million, as well as $15 million in damages for past water underdeliveries; Tohono O'odham, approximately $162 million in water acquisition and development costs; Salt River Pima–Maricopa, $47.5 million for an Indian community trust fund; and Fort McDowell, $23 million for a similar community development fund, as well as uncertain additional amounts for water acquisition.

The federal government is obligated to provide $30 million for a development fund for the San Luis Rey Indians, plus additional amounts to line the All American Canal, develop a groundwater recharge program, and pay for the use of water delivery systems. The federal government pledged to pay 60 percent of the cost of the ALP, benefiting the Colorado Utes and other local users, a dollar amount that remains to be precisely quantified. Federal contributions for other settlements have been $4.5 million for the Florida Seminoles, $22 million for the Shoshone-Bannock tribes of the Fort Hall Reservation, $43 million for Fallon Paiute-Shoshone tribal development, $40 million for Pyramid Lake Paiute economic development as well as $25 million for fisheries restoration, $7 million for the Jicarilla Apache settlement, $24 million for the Shivwits Band in Utah, and an almost $400-million package for the Northern Utes (including $198 million as damages for breach of an earlier agreement with the tribe). These federal funds are often earmarked for specific purposes, such as reservation water development, water acquisition, economic development, water project operation and management (O&M) costs, and environmental restoration expenses.

Cost Sharing

Most settlements have included money or in-kind contributions from the state government, local water users, and even the tribe, in addition to the usually much larger federal share. In Arizona, the state and local contributions have ranged from $200,000, defraying the cost of the Yavapai-Prescott Indian Community's water service agreement with the City of Prescott, to a $68-million contribution to the Salt River Pima–Maricopa Indian Community agreement ($3 million cash, $9 million to acquire water, and $56 million as the in-kind value of 32,000 acre-feet of water). Tribal contributions have included money for on-farm irrigation improvements ($1 million in the case of Tohono O'odham; $13 million from the proceeds of a federal loan in the case of Fort McDowell).

In Montana, the state committed $9.2 million to assist in the enlargement of the Tongue River Dam and to repay a tribal loan related to the project in the amount of $11.5 million. The Crow Reservation settlement includes the state's payment of $15 million to settle coal tax litigation between the state and tribe. The state and local contribution for the Fort Belknap settlement will be finalized when Congress approves the compact. The Fort Peck settlement, because it did not contain an economic package, has no provision for a state, local, or tribal contribution.

Where regional water supplies are inadequate to satisfy the water entitlements of all parties, monetary payments may be offered to non-Indian rights holders or to tribes as part of a water settlement agreement. In other instances, monetary payments are offered as compensation for past damages in settling water disputes. Settlements have included funds for improving reservation infrastructure, such as more efficient water delivery systems, and for economic-development projects.

Many settlements involve leases of tribal water for off-reservation use where payments for leased water are made over a number of years. Compensation agreements must take into account how the value of the water will change over time. If a discrepancy emerges over the years between the market value of water and the lease payments, the stability of the agreement may be threatened. To overcome this problem, the lease agreement should provide that lease payments be adjustable periodically. The adjustment factor should reflect changes in water values over time, be readily measurable, and not be subject to manipulation by parties to the agreement. The adjustment factor may be based on energy costs in the region (since energy is one of the primary costs of supplying water), on water rates charged by regional water providers, or on a general price index, such as the consumer price index. The adjustment factor should be acceptable to all parties and specified in the lease agreement.

Some parties to conflicts have refused to consider money as a substitute for land or water.[1] Having won lengthy and expensive litigation or spent significant effort and money to assert water rights in a negotiation, tribal leaders may find it difficult politically to ask their people to accept money instead of receiving all the water to which they believe they are entitled. While monetary compensation may seem a practical remedy for impairment of tribal water resources, some tribal members have expressed concern that the money would be gone within a generation, whereas land and water remain forever.[2] Likewise, non-Indian rural communities threatened by loss of agricultural water supplies often believe that although money helps, water is irreplaceable in assuring their community's future.

The cost-sharing features of other western settlements are uniquely tailored to the circumstances facing the negotiators. In the San Luis Rey settlement, state and local parties agree to provide water and the use of local delivery systems, as well as the costs associated with the Warner Well Field ($1.5 to $3.18 million). Non-Indian parties have pledged 40 percent of the cost of the ALP (calculated at $200 million before the project was reformulated in 2000). Florida committed $500,000 in water-management services toward the Seminole settlement. In some of these settlements, tribes have pledged to cover O&M costs for water delivery (San Luis Rey) and a share of capital costs in the event tribal water is used on off-reservation lands (ALP).

Only two congressionally approved settlements are entirely funded by the federal government. These settlements, with no provision for local cost sharing, are the Ak-Chin Indian Water Rights Settlement and the Northern Ute's settlement.

Off-Reservation Leasing of Tribal Water

The economics of a settlement may be enhanced for all parties by agreements for off-reservation leasing. Some non-Indian parties have agreed to lease tribal water as part of the settlement, thereby providing an ongoing flow of water lease revenues to the tribe and improved water supply reliability for the non-Indian parties.

Tribes have never been authorized to permanently alienate (sell) their reserved water rights, but they can, with congressional approval, lease water for use off reservations. The need for congressional consent stems from the Indian Nonintercourse Act, which establishes federal control over purchases of land and other resources from Indian tribes.[7] Congress has delegated to the secretary of the Interior the authority to approve leases of Indian land to non-Indians, and some interpret this to include the water needed to fulfill the purpose of the lease.[8] This makes leasing Indian land, along with the water to be used on the land, a relatively straightforward process that can be accomplished without the involvement of the Congress. In contrast, Congress has not granted such general approval for off-reservation water marketing, making such leases more complicated.

A pragmatic problem facing tribes who wish to lease their water is the lack of incentive for non-Indians to pay for Indian water when they already are using it without cost. This situation is prevalent in the West, because tribes typically lack the capital to develop new on-reservation irrigation activities and other water-intensive projects. Non-Indians who have been using Indian water without cost are reluctant to pay for it unless tribes construct diversion and storage facilities, or in some other way withhold tribal water. Nevertheless, for many tribes, water leasing is a promising way to derive near-term economic benefit from their entitlements and to build up capital for future reservation-development projects.

In the early years of tribal water settlement negotiations, there was widespread opposition by western state governments to off-reservation leases of tribal water. Western states argued that under state law, jurisdiction concerning water use is vested in state agencies. This principle is still articulated but is no longer a major barrier to leasing arrangements, because state and local governments appreciate the growing demands on water and the important role tribal water can play in helping municipalities meet their water needs. Where states continue to vigorously draw the line is in their opposition to interstate marketing of tribal water rights. States oppose such marketing because they believe it will disrupt carefully crafted interstate apportionments. The Jicarilla settlement and many of the Arizona settlements include such a prohibition on interstate marketing.

Most settlements include some provision for off-reservation use of tribal water, although the specific arrangements vary considerably. In some cases, off-reservation use is a material part of the agreement, as in the Salt River Pima–Maricopa and Fort McDowell

settlements, in which Phoenix-area cities agree to lease certain water for ninety-nine years. Some settlements specify only that off-reservation marketing be pursuant to state law (Fallon Paiute-Shoshone, Truckee-Carson–Pyramid Lake) or that the terms and conditions strip the marketed water of its reserved rights characteristics (Northern Ute). Other settlements allow tribes to market their water in the future (Ak-Chin, San Luis Rey, ALP). In Idaho, off-reservation leasing must occur through the state's own water bank. Arizona officials have encouraged the tribes in that state to make use of the Arizona Water Bank. The Fort Peck tribes may even engage in out-of-state marketing, but they must first afford Montana state government an opportunity to share in the sale. (The state has its own water-marketing authority.)

The Fort Hall settlement limits transfers of water within the reservation to consumptive use. In recent Arizona settlements, tribes may lease only their CAP entitlements, and only within designated portions of the state. In the Colorado Ute settlement, the tribes may lease their water under criteria similar to those governing transfers of water rights held under state law.

In some basins, a tribe's full use of its *Winters* rights would disrupt non-Indian water users only in times of shortage. In these instances, contingent (dry year only) water use contracts could be attractive to both tribes and junior non-Indian water users. Under such agreements, a tribe might consent to share shortages with non-Indian water users rather than to exercise the full seniority of the tribal right, thereby protecting non-Indian water users during dry years. The Navajo Nation's agreement in the 1960s with proponents of the SJCP involved sharing shortages when flows are insufficient to satisfy both the SJCP and the NIIP.[9] The Wind River tribes and the State of Wyoming entered into a 1989 interim agreement for equally sharing surpluses and shortages in the basin.

Economic Efficiency Considerations

A key policy objective driving federal participation in Indian water settlements is to fulfill the promise of permanent tribal homelands by honoring and protecting the reserved water rights of Indian tribes. To provide permanent homelands, reservations must be sustained by viable reservation economies over successive generations with opportunities for tribal members to maintain a reasonable standard of living. In implementing this equity-based federal policy, a number of efficiency issues emerge concerning new irrigation projects, new water-development projects, and the high costs of reaching settlements.

Economic efficiency is evaluated by comparing the costs and the benefits of proposed water projects and other features of settlements. The federal OMB conducts economic analyses of proposed settlements.

New Water Development

Indian water rights settlements typically serve non-Indian goals and objectives, as well as benefiting tribes. Some settlements involve federal support for new water projects that mainly supply non-Indians. This so-called "Indian blanket" approach of wrapping together Indian and non-Indian project components has been effectively pursued by many western states to obtain federal appropriations for projects that cost-conscious administration officials otherwise might reject. For instance, in 1965 proponents of the Central Utah Project (CUP) entered into the 1965 deferral agreement with the Northern Ute Tribe in an effort to bolster support for the project. Under the agreement, the tribe was promised a large water project in exchange for deferring use of the water until 2005. Despite millions of dollars in subsequent funding for CUP, the Indian unit of the project was never built.[10] Ironically, another portion of CUP is designed to transport water away from the Uintah and Ouray Reservation of the Northern Utes for use by non-Indians in a heavily populated neighboring basin. The Northern Ute settlement, passed in 1992, provides the tribe with money as compensation for the exported water.

New water projects often are not the most cost-effective means of satisfying the *Winters* entitlements of tribes or providing additional water for non-Indian use. Alternatives such as agricultural and urban water conservation, improved ditches and canals, exchanges, leases, and use of treated wastewater may be economical substitutes for developing new supplies. Where water is being used by non-Indians to irrigate marginal lands, these water supplies may be acquired to satisfy tribal entitlements. Acquisition of

existing water supplies may be far more cost effective than constructing new dams and canals. This approach was taken in the Fort McDowell settlement in Arizona, under which the water supplies of a financially troubled irrigation district were acquired and made available to the Fort McDowell Indian Community.

New Irrigation Projects

Although the PIA quantification standard encourages tribes to view new irrigation projects as the logical use of their water, bringing new lands under irrigation may not be the best use of tribal resources. New agricultural development can disrupt wildlife habitat and archeological sites as well as degrade air and water quality. In addition, employment of members typically is a key objective of tribes, and the capital-intensive nature of modern agriculture results in relatively few, low-paying, and seasonal jobs. On the other hand, for reservations located in isolated areas with limited potential for tourism, industry, and other economic activities, irrigated agriculture may provide reservation households with livestock forage, some jobs, and enhanced prospects for sustainable tribal homelands.

As with non-Indian farms, tribal farming enterprises typically rely on crops that are eligible for federal commodity payments to enhance farm profitability. Likewise, under the terms of many settlements, tribes receive water at costs well below the actual cost of delivery, leaving federal taxpayers to pick up the tab for both water deliveries and commodity payments.

Congress has gradually reduced water subsidies and commodity payments for non-Indian agriculture. The OMB opposes Indian water settlements that include a water project whose economic feasibility depends on the production of surplus crops. Accordingly, federal and tribal policy makers would do well to avoid relying on subsidized water pricing and farm programs in efforts to satisfy tribal water entitlements.

Costs of Settlement Processes

Settling Indian water claims can be extremely expensive and result in high associated costs. In the early 1980s, the Justice Department estimated that an average of $3 million was spent in preparation to litigate each Indian water rights case.[11] It was estimated that by mid-1990, the State of Wyoming spent $14 million, and the U.S. government spent $10 million, to litigate the water rights of the Wind River Reservation.[12] These figures do not include the cost of tribal attorneys, and litigation expenditures have increased since then as unresolved issues have emerged. The special master for the case noted in 1988 that no case in his experience has carried so many hours and so many thousands of pages of discovery proceedings involving unprecedented expense to parties on all sides.[13]

The costs of litigated settlements tend to be especially high, but the same type of technical studies and preparation usually are required for negotiations. In both litigation and negotiation, the parties typically retain attorneys, engineers, hydrologists, and other experts. Many of these costs are necessary to sort out ambiguous water claims and to obtain better information about hydrology, fisheries, cropping patterns, and other technical details essential to a well-informed resolution. Nevertheless, both litigation and negotiated settlements take a heavy financial toll on participants and taxpayers.

Tribal Administration of Water Resources

Some settlements anticipate how water will be administered on the reservation; many are silent on the subject. Most of the Montana settlements require the tribe to adopt a tribal water code, to be approved by the secretary of the Interior, setting forth the procedures to be used for permitting uses and changes in uses of the tribal water rights (Fort Peck, Fort Belknap, and others). Typically, these settlements also recognize state authority to regulate state water rights on or off the reservation. Tribal regulatory authority has also been recognized in the Florida Seminole, Fallon Paiute-Shoshone, and Truckee-Carson–Pyramid Lake agreements (tribal management plans). The San Luis Rey settlement establishes an Indian Water Authority to market water and administer the $30 million development fund. Several Arizona settlements require the tribes or Indian communities to develop groundwater-management plans consistent with the state's own groundwater-management act (e.g., Yavapai-Prescott).

Enforcement and Dispute Resolution

Even the most wisely crafted settlement cannot resolve problems for all time. Time and changing circumstances may produce problems and disputes that were not anticipated by the original negotiators of the agreement. To enable settlements to be more viable documents, some parties have incorporated dispute-resolution processes into their agreements. Montana and its compacting tribes have pioneered the use of these dispute-resolution procedures in their agreements. These procedures have been used on occasion with satisfactory results. Usually, a compact board of three members is established in the agreement. One member is appointed by the governor, one is appointed by the chair of the tribe, and the third member is appointed by the other two. The recent Fort Belknap compact sets forth a typical statement of the board's dispute-resolution procedure: "The Fort Belknap-Montana Compact Board shall have the jurisdiction to resolve controversies over the right to the use of water between Persons authorized to use any portion of the Tribal Water Right and Persons holding any water rights Arising Under State Law" (capitalized words have detailed definitions in the compact).[14] A similar three-person intergovernmental board is created in the Fort Hall agreement for dispute resolution. Most other settlements do not specifically provide for dispute-resolution methods short of litigation. Since many settlements will be incorporated into general stream adjudication decrees (usually issued by state courts), the provisions may be enforced in those courts. The Florida Seminole agreement specifically recognizes that the tribe may resort to federal court to enforce its rights.

Other Settlement Features

Almost every Indian water settlement requires the tribe to waive all existing and future claims to water, except for water supplies dedicated toward the settlement. The waivers usually benefit all non-Indian water users, even ones that did not participate in or contribute to the settlement. The waivers also waive damage claims against other water users, for impermissibly using tribal water in the past, and against the United States, for failing as trustee to protect the tribe's water

Economic and Financial Considerations for Settlements

(All examples below are illustrative and not intended to describe actual cases.)

1. Does the settlement specify well-defined baseline performance standards and measurement protocols for actions that parties must undertake?
   EXAMPLE: "Irrigators will reduce their water use by half" vs. "Irrigators will reduce their water diversions to 150,000 acre-feet per year (50 percent of their 1990 diversions), as measured weekly at Irrigation District Pumping Station 1A with records to be compiled by the Bureau of Reclamation."
   EXAMPLE: "The irrigation district must implement the five best management practices for water conservation detailed in Bureau of Reclamation Manual 1996B, with full implementation to be certified by the Bureau no later than December 31, 2004, and monitored monthly thereafter."

2. Are the mechanisms selected the most cost-effective means to achieve goals? Incentive-based mechanisms generally are more cost effective and flexible than mandating a specific technology or management practice. If costs change or new technologies become available, then the specific actions that seemed most desirable when the agreement was drafted may become outmoded.
   EXAMPLE: "The irrigation district agrees to alter its water-rate structure to promote water conservation and to establish trading mechanisms for water permits, in order to promote more efficient water management and to comply with the annual cutback in water use mandated in the negotiated agreement."
   EXAMPLE: "The municipalities who are parties to the settlement agree to alter their water rate structures to encourage water conservation. They will implement increasing block-rate pricing and summer surcharges for excessive water use."
   NOTE: An agreement that requires parties to undertake specific expenditures and alter pricing structures can assist them in getting approval from regulatory authorities (if needed) for new expenditures and changes in pricing structures. Such regulatory authorities could include state corporation commissions or water boards, for instance.

3. Are the types of costs involved in implementation fully identified, including direct monetary outlays, contributions of staff time and other resources, costs of borrowing and raising money, and transaction costs?

4. Are the costs to all affected parties considered—stakeholders at the table, public agencies and taxpayers, and dispersed interests not at the table who may be affected?

5. Are cost-sharing principles and compensation packages well defined? Keep in mind that costs include not only monetary outlays but also reduced access to natural resources.
   EXAMPLE: "Historical fish catch quotas will be cut 20 percent during the next five years to allow fish stocks to improve. Job retraining will be provided to all persons employed on fishing boats during the past three years along with an expanded unemployment compensation program. Economic development grants will be provided to towns in which 10 percent or more of the employed population has been employed in the fishing industry over the past three years. The federal government will provide economic-development grants and unemployment compensation. The state will provide job retraining."

6. Are the costs assigned to various parties realistic in terms of the parties' ability to pay and the financial mechanisms available to each of them? Are loan repayment assumptions based on realistic projections about economic growth, future costs of inputs (inexpensive water or electric power), access to subsidies, others?

7. Are the financial instruments necessary to raise implementation money specified and is the overall mix of financial instruments cost effective given the powers of the various parties to levy taxes, issue bonds, and otherwise raise money?
   EXAMPLE: "The municipality will issue bonds, the

public utility will obtain a low-interest public loan, the water agency will increase its pumping tax on groundwater use, and the nongovernmental organization (NGO) will provide donor money to begin the most urgent habitat-restoration projects."

8. Do cost-sharing agreements provide a contingency fund (as with construction projects) for unanticipated costs, and do they specify the share of such unanticipated costs to be paid by the parties?

9. Are sanctions for noncompliance specified, including deadlines, performance benchmarks, and assessment of penalties? For instance, the 1978 Ak-Chin settlement provided that the federal government be liable for the replacement cost of the water supply promised if delivery obligations were not satisfied. Subsequently, the federal government did make payments to the tribe in recognition of its failure to make timely delivery of water.

10. Has an implementation team been designated with authority to monitor compliance, impose sanctions, and evaluate progress toward achieving the goals specified?
EXAMPLE: "The state engineer shall monitor daily water diversions of parties to the settlement and issue monthly reports. The tribal water quality program shall monitor dissolved oxygen levels weekly in the rivers that are the subject of the agreement and issue quarterly reports. A settlement implementation team shall meet quarterly to examine compliance and initiate enforcement actions in the case of noncompliance."

11. Is there an adaptive-management team and process to respond to unexpected changes in natural, political, or economic conditions that affect implementation?

12. Have decision-making structures (that have proved effective and acceptable to the parties) been institutionalized in the agreement so that the parties return to these venues for problem solving and these processes become the new way of doing business?
EXAMPLE: "A settlement implementation team composed of one appointed representative from the tribe, the state, the city, and the U.S. Department of the Interior shall convene quarterly to examine settlement progress and to provide a problem-solving venue."

13. Are documentation protocols that are incorporated into the agreement (such as monthly reporting of expenditures associated with implementation) compiled by a central recorder? Documentation should also include changes in resource pricing and subsequent changes in resource use.

rights. In a rare instance, claims against certain nonsettling parties or for specific past damages may be reserved.

These waivers provide states and non-Indian water users with certainty concerning the extent of the tribes' water rights. The waivers may also simplify pending general stream adjudications by removing some of the major parties and issues from the litigation. The Fort Peck compact, for example, states, "Tribes hereby relinquish forever any and all existing and future claims to water from any source and for any purpose."[15] The Colorado Ute settlement includes a tribal waiver of claims for past damages or injury as well as to future claims.

Justice Louis Brandeis once recognized states as laboratories of experimentation when it came to the development of the law. The quarter-century of Indian water rights settlements demonstrates the benefit of having allowed western states and tribes to develop different approaches to the quantification of these rights. We have gained a better understanding of what works, what does not work, and under what circumstances. (See sidebar 7.2 for a useful checklist of the type of considerations negotiators should keep in mind during their discussions and drafting.)

In the arid West, negotiators of Indian water rights seek to find water for tribal groups who have senior claims but are developing their water last. The potential of new uses on already strained water sources has serious implications for other water users and ecological systems. Since the feasibility of new water projects has declined, settlement water must likely come from improved water management. Fortunately, innovative water management promises to bridge for a while the deficit between limited supplies and increasing demands. In the process, water users are becoming more interdependent, and these relationships may produce more water supply reliability and social equity over the long term.

Negotiation processes and settlement terms may always vary in different parts of the West, but we are now in a position to move toward more standardized terms and language in these agreements. Settlements are always site specific and necessarily tailored to local water availability and competing water needs. Unfortunately, diverse approaches in the past have produced large inconsistencies in the amounts of water and money dedicated to settlements. As all parties learn more about how other settlements have been structured, possibly a more consistent and equitable approach will emerge.

PHOTO 8.1 Old shed and windmill. Photo: University of Arizona Agricultural Communications

CHAPTER 8

Making Water Available for Indian Water Rights Settlements
James P. Merchant

The fisheries, the wildlife, the trees here are part of us. Our ceremonies depend upon them. Our culture depends upon water being in the river. Without the water, the fisheries, the wildlife, which are our heritage, we cease to be Indian people.

Wes Martel, former tribal council member, Wind River Reservation

Settlement of Indian water rights claims typically requires thousands of hours of stakeholder effort and many years of difficult, and sometimes hostile, litigation and negotiations. In many cases, settlements are elusive because the water claimed by the Indians has already long been developed and used by other parties. This is due to the difference between Indian and non-Indian water rights (as explained in greater detail elsewhere in this book). On one hand, tribes have a federal reserved right to an amount of water sufficient to achieve the purpose of their reservation of land. This right can lie dormant until the tribe is ready to use its water. Unfortunately, the treaties, statutes, and executive orders that establish Indian reservations do not state the quantity of water to be reserved along with the land. On the other hand, since the late nineteenth century, non-Indian irrigators in the West generally have developed water under a system of prior appropriation: a first-in-time, first-in-right system of property rights. This system has given non-Indian irrigators every incentive to develop an area's water resources as rapidly as possible, despite any unquantified tribal claims to that water. As a result, by the time real efforts were initiated to resolve tribal water claims, the supply in many areas could not satisfy those claims without affecting non-Indian users. This chapter describes how past Indian water rights settlements have dealt with this problem and explores the extent to which agricultural water conservation can provide a solution.

Water Sources in Past Indian Water Rights Settlements

Past Indian water rights settlements have largely been achieved by reducing competition for local water, thus minimizing the potential impact of tribal claims. Settlements have targeted both the supply and the demand for local water supplies.

On the supply side, the emphasis has focused on importing additional water from outside an area and on developing additional local water supplies. On the demand side, settlements have reduced tribal water claims in exchange for an economic-development fund established for the benefit of the tribe, or have reduced non-Indian demand by paying one or more parties to reduce their existing water use. Agricultural water conservation measures to make water available to satisfy tribal claims have been used in only a few settlements.

Water Supply-and-Demand Management Approaches

A review of water supply-and-demand measures, including conservation, that have been employed to achieve those settlements is helpful in understanding the reasons for limited use of agricultural conservation.

Import water supplies from outside the local area. Several past settlements have relied on importing water or water rights into an area in order to increase the size of the water supply pie being divided.[1] The additional water is intended to reduce competition for limited local water resources by providing enough water so that the parties can reach a mutually beneficial agreement. While this approach was essential to the Rocky Boy's settlement in Montana and the Jicarilla Apache settlement in New Mexico, most examples have involved transfers of CAP allocations.[2] One reason that CAP allocations have been available for Arizona settlements is that many of the agricultural districts that signed up for the allocations have found the water to be too expensive. Consequently, some districts relinquished their CAP contracts to the federal government, making that water available for other purposes. The use of these allocations for tribal settlements has improved the financial position of CAP because the federal government assumed responsibility for the associated CAP capital and operating costs.

Develop new local water resources. A few water rights settlements have relied on the expansion of existing local water supplies.[3] The Northern Cheyenne settlement in Montana facilitated the reconstruction and enlargement of the Tongue River Dam, which not only corrected a hazardous condition at the dam but also created 20,000 acre-feet of new storage for the benefit of the tribe. The Northern Cheyenne Tribe agreed in the settlement to lend the State of Montana $11.5 million to finance the project using federal money appropriated for the tribe as part of the settlement.

The Colorado Ute settlement provided for the construction of an entirely new off-stream reservoir at Ridges Basin to store Animas River water for use by the Ute Mountain Ute and Southern Ute tribes as well as by several rapidly growing local non-Indian communities and the Navajo Nation. One common theme in the Colorado Ute, Northern Cheyenne, and other settlements is that new water development helped resolve non-Indian water supply problems in addition to providing water for tribes.

Focus on the broader tribal objective of economic development. In some instances, tribes are willing to accept a reduced water supply in exchange for monetary payments that promote the tribe's economic development. The goal of many tribes is not to secure additional water per se, but to enjoy the economic development made possible by that water. Accordingly, some settlements have provided an economic-development fund in lieu of new water projects. This approach may provide a tribe with greater economic value than the tribe could have realized from the water foregone.

Providing money in lieu of water, however, is not a suitable solution for all tribes. Many tribes desire to increase on-reservation employment for tribal members. Some reservations have few economic-development opportunities other than water-intensive agriculture. Although income from off-reservation water leases and investments may help raise on-reservation

living standards, it may do little to provide employment to tribal members. Each tribe needs to weigh these considerations before accepting money in lieu of water.

The Northern Ute Indian Tribe is an example of a tribe that negotiated a preliminary settlement intended to compensate the tribe for accepting a smaller amount of water rights. In 1965, the United States promised to develop a unit of CUP for the benefit of the tribe. The Bureau of Reclamation failed to locate a feasible reservoir site for the tribal project, and Congress never authorized construction. Consequently, the 1992 Ute Indian Rights Settlement Act attempted to put the tribe in the same economic position as it would have been were the CUP Indian unit constructed.[4] The settlement act authorized payment to the tribe of an annual income based first on a share of the project's capital repayment had it been built and later on the fair market value of the water the tribe relinquished. The overall settlement of water rights between the tribe and the State of Utah, however, remains unresolved.

Purchase off-reservation water rights. Another means to secure water for settlements has been to purchase water rights from willing sellers. The Ak-Chin settlement in Arizona transferred to the tribe 50,000 acre-feet per year of water rights that were previously authorized for the Yuma Mesa Division of the Gila Reclamation Project. The irrigation districts that would have been entitled to use the transferred water were given $9.4 million to pay for water conservation and drainage measures and for improvements to their water delivery systems. The water transferred from the Gila Project was to be conveyed to the Ak-Chin Community through CAP.

Two Indian water rights settlements in western Nevada also have incorporated water rights purchases from willing sellers to make enough water available for the parties to reach an agreement. The Fallon Paiute-Shoshone Indian Tribes Water Rights Settlement Act provided federal funds to the tribe and authorized the tribe to acquire from willing sellers and put into trust rights up to 8,454 acre-feet per year of water. The tribe can use these rights for any beneficial activity, including irrigation, fish and wildlife, municipal and industrial, recreation, or water quality improvement. There have been few willing sellers, however, and the price

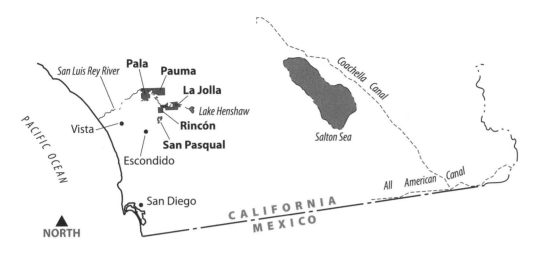

MAP 8.1   Selected reservations in Southern California

for water rights has exceeded what was anticipated in the settlement.

The Truckee-Carson–Pyramid Lake water settlement authorized the federal purchase of water rights for the purpose of sustaining 25,000 acres of wetland habitat that was previously supplied only from flood flows, spills, and irrigation return flows. This purchase program is currently being implemented largely with water rights purchased from the Newlands Irrigation Project. These settlements are examples of how negotiators found locally acceptable approaches for reducing regional competition for water that made it possible to reach an overall agreement.

Conserve water resources to provide settlement water. Only two settlements have relied on water conservation to provide some of the water needed to reach an agreement. In 1988, the San Luis Rey settlement provided the La Jolla, Rincón, San Pasqual, Pauma, and Pala bands in Southern California (see map 8.1) with a promise of 16,000 acre-feet per year. The federal legislation indicated that conjunctive use of groundwater or lining of the All American Canal could generate the promised water but did not commit the United States to any particular source. In 2000, the Imperial Irrigation District (IID), Metropolitan Water District of Southern California (MWD), San Diego County Water Authority, and Coachella Valley Water District reached a tentative agreement on several water conservation and transfer terms, one of which was to provide 16,000 acre-feet per year of water conserved from lining the All American Canal. This set of agreements

was reviewed in 2002 by California's State Water Resources Control Board but has not yet been ratified. The implementation of the canal-lining project and the availability of any conserved water are likely still years away.

The Truckee-Carson–Pyramid Lake settlement envisioned water supply enhancement through conservation by farmers and on the irrigated lands of a naval base. The settlement act directed the navy to "develop land management plans or measures to achieve dust control, fire abatement and safety, and foreign object damage control . . . to reduce direct surface deliveries of water."[5] This settlement also directed nearby cities to install water meters and charge customers by the quantity of water they use instead of a flat fee in order to improve urban water management.

The fact that agricultural water conservation has played a role in only two of the seventeen Indian water rights settlements reviewed is significant. The next section will identify some of the impediments to using conserved water in Indian water rights settlements and will explore the prospects for using this approach in future water rights settlements.

Use in Future Settlements of Water Conserved by Agriculture

Irrigated agriculture is the biggest water user in most of the western United States. In principle, agricultural water conservation could facilitate Indian water rights settlements in two different ways. First, on reserva-

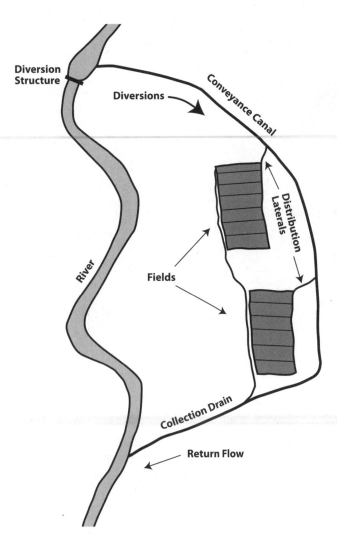

FIGURE 8.1 Schematic of irrigation project

tions with more water available than is needed to irrigate the irrigable land, greater water use efficiency in a proposed tribal irrigation project would reduce the water needed to implement that project and satisfy the tribal claim. Second, off-reservation conservation could free up water needed by tribes.

Water Conservation Considerations

A review of some aspects of water use and conservation will provide a context for these issues of agricultural water conservation in water rights settlements. Factors such as how water is used to irrigate crops, how this irrigation water can be conserved, and the possibilities for water conservation in new irrigation

projects on reservations as well as in existing agricultural districts all inform the issues.

How water is used to irrigate crops. Figure 8.1 shows how water is first diverted from a surface or groundwater source, conveyed to an irrigation project, then distributed to individual fields. Figure 8.2 shows how water is applied to the fields, where some evaporates from the soil surface and some is transpired by the crops (these uses together make up *evapotranspiration*, or ET). Some of the applied water may run off the field and could be collected in a drainage ditch. Other applied water may percolate below the root zone and make its way to an aquifer or be intercepted by subsurface drains and conveyed to a drainage ditch. Surface runoff or subsurface drainage water that returns to the original water source is called *return flow*.

Some of the diverted water can be lost (but not necessarily consumed) at any point in the conveyance and distribution systems.[6] Some of the water conveyed in an open canal may evaporate. If the canal is not lined, water will seep through the canal into the ground. If more water is diverted than actually used, the canals may spill excess water. Water-loving plants known as *phreatophytes* tend to flourish along canals and ditches if their roots can reach a water supply. While water evaporated from open canals or transpired by phreatophytes is consumed, seepage and spill water may remain available for use. To the extent that the seepage and spill water return to the original source (or another water body useable for irrigation), that water is not consumed. If the seepage or spill water flows to a saline body unusable for irrigation, it is considered consumed and unavailable for irrigation. Similarly, applied water beyond that needed for ET sometimes returns to a useable water body and is available for further use. If surface runoff or deep percolation joins a useable water body, then it can be reused elsewhere for additional irrigation.[7]

How irrigation water can be conserved. There are opportunities to conserve water at almost every phase in crop irrigation. As discussed above, only some savings actually reduce the amount of water consumed, thereby making additional water available for other uses. Reducing canal evaporation by converting open canals to pipelines and controlling phreatophytes are two methods of reducing water consumption during

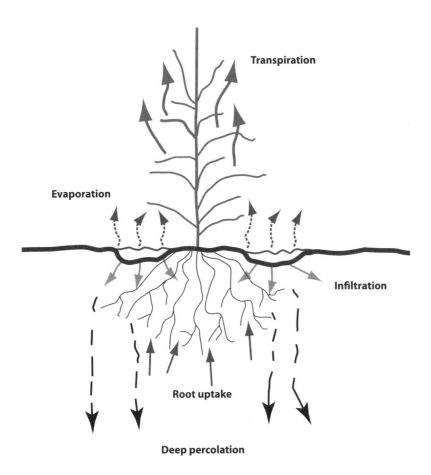

Transpiration

Evaporation

Infiltration

Root uptake

Deep percolation

FIGURE 8.2 Schematic of crop evapotranspiration, infiltration, and deep percolation

conveyance. Lining canals to reduce seepage or building small reservoirs to capture canal spills only reduces consumption if these water losses would otherwise fail to return to a useable water body. If these seepage losses or spills flow to a useable water body, they are already available for additional uses without the conservation effort.

Water applied to a field is consumed by evaporation from the soil surface and by crop transpiration. Evaporation losses become a smaller percentage of total ET as a crop becomes established. Evaporation losses could be minimized with less frequent irrigations or by using irrigation systems (such as surface or subsurface drip, microsprinkler, or alternate furrow surface irrigation) that reduce the wetted soil surface. Drip and microsprinkler irrigation systems are expensive and not suitable for all crops.

Crop transpiration is the major consumptive use of irrigation water and is, in fact, the main purpose of irrigation. Generally, the more water available for a plant, the higher its yield up to the point of the maximum attainable yield. On a field-wide level, however, crop yields exhibit a diminishing return relationship to applied water because of soil or irrigation application variability. To maximize profits, an irrigator should apply water to the point that the cost of the next increment of water equals the profits from the increased crop yield. Applying more water would increase net returns by less than the cost of irrigating, and much of the water would go to return flows or deep percolation. Applying less water would cause the irrigator to lose potential profits because the foregone net returns would exceed the saved irrigation cost. If the irrigator is applying the correct amount of water, cutting back water use will reduce irrigator profits. A field study of several hundred irrigators in California's Central Valley found that approximately one-third of the irrigators are actually applying too little water, one-third too much, and the remaining one-third are applying the correct amount. The study concluded that because many irrigators are applying too little water, improvements in irrigation management might actually increase water use.[8]

Runoff and deep percolation are two losses that constitute the part of applied water not consumed by ET. If these losses flow to saline water bodies, they are unavailable for reuse in irrigation.[9] Consequently, reducing the runoff and deep percolation under those circumstances can provide additional useable water.

Runoff primarily occurs in surface irrigation systems. Sprinkler and drip irrigation systems can be designed to avoid "ponding" of water and runoff. Some surface irrigation systems also minimize runoff. Level basins, for example, capture the applied water within a berm area, allowing all water to infiltrate into the soil. The most common surface irrigation system, furrow irrigation, incorporates runoff into its design. In order for water to infiltrate into the desired depth of soil, it must be available over the soil surface for an adequate length of time (opportunity time). Unless the furrows are completely level, the applied water will advance toward the tail end of the furrow, and some water will necessarily run off the field if the entire length of the furrow has water for an adequate opportunity time. Good management can minimize the runoff, but the runoff cannot be completely eliminated without underirrigating the tail end of a field. Runoff can be captured in tailwater ponds and reused on the same or different fields, but such a collection and reuse system can cost $120 to $190 per acre-foot of saved water.

Deep percolation refers to the water that percolates below the root zone of the plants. Deep percolation can occur with any type of irrigation system and is due to a combination of factors, including the need for leaching, nonuniform soils and irrigation rates, and management practices. Leaching is the practice of applying extra water (beyond that needed for ET) to a field in order to drive salts below the root zone. Salts interfere with a plant's ability to use water, and high salt concentrations can reduce crop yields. Leaching is a crucial practice in areas where salts tend to accumulate to harmful levels. Even without any leaching, it

is nearly impossible to irrigate a crop adequately with no deep percolation. Unless a field is perfectly uniform in both soil texture and water application rate, water will percolate beyond the root zone in some parts of the field before the root zone is filled in other parts. Figure 8.3 shows how deep percolation occurs under both furrow irrigation and irrigation methods that minimize runoff. Some or all of the deep percolation may return to a useable water body and be available for reuse.

Prospects for conserving water in new irrigation projects on reservations. A new irrigation project can be designed for high water use efficiency, thus reducing the amount of water necessary to satisfy a tribal claim and easing competition for local water supplies. In fact, new irrigation projects designed for reservations already incorporate efficient practices, and so additional water savings may be elusive. One reason for the high efficiency is that modern engineering technology has encouraged increasingly more efficient irrigation designs as our knowledge of hydrology, soil science, and plant science has progressed. High efficiency in reservation irrigation designs also results from two occurrences often found on Indian reservations.

First, reservation irrigation projects usually are designed to irrigate challenging land (land with low water-holding capacity, steep slopes, or other conditions that would be difficult design parameters for traditional surface irrigation systems). Many reservations were established after non-Indians had claimed the most irrigable land, leaving the Indians with land more difficult to irrigate. The San Carlos Apache Reservation in Arizona and the Tule River Indian Reservation in California are two examples. In addition, some reservations with a desirable land base lost these lands after the General Allotment Act was enacted in 1887. Some of these reservations were opened for non-Indian settlement after portions were allotted to tribal members (e.g., Rosebud Sioux Indian Reservation in South Dakota). On some reservations the land allotted to tribal members was later sold or otherwise lost. In addition, tribes asserting a claim to a reserved water right are usually interested in exploring the limits of what can be considered "irrigable." Accordingly, an irrigation project design will at least consider irrigating land that requires modern technologies, such as drip or microsprinkler irrigation. Al-

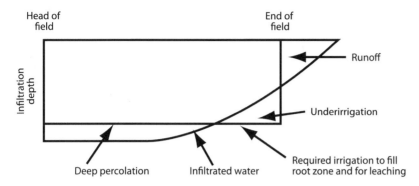

Furrow Irrigation

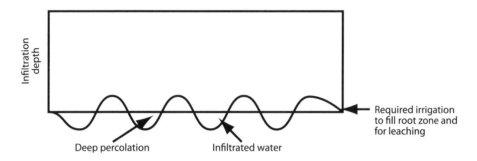

Level Basin or Sprinkler Irrigation

FIGURE 8.3   Schematic of runoff and deep percolation for furrow irrigation and level basin or sprinkler irrigation

though well-managed surface irrigation systems can reach high efficiencies, these modern low-volume systems typically operate with even higher efficiencies.

Second, for some of the same reasons that land with substantial development challenges is evaluated in Indian irrigation projects, these same projects often rely on relatively expensive water. Indian projects sometimes need to include long water conveyance systems, high pump lifts, or new storage projects that neighboring non-Indians were able to avoid. This increases the relative cost of water for tribes, giving irrigation engineers an incentive to design highly efficient projects. Both the availability of modern irrigation technology and the potentially high cost of water delivery motivate design engineers to maximize system efficiencies.

Prospects for conserving water in off-reservation agricultural districts. Existing off-reservation agriculture may offer attractive opportunities to conserve water. The best opportunities may occur in older irrigation projects that convey water through unlined canals and ditches and apply it through surface irrigation methods. Irrigators do tend to make progressive improvements in their systems, not only to reduce water costs but also in the expectation of higher yields and lower labor or chemical costs. Nevertheless, the incremental cost of saving additional water in existing irrigation systems may be less than the cost of reducing water use even further with newly designed systems.

Capital improvements that have proved to increase water use efficiency include lining canals (reducing deep percolation), constructing small regulating reservoirs along a canal (reducing canal spills), leveling fields (reducing runoff and deep percolation), converting surface to sprinkler or drip irrigation systems (reducing runoff and deep percolation), and building tailwater pumpback systems (reducing runoff).

Management decisions also affect water use. At the most basic level, a grower must make the choice of planting a crop or leaving a field fallow. Water use varies widely among crops, so the choice of a particular crop affects both crop ET and the ancillary water uses such as leaching (salt-sensitive crops would require more leaching than salt-tolerant crops) and water application losses (deep percolation and runoff on a particular field would be roughly proportional to ET). The scheduling of irrigation is another management decision, and use of information on weather and field-level soil moisture can greatly increase the accuracy of decisions on when and how much to irrigate.

Many of these conservation practices have been applied to provide water for urban growth. In Southern California, for example, despite rapid population growth over the last several decades, significant new water supplies have not become available since the State Water Project began delivering water to the region in the 1960s.

The MWD provides wholesale water to member water utilities that serve about 17 million people in the region. With the growing population in its service area and pressure from other Colorado River states for California to reduce its use of Colorado River water, the MWD has been actively seeking new water supplies. For example, it reached an agreement in 1989 with the IID to fund water conservation measures within the IID in exchange for the conserved water. The agreement includes canal lining, canal-regulating reservoir construction, a pilot tailwater pumpback system project, and some management improvements such as system automation and a twelve-hour (instead of twenty-four–hour) water delivery schedule. The MWD has spent over $100 million implementing these measures, and the water savings total more than 100,000 acre-feet annually. The improvements were designed to capture water that would otherwise be spilled or drain to the Salton Sea, a water body too saline for irrigation use. These water savings increase the water available for various uses.[10]

The MWD also negotiated an agreement with the Palo Verde Irrigation District (PVID) to pay district growers to fallow land, giving the MWD access to the water that otherwise would have been consumed by crops. The agreement allows the MWD to dictate annually the acreage to be fallowed and the water to be conserved based on the MWD's year-to-year water needs, with the annual water transfers varying from 25,000 acre-feet to 111,000 acre-feet. The cost of this water to the MWD will range from $153 to $206 per acre-foot, depending on how much water is actually conserved. In contrast to the conservation approach in the MWD's agreement with the IID, the agreement with the PVID saves water by reducing crop water consumption (via ET). The MWD will receive only the water that would have been consumed on the fallowed land. Although the PVID diverts from the Colorado River substantially more water than it actually consumes, the district gets credit for return flows to the river. Unlike the MWD and IID case, water conservation from lining canals or reducing field runoff in the PVID would not produce any additional water savings that could be transferred to the MWD.

The MWD's agreement with the PVID highlights a complication in the use of fallowing to conserve water. Most water rights in private irrigation districts are held by either landowners or the irrigation district (whose members are landowners), so landowners are the parties receiving payments under a water conservation and transfer agreement. Two other groups of people are financially affected by land fallowing and may not be represented in the negotiations or payment arrangements—the farm workers employed on the affected farms and businesses who rely on trade with local growers. The MWD agreement did recognize these third-party impacts and sought to mitigate them by (1) limiting the fallowing offer to a maximum of 29 percent of irrigated acreage, (2) promising $6 million for local community improvement programs, and (3) demonstrating in a pilot project that 93 percent of the money paid to the PVID grower would likely be spent in on-farm investments, purchases, and debt repayment, and that most of this spending would occur in the local area.

Agricultural water conservation has played a limited role in providing water for past Indian water rights settlements and is likely to facilitate future settlements only under specific circumstances. Although the parties should continue to seek opportunities to apply conservation as a means of reducing competition for water, they need to recognize the limitations of this approach:

- Most Indian water rights settlements have used means other than conservation to solve the problem of water shortages. Examples include developing new water supplies, importing water, purchasing non-Indian water rights, and compensating tribes for reducing their water claims.

- Improving irrigation efficiency to save water is usually expensive, and the parties must be willing to bear the cost. Recent efforts in California, for example, have achieved conservation costing about $120 to $200 per acre-foot.

- Some efficiency measures will work only under certain conditions. Some highly efficient irrigation systems, for example, are not well suited to all crops or soil types; and canal lining may not save much seepage if the canal is located in relatively impermeable soils.

- Additional conservation efforts to stretch water supplies may be particularly problematic on new Indian projects. Such projects are often already designed to achieve high efficiencies due to the challenging land being irrigated and expensive water supplies, both of which give the design engineers an incentive to conserve water in order to minimize costs.

- Past experience in implementing improvements to save water shows that the results can be somewhat unpredictable and may take years to achieve. The 1988 MWD-IID agreement achieved nearly twice the savings expected for some measures (twelve-hour delivery schedule) but less than 65 percent of the savings expected on other measures (canal lining).

- Other parties may already have a claim to the water being conserved. If the conserved water was previously runoff or deep percolation that was being reused by others, then those users may have enforceable rights to the water. The only source for conservation that is clearly without competing claims is the water presently being consumed by crops. Fallowing is therefore an appealing method to conserve water because no other party has a claim. Fallowing has other problems, however, due to the importance of irrigation to a region's overall economy and the high cost to compensate landowners for fallowing their land.

PART 4

Learning from Collective Experience

When westerners work hard together on issues that affect their homeland, it feels to them that what they are doing *is* democracy in the most fundamental, the most meaningful, the most enduring sense.

Daniel Kemmis, *This Sovereign Land*

PHOTO 9.1   Headgate awaits the gift of water. Photo: Todd Sargent

CHAPTER 9

Representative Settlements and Settlement Efforts

> In scarcity lies the opportunity for community. The native peoples of the Americas practiced the art of water works construction out of ingenuity and necessity, praying to the gods for rain to fill their earth-constructed hope against despair. The native peoples also demonstrated that water supply planning and infrastructure is a core responsibility of those who would govern in the public interest. Westerners always come round to the practical and symbolic value of water for people and the environment.
>
> Justice Gregory J. Hobbs, Jr., Colorado Supreme Court, Manchu Picchu book review

In this chapter we examine a series of settlements and settlement efforts, which are central to our discussion. Most settlement work occurred since 1980, but in several cases agreements were reached earlier. With the increasing number of settlement efforts, it is not possible to profile all of them here. Rather, we present a series of settlements that represent various conditions and solutions. The cross-section of profiles presented here highlights the complexity of the settlement process and the ingenuity of parties seeking to achieve durable and effective settlements. These profiles could be organized in many ways. We have chosen to present most of these profiles based on the venue in which they were achieved or attempted: as the result of strong congressional leadership, as the result of state governmental initiatives, as the result of tribal initiatives, or as the result of other water users' efforts. We begin this chapter, however, discussing litigation rather than settlement as a means to quantify tribal water rights claims. We close the chapter with profiles addressing two major problems confronting settlement efforts today: how the ESA complicates negotiations, and when, if ever, a settlement is finally settled.

Quantification Resulting from Litigation

The water rights of tribes are legally based, and litigation is the traditional method to recognize and quantify such rights. When and how litigation is used depends on the circumstance. In some areas, like South Dakota, all water users seem content to avoid litigation. In other settings, states have initiated large general stream adjudications in order to obtain jurisdiction over and quantify federal reserved water rights. Some tribes, like Arizona's White Mountain Apache Tribe, have resisted state court jurisdiction. Other tribes, like the Gila River Indian Community, have decided that even state court litigation of their water rights can be a tool for securing settlement. Finally, states, tribes, and federal agencies can tacitly agree to litigate in both state and federal courts, as has happened in Oregon and New Mexico.

Even when well managed, litigation is expensive, yields narrow results, and can foster lasting ill will in the community. Wyoming's Bighorn River adjudication, also known as the Wind River litigation, is often used as the poster child for the disadvantages of using litigation to determine Indian water rights.

Wind River Litigation

Ramsey Kropf

> The result of the court is fragmented, providing no clear guidance to the parties. Pragmatically, it is difficult to imagine how this opinion can be implemented ... All that is really clear from this narrow opinion is that the parties will continue to litigate their conflicts.
>
> Justice J. Golden, Wyoming Supreme Court, referring to 1992 Wind River ruling

The decades-long Wind River litigation has been bitter and expensive, and leaves a legacy of continuing uncertainties over water supplies and strained intergovernmental relations. A series of court rulings, however, has clarified specific issues, including the quantity and seniority of tribal water claims. The courts recognized a large and senior tribal water right based on the PIA standard. The case, carefully observed by tribes and states throughout the West, serves as a critical reference point for other parties, with its graphic portrayal of the benefits and hazards of litigation. Only the most basic aspects of the litigation and negotiations are presented here.[1]

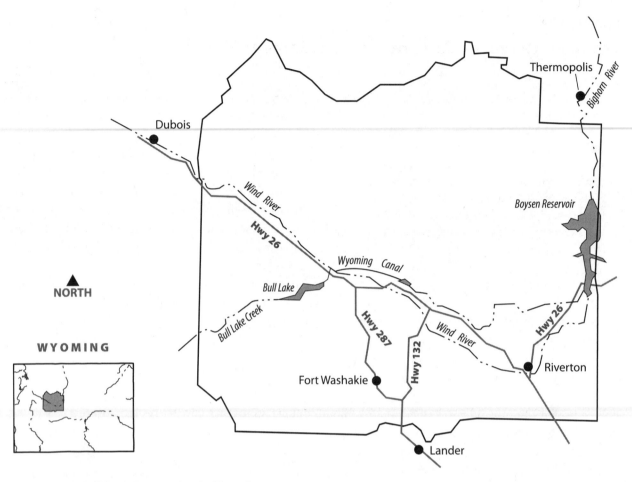

MAP 9.1 Wind River Reservation in Wyoming

Physical setting. In the early 1800s, non-Indians began to enter the traditional homelands of the Shoshone Indians in what is now northwestern Wyoming. In an effort to avert the bloody conflicts erupting elsewhere as Indian homelands were encroached upon, the United States and the Shoshone Indians entered into the First Treaty of Fort Bridger in 1863. The treaty recognized vast portions of the present-day states of Colorado, Utah, and Wyoming as Shoshone territory.

Just five years later, Shoshone lands were reduced substantially under a subsequent treaty that created the Wind River Indian Reservation (see map 9.1). In 1878, the United States moved the Arapaho Tribe from the plains onto the Wind River Reservation despite historic intertribal enmity and vehement objections from both tribes. The Shoshone and Arapaho tribes have jointly occupied the reservation since that time and their Joint Business Council is charged with co-ordinating reservation governance between the two tribes.

Although it comprises only a small portion of the Shoshone's historical territories, the reservation includes fertile river valleys, extensive grasslands and forests, valuable mineral and energy deposits, and numerous lakes, springs, and streams. One of the most productive and well-watered regions of Wyoming, it attracted non-Indian farmers who homesteaded on the reservation during the allotment era (1887 to 1934), when the federal government opened reservation lands to non-Indian settlement. Consequently, land ownership within the Wind River Reservation (as with many reservations) is fragmented among tribal ownership, individual Indian allotments, and non-Indian allotments. This makes tribal regulation of land and water use difficult, given the reluctance of non-Indians to be regulated by tribal governments. Although much of the 2.2 million-acre reservation is tribal land or held by Indian allottees, the most productive agricultural lands belong to non-Indians.

Non-Indian farmers developed extensive irrigation on the reservation under the sponsorship of federal reclamation programs. The reservation encompasses Wyoming's largest canal and irrigation district, with a primarily non-Indian membership. This canal historically diverted the entire flow of the Wind River during periods of intensive irrigation, leaving a dry riverbed below the diversion dam.

Commencement of adjudication. The State of Wyoming initiated the *Big Horn* adjudication in state court in the mid 1970s, in part to clarify the rights of non-Indian water users with respect to the Wind River tribes. A special master was appointed by the court to administer the process, and early in the adjudication, the master divided the case into three phases. The tribes and the United States (acting on behalf of the tribes) each filed water claims. The special master quantified the reserved rights of the tribes based on a broad spectrum of uses, including irrigation, fisheries, wildlife, livestock, mining, commercial, municipal, and domestic. His report was released in 1982 after four years of hearings that involved over one hundred attorneys, 15,000 pages of hearings transcripts, and unprecedented expense to parties on all sides.[2]

The Wyoming District Court disagreed with the special master's findings and concluded that the tribes had reserved the water solely for agriculture. Based on the PIA analysis developed by the special master, the district court quantified the tribes' reserved water rights at 500,717 acre-feet per year, with a priority date of 1868, making them the most senior water rights in the basin. Following appeals by all parties, the Wyoming Supreme Court in 1988 upheld the use of the PIA standard (against the state's opposition), ruled that reserved water rights do not extend to groundwater, and denied reserved water rights for instream flow and other tribal purposes.[3] In 1989, the U.S. Supreme Court, in a split decision (4-4 with one abstention), affirmed the Wyoming Supreme Court's use of the PIA standard in quantifying the tribes' entitlement.[4]

The state and the tribes negotiated a one-year agreement following the U.S. Supreme Court ruling in which all parties accepted equally shared surpluses and shortages of water in the basin. In return for this protection of non-Indian water users, the state paid the tribes $2 million in a compensation fund, granted $1 million for repair and expansion of reservation water delivery systems, and forgave 75 percent of oil and gas severance taxes it collects from reservation energy production. The agreement expired in March 1990 and was not renewed.

Use and development of tribal water. In April 1990, the Wind River tribes, through their water resources control board, dedicated a portion of their quantified *Winters* rights to maintain streamflows and protect fisheries. The State of Wyoming and non-Indian water users objected to this instream flow dedication, because its enforcement might prevent irrigators from receiving their accustomed diversions. The Wyoming state engineer declined the tribes' requests to enforce the instream flow permit and did not require reduced diversions from the river.

The parties returned to state court to contest issues concerning state-tribal jurisdiction to administer water rights and tribal dedication of *Winters* rights for instream flows. In 1990, the Wyoming Supreme Court addressed the issue of the priority dates of non-Indians who owned land formerly held by tribal allottees.[5] Another series of cases was litigated in 1990, 1991, and 1992. In March 1991, the Wyoming District Court found that the tribes had administrative jurisdiction over all water rights exercised on the reservation, including state-permitted water rights. The State of Wyoming and non-Indian water users appealed. In 1992, a highly fragmented Wyoming Supreme Court found in five separate opinions that the tribes could not dedicate a portion of their *Winters* rights to instream purposes.[6] In this ruling, the court also found that the tribal government does not have blanket jurisdiction over non-Indian water users on the reservation and that the state has some jurisdiction over water rights exercised on the reservation (reversing the 1991 district court ruling). The five Wyoming Supreme Court justices split on each substantive issue, thereby intensifying debate about the allowed uses of reserved rights and state-tribal jurisdiction.

Denied the option of using their decreed water for instream flow use, the tribes turned their attention to developing their decreed agricultural right. Disputes about jurisdictional matters, however, were not over.

Allotment and appurtenancy issues. During 1992, another court decision opened another area of controversy concerning the water rights of allotments (often referred to as *Walton* rights) and other specific parcels within the reservation. The district court issued a judgment (and later its decree/order partially amending judgment) concerning *Walton* rights claims. Sovereign control over the administration of *Walton* rights was at issue.

The district court's 1992 determinations on *Walton* rights triggered additional litigation for the next decade. The tribes consider *Walton* claims as incursions on tribal reserved rights, because these claims were largely made by non-Indian successors to Indian allottees, who also claimed the same priority date as the federal reserved right. In 1992, the district court reviewed the special master's report on the first ten original remanded *Walton* claims, laying out a framework by which the parties could evaluate those claims. The court also certified its judgment so that the decision could be appealed in the Wyoming Supreme Court. Other orders emanated from the district court in 1992 addressing claims to groundwater uses and adjudicating small stock and domestic wells.

In 1993, the parties took a hard look at the over four hundred new *Walton* rights claims that had been filed with the court pursuant to the *Big Horn II* decision.[7] The Bluff Irrigation District, holding junior water rights, was joined by other districts in a motion requesting the dismissal of all *Walton*-type claims that were not based on Indian allotments, which would have the effect of reducing the *Walton* claims by half. These "super-*Walton*" claims were based on title derived from the Homestead Act, the Cash Entry Act, the Desert Land Act, and the federal Reclamation Act.[8] These super-*Walton* claimants bootstrapped their claims to the Indian reservation's priority date, because these lands were once within the boundary of the reservation. Unlike other *Walton* rights, the super-*Walton* claims did not derive title directly from an Indian allottee. Before the district court decided Bluff Irrigation District's motion, the Wyoming Supreme Court issued *Big Horn IV*.[9] This procedural order directed the district court to fully adjudicate all *Walton*-type claims prior to reviewing any interim decisions

about the nature of those claims. In early 1994, the district court dismissed all super-*Walton* claims. The Wyoming Supreme Court, in *Big Horn V*, affirmed that claimants who were not successors in interest to Indian allottees could not claim an 1868 federal reservation priority date.[10]

Incremental use of settlement. In 1995, in response to these rulings, the court-appointed special master began to schedule hearings regarding *Walton* claims, including thorny issues related to administration of *Walton* rights. The parties designed a process by which they could look at all the varied factual issues for the *Walton* claims and set aside their disputes on the difficult cross-cutting global legal issues. As hearings were scheduled, many settlement meetings were held to reach agreement on factual issues and identify areas where hearings might be needed later. In August 1996, the parties agreed on procedures to reserve their legal positions in multiple claims for later determination. The district court formalized this process in its *Order Regarding Global* Walton *Issues* (November 1997). This modest but growing use of settlement occurred in other areas of litigation as well.

Other state-based claims were moving forward in the adjudication process on a separate track, without opposition by the United States and tribes. All debates on the effects of state-based claims were put off until the court determined the state-based claims in the third phase of the litigation. Based on the parties' earlier settlement, these smaller and less contentious claims could move forward in a relatively unopposed fashion through the adjudicatory process.

In addition to the reserved global issues, including administration of *Walton* rights, in 1998 a new Petition for Appurtenancy was filed. This raised appurtenancy issues for petitioners who were not *Walton* rights claimants but had claims to 1868 water rights as either fee owners or trust landholders. The petitions claimed that the federal reserved right associated with their property in the *Big Horn I* decree (original decree quantifying federal and tribal rights) should be determined as appurtenant, or assigned to their lands. They feared that the tribes would move the overall federal reserved rights among various lands so that current irrigators would be unable to use the amount associated with their property. Petitioners were concerned that they would be unable to secure financing if their lands were valued as dry. Because these petitioners were not *Walton* claimants, the special master put the Petition for Appurtenancy on a different schedule than the *Walton* claims.

Between 1995 and 1998, the *Walton* cases progressed largely by stipulated settlements. Because the global legal issues were reserved for a later date, the parties were able to reach settlement in almost all cases on most factual matters. By June 1998, the factual determinations were largely complete. At that time, the special master held a hearing on the disputed facts regarding administration and appurtenancy, in addition to hearing a variety of the other reserved legal issues. The special master's report was filed after this hearing in 1999, and the district court upheld a majority of the report in 2000. This decision provided a tabulation of all *Walton* rights granted and identified those denied. In addition, the court issued an administration strategy: Non-Indian *Walton* rights holders would be subject to state administration, but once at the Indian headgate, the tribes would administer *Walton* rights. Any dispute would go first to the state engineer to resolve and then to the district court if the state engineer's solution was unacceptable. The few *Walton* rights claimants who were not granted *Walton* rights by the district court appealed to the Wyoming Supreme Court. The court issued its opinion, *Big Horn VI*, in June 2002.[11] The court held that, since the Wind River Irrigation Project was intended to benefit allottees and their successors, *Walton* claimants were entitled to share in the reserved right if they could demonstrate beneficial use of the water within a reasonable time.

Settlement of appurtenancy issues. The separate Petition for Appurtenancy proceedings rekindled old distrust among the parties, and the special master set a hearing for the matter in Spring 1999. After some discovery decisions, the parties were able to present the court with a stipulated settlement and consent decree regarding the Petition for Appurtenancy. Both the tribes and the petitioners agreed that the water right, regardless of how it might be administered, should be appurtenant to the land. The district court held a hearing for objections on this matter in 2001, dismissed several objections, and finally accepted the settlement.

Pursuant to the consent decree, tribal members and successors-in-interest to trust or fee-owned lands will be treated the same as long as the lands where included in the quantification of the tribes' federal reserved rights in the 1980s. These rights will be permanent unless they are abandoned or not beneficially used in accordance with applicable law. The consent decree does not address regulation or administration.

Reflections. Active for over a quarter-century, the Bighorn River general stream adjudication continues. Although Wyoming's courts have decided many issues in the *Big Horn* case, the parties have resolved many other issues by themselves. The special master's original decision to break the case into three phases has enabled the parties to settle some issues, leave intractable problems for the courts, and allow the adjudication to progress. In contrast to settlement efforts elsewhere in the western United States, comprehensive settlement processes have not been used in the Wyoming adjudication. Rather, discrete issues have been settled through negotiations, and the battles over broader legal principles have gone through the judicial process.

The permits granted by state law to large irrigation districts have not been reported to the court, and it is unclear whether the tribes or federal government will dispute these rights. Until the final Phase III claims are completely adjudicated, and until any tribal and federal claims disputing these rights are resolved, the adjudication will continue. While waiting for the Phase III claims to be addressed, the parties continue to discuss strategies to obtain additional water storage and federal appropriations to address water-management issues. Under the auspices of the court and the state engineer, the major parties have also begun discussions on the form the final decree in the adjudication will take. Wins and losses for both sides have brought the parties together to settle some issues, an approach that seemed impossible two decades ago.

This profile illustrates the federal government's responsibility in producing the current conflicts. The United States ratified treaties with the Shoshone that guaranteed extensive land reservations but later diminished the size of the reservation, settled another tribe on those lands, encouraged non-Indian settlement, and subsidized irrigation development for non-Indian farmers on the reservation. Federal agencies, however, are now playing a positive role in searching for solutions. The FWS has provided critical information on reservation fisheries and is working in cooperation with tribal and state wildlife officials. Federal agencies are also participating in joint tribal, state, and federal efforts to improve water supplies for water users in the Wind River basin through better water management and new storage development.

As former Wyoming state engineer Jeff Fasset said in 1992, "Courts provide narrow answers to narrow questions, yielding a crop of new questions."[12] This certainly has been the case concerning the management of reserved rights and the significance of *Walton* claims in the *Big Horn* adjudication. The courts have failed to resolve the question of management jurisdiction, and ramifications continue, leaving the future of Indian and non-Indian communities clouded by uncertain access to water and lack of coordinated water management. Although court decisions may guide them, parties are ultimately forced to deal with each other in resolving their shared use of water in the Bighorn basin.

Settlements Resulting from Strong Congressional Leadership

Some of the first Indian water rights settlements resulted from strong federal government leadership with modest participation by state government. This was an era when western members of Congress, such as Senator Barry Goldwater (R-AZ), Senator Clinton Anderson (D-NM), and Representative Wayne Aspinall (D-CO), held powerful committee positions. Representative John Rhodes (R-AZ), in particular, was influential in securing early settlements in Arizona, such as the Ak-Chin settlement (1978) discussed below. These early settlements were not isolated initiatives, however, but often necessary steps in enabling southwestern states to develop their allocations under the Colorado River Compact. For example, the 1962 Navajo Indian Irrigation Project (NIIP), discussed in a later section, allowed New Mexico to proceed with its SJCP diverting water from a Colorado River tributary.

The Truckee-Carson–Pyramid Lake water settlement (1990), also profiled below, is a more contemporary example of a settlement forged by the personal leadership of a United States senator. This settlement was in response to a complex set of problems and, thus, mirrors the growing complexity of western water issues. Because of the time and resources necessary to

craft a settlement in today's complex water arena, we are unlikely to see members of Congress as involved in these negotiations as in the past. Settlements still need congressional champions in later stages of the process, however, to secure final approval and federal money.

Ak-Chin Water Settlement

> It is impossible to understand the appeal of negotiated settlements . . . without first understanding this long and frustrating struggle to obtain water for Indian reservations. Indian tribes won many court battles, but Anglos nearly always ended up with the water.
>
> Daniel McCool, *Native Waters*

The 21,840-acre Ak-Chin Reservation was established by executive order in 1912 for scattered bands of Pima and Papago Indians. The reservation is located in the midst of a productive agricultural area in south-central Arizona (see map 9.2). Prior to completion of CAP, neighboring irrigators, as well as the Ak-Chin Indian Community, were wholly dependent on groundwater for irrigation and domestic purposes. By the 1960s, the Indian community was irrigating approximately 10,000 acres with groundwater pumped from depths of forty to fifty feet. Due to the outstanding success of the tribal farming enterprise, the Indian community had achieved near economic self-sufficiency. Extensive off-reservation pumping nearby caused sharp declines (approximately twenty feet per year) in groundwater levels beneath the reservation, and the Indian community's irrigated acreage declined from 10,000 to less than 5,000 acres.

Negotiations. The Indian community first turned to the United States, requesting in 1976 that it file suit against the non-Indian pumpers on behalf of the community. In recognition of its trust responsibility to provide the Ak-Chin with a reliable water supply, the federal government entered into negotiations with the community to settle its water claims. This approach was supported enthusiastically by the State of Arizona and local non-Indian water users.

Settlement agreement. After two years of negotiations and before the lawsuit was filed, the Department of the Interior reached an agreement with the Indian community. The settlement provided for both an interim water supply to meet the emergency needs of

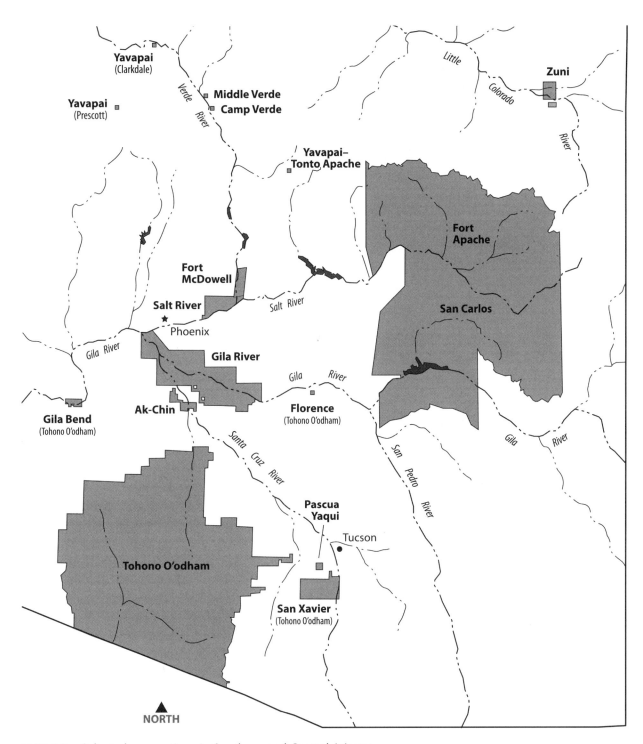

MAP 9.2 Selected reservations in Southern and Central Arizona

the Indian community and a permanent water supply within twenty-five years. The settlement envisioned developing a well field on nearby federal land to provide the interim supply. Although not clearly identified, the permanent supply (85,000 acre-feet annually to irrigate 16,725 acres) was to include groundwater developed from nearby federal lands, groundwater underlying the reservation, the Ak-Chin's previous CAP allocation, and other sources as needed. Under the act, the federal government would be liable for the replacement cost of the water if it failed to meet the delivery obligations.

Although the federal administration was supportive of the Ak-Chin's claim to water, it was concerned about overall cost and federal liability, particularly in light of the uncertain nature of the water supply. Despite these concerns, the settlement was passed by Congress and signed by President Carter in 1978.[13] Although enjoying the support of the State of Arizona and local water users, this settlement was opposed by most other western states.

Settlement amendments. The settlement was amended in 1984 when the anticipated water supplies proved insufficient and too costly. The revised agreement, negotiated with the active involvement of Arizona's congressional delegation (Senator Barry Goldwater, Representative Morris Udall, and Representative John McCain) provided for the federal government to pay damages for failure to make timely delivery of the interim water supply and modified the funding and delivery schedules for the permanent water supply. The federal government provided the community with $15 million to meet interim water needs, contributed other economic-development grants and loan forgiveness worth $28.7 million, and moved the permanent supply deadline up to 1988. In exchange, the Indian community relieved the federal government of its responsibility to provide an interim water supply and agreed to an overall reduction in its permanent water entitlement. Under the revised settlement, the community receives 75,000 acre-feet of water in normal years, as little as 72,000 acre-feet in dry years, and up to 85,000 acre-feet in wet years.

The water supply was secured for the revised settlement by reallocating 50,000 acre-feet per year of Colorado River water from the Yuma Mesa Division of the Gila Project to the Ak-Chin Indian Community.[14] This water, which is delivered to the community through the CAP canal, was an unused portion of a 300,000 acre-feet allocation available to the Yuma Mesa Division under contracts entered into according to the Boulder Canyon Project Act of 1928.[15] The transferred Colorado River water retains its priority date, a priority superior to that of CAP, making the entitlement senior by Arizona standards.

The federal government agreed to provide the Yuma Mesa Division with a $9.4 million grant for im-

provements and conservation measures and to forgive federal loan obligations worth approximately $17.8 million in exchange for transferring 50,000 acre-feet of its CAP allocation. The State of Arizona vigorously opposed the transfer provision of the amended settlement, arguing that the unused portion of the Yuma Mesa Division's Colorado River entitlement should be reallocated to CAP in perpetuity since CAP is the junior appropriator next in line.

The balance of the tribal community's water entitlement is to be provided from the Ak-Chin's 58,300 acre-feet CAP allocation.[16] The portion of these supplies not needed to meet the obligations of the settlement is to be reallocated on an interim basis to CAP, potentially making additional water available to central and southern Arizona water users. In the secretary of the Interior's view, this provision makes excess Ak-Chin water available for future Indian water settlements in Arizona.[17]

The federal government bears the entire financial obligation under this settlement and also is responsible for the replacement cost of any water that it fails to deliver to the community. The federal OMB has strenuously opposed federal liability for damages in more recent Indian water settlements and also insists on reasonable local contributions.

Off-reservation leasing. The original settlement did not provide for off-reservation leasing of any portion of the Indian community's entitlement, due to strong opposition to the principle of off-reservation marketing by the state, western governors, local irrigators, and other non-Indian interests. In 1992, fourteen years after the original legislation's enactment, Congress passed a bill, supported by the State of Arizona, the Indian community, and local water users, that amends the settlement to allow off-reservation leasing of portions of the water entitlement in select areas of the state.

The 1992 amendment clarified the tribe's ability to lease some of their water.[18] In an innovative agreement, the Ak-Chin leased part of their water rights under a one hundred–year contract to a large Arizona-based developer. By increasing their water efficiency through drip irrigation and computer monitoring systems, the community was able to lease 10,000 acre-feet annually to provide the one hundred–year assured water supply to developer Del Webb Corporation for a planned community of 40,000 people north of Phoenix. With a contract directly with the developer, this is the first tribal water–leasing deal that bypasses a subcontracting irrigation district.

In addition, the ADWR promulgated a new rule to specifically accommodate transactions like the Ak-Chin–Del Webb deal. Under the current Arizona law, a developer needs a one hundred–year perpetual assured water supply before its development can be approved. Conversely, most tribal settlements restrict tribal water leasing to contracts not exceeding one hundred years. Thus, if a developer leases one hundred years of water from a tribe to meet its assured supply, the developer must find replacement water for the last years of the one hundred–year period. Under the new rule, developers and tribes may renew one hundred-year leases each year to satisfy the state requirement of one hundred–year assured supplies. The new ADWR rule gives flexibility to providers using Colorado River or CAP water leased from an Arizona Indian community to meet their assured water supply requirements.[19] If the leased water initially satisfies the one hundred-year assured supply requirement, the department will wait until the fiftieth year to review the developer's assured supply certificate. At that time, the developer must show evidence of active negotiations with the tribe to renew the lease. To ensure security to customers, tribal leased water can account for only 15 percent or less of the provider's total water supply.[20]

Reflections. The Settlement of Ak-Chin Water Rights Claims of 1978 was among the first Indian water rights disputes resolved through a legislative settlement. This settlement has several interesting features:

- The original settlement agreement was between the United States and the Ak-Chin Indian Community and did not involve the State of Arizona or local water users directly.
- This is one of only two Indian water settlements passed by Congress in which the federal government bears the entire financial burden.
- Imported surface-water supplies were used to satisfy the community's entitlement.
- The Ak-Chin settlement had to be amended in 1984, six years after its enactment, and further amended in 1992, illustrating the difficulty of achieving finality on these complex issues.

- The active involvement of key members of Arizona's congressional delegation, who held leadership positions in Congress, greatly assisted in the formulation and passage of this settlement and amendments.

The Ak-Chin settlement is viewed as having been successfully implemented, partly due to updated provisions when it was amended in 1992. The Ak-Chin Community is upgrading residential water supply infrastructure and sewage facilities, as well as exploring new strategies for water conservation in reservation agriculture.

Truckee-Carson–Pyramid Lake Water Settlement

> The ESA is a great concern to tribes. When balancing of tribal and environmental issues occurs, tribes tend to lose out. We need to require, as part of ESA consultation, the consideration of unused tribal rights when new development is proposed. We need to include tribal (unexercised) rights when developing the environmental baseline in ESA consultations. We need to be able to develop tribal rights without triggering a jeopardy opinion, and we need to consider tribal rights when designating critical habitat and developing habitat conservation plans.
>
> Jeanne Whiting, attorney representing tribes

The Truckee-Carson water settlement involves the Pyramid Lake Paiute Tribe, the state of Nevada, federal interests, western Nevada water users, and environmental advocates. The settlement highlights the role of tribal bargaining power in motivating conflict resolution, the importance of including environmental concerns in crafting a settlement, and the crucial role of effective leadership in resolving water disputes.[21] Only certain features of the settlement are discussed here.

The Truckee and Carson rivers, which flow into the western Nevada desert from their headwaters in the Sierra Nevada range of California, provide water for Indian tribes, cities, fisheries, wetlands, and the Newlands Irrigation Project, a large federally developed irrigation project (see map 9.3). The Pyramid Lake Indian Reservation, the ancestral home of the Pyramid Lake Paiute Tribe, surrounds Pyramid Lake, residence of the cui-ui, a rare fish species, and the threatened Lahontan cutthroat trout. This unique high desert lake, which along with the fish is of special cultural sig-

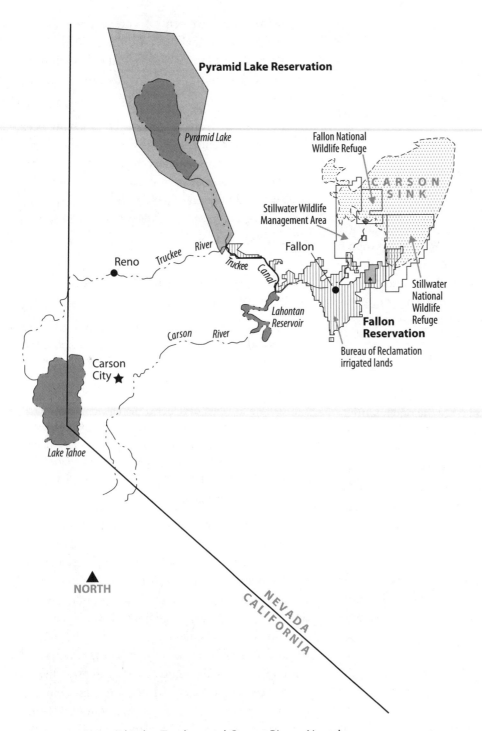

MAP 9.3 Pyramid Lake, Truckee and Carson Rivers, Nevada

nificance to the tribe, is the terminus of the Truckee River and depends solely on the river for inflows.

The long history of conflict in the Truckee and Carson basins began in the early 1900s, due to numerous diversions of water from the Truckee River.[22] The most important impact arose from diversions for irri-

gation purposes. These diversions are accomplished mainly through the Truckee Canal, completed in 1905, which until recently transported approximately half the flow of the Truckee River into the neighboring Carson basin. Diverted water is held in Lahontan Reservoir, along with Carson River inflows, for irrigation deliveries to the Newlands Project and other smaller irrigation projects. The Newlands Project irrigates about 60,000 acres in the Carson basin, including several thousand acres on the Fallon Paiute-Shoshone Indian Reservation.

Reductions in Truckee River flows led to precipitous declines in Pyramid Lake of more than seventy feet since 1906, threatening the fisheries and depriving the Pyramid Lake tribe of fish and water upon which they had relied for centuries. The situation is complicated further by the fact that the Stillwater National Wildlife Refuge and surrounding Lahontan Valley wetland, one of the most important wetland areas in Nevada and a key staging area for Pacific Flyway waterfowl, are dependent on return flows from the Newlands Project and thus, to some extent, on Truckee River diversions.

The tribe pursued negotiations and litigation for decades in order to restore stream and lake levels for fisheries. The United States filed suit in 1972 against water users on the upper Truckee River who are party to the Orr Ditch Decree, which allocates river waters, claiming reserved water rights on behalf of the tribe.[23] Following ten years of litigation, the U.S. Supreme Court dealt the tribe a serious blow by rejecting its reserved water rights claim to Truckee River flows.[24]

Negotiations. In spite of numerous efforts to resolve this conflict, no real progress was made until Senator Harry Reid (D-NV) intervened in the settlement process after he was elected to the Senate in 1986. Through his commitment and the hard work of his staff, a new round of negotiations began in early 1987. The success of these negotiations illustrates the importance of constructive leadership in resolving complex water disputes. In addition, various court decisions were essential to convince the parties to negotiate fundamental rights in order to reach an acceptable compromise.

The ESA, under which the rare cui-ui were federally listed as endangered, also was very important in paving the way for a negotiated settlement. A 1985 court decision found that uncommitted storage water in a federal storage facility on the upper Truckee could be used only to protect endangered fish in Pyramid Lake, and not to satisfy the growing urban water needs of the Reno-Sparks area.[25] Consequently, other water users began to recognize the threat to their own water diversions and sought to negotiate with the tribe and the United States. The FWS, responsible for both endangered fish and wetlands, became increasingly involved, as did environmental organizations on behalf of Pyramid Lake and the Lahontan Valley wetland.

The negotiations aimed at satisfying the seemingly incompatible water demands of Indian tribes, irrigators, endangered species, wetland protection, and urban growth. The settlement legislation, passed by Congress in 1990, ratified the settlement agreements of both the Fallon Paiute-Shoshone and the Pyramid Lake Paiute tribes. Indeed, the very existence of the Truckee Canal closely links the interests of these tribes, and their ability to recognize and respond to this interconnection in creative ways was important in reaching settlement agreements.

Settlement agreement. The Truckee-Carson–Pyramid Lake settlement provides protection for Pyramid Lake and Truckee River fisheries, continued water deliveries for irrigators and cities, and federal money to buy out irrigation rights and promote agricultural water conservation in order to assure water for wetlands. The various water rights acquisition mechanisms contained in the settlement have played a crucial role in diffusing conflicts and reconciling endangered species and wetland concerns. In particular, the legislation includes authorization and funding for the acquisition of active Newlands Project water rights to benefit the Fallon tribe, to protect and restore the Lahontan Valley wetland, and to promote recovery of the Pyramid Lake fishery. The federal government, local conservation groups, and the Nature Conservancy, a national organization specializing in habitat preservation, have made a number of water rights acquisitions. Although essential tools to implement the settlement, these acquisitions are also controversial within agricultural communities due to decreases in irrigated acreage.

Reflections. Dissension between parties in the area, particularly between agricultural interests and the tribe, has not abated. Competition for water is aggravated by the rapid population expansion of the Truckee Meadows and Lahontan Valley areas. In the 1999 Nevada legislative session, parties representing the Fallon area agricultural interests introduced a bill that would change state law to allow farmers to overcome the consequences of ongoing litigation with the tribes over water use. This political move stimulated intense negotiations among rural lawmakers, tribal representatives, and utility lobbyists. Senator Reid constructed an agreement that obligated the state and federal government to purchase $13 million worth of water rights on Fallon area farmland, thereby increasing the amount of water that the Pyramid Lake Paiute Reservation would receive.

These water rights, once acquired, will be transferred to the tribe and the local county to be used largely for environmental purposes. Part of the negotiated compromise requires the parties to dismiss pending litigation. Another part of the agreement allows local farmers to move water rights from one part of their property to another. In 2004, the major parties reached agreement on the key features of Truckee River operations and water rights acquisitions continue, with the goal of improving wetlands, water quality, and flows for fisheries. Ongoing regional drought confounds achievement of goals established in the 1990 water rights settlement and in subsequent intergovernment water management agreements. Still pending is a final agreement on how the Truckee River will be managed to accommodate competing needs. A finalized operating agreement between the state of California and the tribe is intended to improve the river's management, stabilize water availability, help protect fisheries, and end any remaining litigation.

The leadership provided by Senator Reid proved crucial in resolving the many interrelated issues concerning the Truckee River. Reid's involvement focused the attention of regional decision makers and federal officials. Even after the main agreement was reached, he and his office have monitored implementation and have intervened to help the parties address new problems that emerge.

The operating rules for federal water storage and conveyance facilities have proved to be a crucial element in resolving water conflicts in this basin. Operating criteria have been reworked with direct input from tribal and environmental interests so that reservoir releases will address fishery and wetland needs as well as supplying farms and cities. Changes in operations of storage and conveyance infrastructure doubtless will be a key ingredient in ongoing settlement implementation.

Several other aspects of this settlement are relevant to ongoing tribal water conflicts. The tribe's negotiating position was strengthened not only by the ESA, but also by its insistence that urban and agricultural water users make more efficient use of water supplies. The demand, although met with strong initial resistance by urban water providers, placed the tribe on high ground in the negotiations, as few could argue that this request was unreasonable given water conservation programs being implemented in other western cities. The resulting settlement agreement required the municipalities to install water meters and, for the first time, charge water users according to the quantities used.

The decades of water-related disputes in this basin could have been partly avoided if the fisheries component of tribal water needs had been recognized and accommodated when water rights for the tribe initially were quantified in the 1940s. The federal government (on behalf of the tribe), however, obtained water rights for only a small amount of irrigated acreage, and fishery needs were neglected until the tribe invoked the federal trust responsibility to tribes and the ESA decades later. To achieve an enduring settlement, quantification efforts must consider the entire range of tribal water needs.

State Government Settlement Initiatives

Settlements are reached for many reasons, and it is difficult to assess the cause-and-effect relationships that produced an agreement. Most settlements, however, have been reached as the result of processes initiated by state governments. Of course, the agreements could not have been obtained without the participation of the tribes, federal government, and many other parties. All these parties ultimately concluded that settlement was preferable to the next best alternative. Without state government initiative, the settlements probably would not have been reached at all.

The first agreement we examine is the Navajo Indian Irrigation Project (NIIP), illustrating the complexities of an interstate river, a large agricultural development on reservation, and downstream urban demands. As previously mentioned, the agreement is also an example of congressional leadership (specifically, by Senator Clinton Anderson of New Mexico), and many tribal leaders maintain that it is not a water rights settlement at all. We discuss it here as an early example of how states address Indian water rights in an effort to achieve other water-related goals.

We also examine three settlements that were reached in the context of a state court general stream adjudication: the Fort Hall settlement in Idaho (part of the Snake River basin adjudication), the Northern Cheyenne settlement in Montana (part of a statewide adjudication), and the Warm Springs settlement in Oregon (part of a statewide adjudication of mostly pre-1919 water rights). States commence these adjudications to clarify federal- and state-law water rights on major river systems and to develop information to better manage these water resources. These cases, however, guarantee decades of litigation, millions of dollars in attorney and consultant fees, and uncertain results for all major participants. Montana developed an alternative to complex litigation by establishing its Reserved Water Rights Compact Commission in 1979. This agency negotiates with tribes and federal agencies over their water rights claims, and litigation concerning these claims is stayed while talks continue. This process produced its first major settlement, the Montana–Fort Peck Compact, in 1985. Because this pioneering compact is well documented elsewhere, it is not discussed here.[26]

Navajo Indian Irrigation Project

> If our access to our water is taken away, our hope for the future is taken too.
>
> Peterson Zah, former chair, Navajo Nation

The Navajo Nation, which holds the most senior water rights on the San Juan River, agreed in 1962 to share shortages during droughts in order to obtain federal authorization for the NIIP. This deferral agreement paved the way for construction of the SJCP, which delivers transbasin water into the Rio Grande basin primarily to serve water users in the city of Albuquerque. While not a comprehensive water rights settlement, this accord is an early example of a negotiated arrangement between an Indian nation and non-Indian water users.

Negotiations. Under the Upper Colorado River Basin Compact of 1949, the State of New Mexico was apportioned just over 11 percent of the consumptive uses of Colorado River water allocated to the upper basin.[27] Because most of New Mexico's water users reside outside of the Colorado River basin, the state sought to divert water from the San Juan River, a major tributary of the Colorado River, across the Continental Divide and into the Rio Grande basin. The San Juan River basin includes portions of three Indian reservations—the Navajo, the Ute Mountain Ute, and the Jicarilla Apache. In seeking to accomplish this diversion, the state understood the need to placate the Navajo Nation, which held the paramount (though unquantified) water rights to the San Juan River. In order to obtain Navajo consent for a large transbasin diversion, the State of New Mexico supported the Navajo Nation's efforts to obtain federal backing for a large-scale irrigation project near Shiprock, New Mexico. State engineer Steve Reynolds and Senator Clinton Anderson were active proponents of this means to allow New Mexico to develop its Colorado River entitlement.

In return for the development of the NIIP (a 110,630-acre project authorized to use 508,000 acre-feet of water per year), the Navajo Nation agreed not to oppose the state's 110,000 acre-feet per year diversion from the San Juan River. This amount of water would be diverted annually through the SJCP for water users in the Rio Grande basin. New Mexico understood the enormity of the potential reserved water rights of the Navajo Nation to San Juan River water and insisted on including in the legislation authorizing the project certain provisions for sharing shortages. These provisions require NIIP to share shortages proportionally with the SJCP in the event that water is not available for both projects. Without this provision, water for the transbasin diversion would be unavailable if the Navajo Nation were to fully develop all its reserved water, including water for municipal and industrial uses. In 1962, Congress jointly authorized NIIP and the SJCP to be built.[28]

Project development. The Department of the Interior enthusiastically supported the SJCP, completing it on schedule in 1967 with twice the capacity needed to accommodate its 110,000 acre-feet annual allocation. In contrast, federal support for NIIP has been tepid. Originally authorized in 1962, the project is now about 60 percent complete.

The NIIP is the preeminent water-development project for the Navajo Reservation and is being developed exclusively for Indian use on lands that lie on or adjacent to the reservation. When the NIIP is completed, it will be one of the largest Indian irrigation projects in the country. Situated on a mesa south of the San Juan River in northwestern New Mexico, the federal government scheduled the NIIP to be built in eleven stages. At inception, economic projections indicated that the project could create more than 6,550 farm and related industry jobs, raising the standard of living for over 33,000 Navajo Indians. NIIP operations began in 1973 when the project first watered about 10,000 acres of farmland.

Part of the enabling legislation for the project established the Navajo Agricultural Products Industry (NAPI) and provided in a forty-year contract signed in 1976 that 508,000 acre-feet annually could be diverted from Navajo Reservoir on the San Juan River for agricultural use. This amount of water was calculated to be able to irrigate 110,630 acres annually. To date, the BIA, in cooperation with the nation, has developed the farm units, farm distribution systems, drainage, and farm-to-market roads. Expenditures for the NIIP total over $400 million thus far.[29]

The project fell behind in the last decade when the government listed species of fish on the San Juan River as endangered. The FWS concluded in July 1999 that the project could be completed without jeopardizing the recovery of those fish.[30]

Currently, NAPI is using only enough water to irrigate about 64,000 acres, growing barley, corn, oats, and wheat. Prior to 2001, the farm had not turned a profit. It is New Mexico's largest recipient of federal farm subsidies. Between 1996 and 2000, NAPI received $7.4 million in subsidies. These subsidies from the USDA help farms pay loan deficiencies and for market loss. "[The farm] wasn't producing the way it was meant to produce. It wasn't as profitable as we'd imagined it to be," says Merle Pete, spokesman for former Navajo Nation president Kelsey Begaye.[31] In March 2001, the Navajo Tribal Council agreed to pay some of NAPI's short-term debts and bills with $10 million out of a fund originally reserved to build a frozen potato product-processing plant on the reservation.[32] In exchange, the NAPI board of directors underwent a major change. In an unprecedented decision, two of the new directors would be non-Navajo agricultural specialists.

Reflections. The NIIP resulted from New Mexico's goal of developing some of its Colorado River water allocation. The state's goal meshed with tribal desires to develop water and create on-reservation employment. Although some commentators have argued that the NIIP legislation represents a settlement of the Navajos' water rights to the San Juan River,[33] the authorizing legislation makes no reference to a settlement of the water rights of the Navajo Nation. The Navajo Nation itself rejects any suggestion that the NIIP legislation even partly settled its *Winters* rights in the San Juan River basin. The rights of the Navajo Nation to water within the San Juan River basin, already a controversial river basin as the result of the ALP, will be quantified as part of the San Juan River general stream adjudication.[34]

Moreover, some Interior officials have suggested that NIIP be reconsidered.[35] As a result of construction delays and federal ambivalence toward the project, it is estimated that an additional $500 million will be needed to bring the full 110,630 acres under cultivation. Although NIIP was not a financial success for the first decade of irrigated crop production, profitability of the large farms has been improving. Although the project achieves excellent crop yields and is now turning a profit for the nation, it has not generated the jobs and revitalization of the reservation economy that was envisioned. The disappointing performance of this project in its early years may be instructive for tribes considering alternative uses of their water and land resources.

In an effort to head off interminable litigation in the San Juan River adjudication, the Navajo Nation and the State of New Mexico have engaged in settlement discussions that in December 2003 produced a proposed settlement agreement that has major potential implications for the NIIP. The agreement, which was distributed for public comment in early 2004, has not been signed by either party and is contingent on, among other things, congressional authorization of basin water-development projects totaling $870 million. Under the settlement, the Navajo-Gallup Water Supply Project, costing $463 million, would be constructed to deliver domestic, municipal, and industry water (22,650 acre-feet per year) to serve 200,000 people on the Navajo Reservation and within the city of Gallup, New Mexico. The agreement also would recognize a water right to 508,000 acre-feet per year for NIIP in the San Juan basin, allowing the irrigation of over 110,000 acres. Congress would authorize $277 million for this expansion of the project. While the negotiators have prepared draft legislation, a bill has not been introduced in Congress.

In a related development, the Navajo Nation filed a federal lawsuit against the Department of the Interior in March 2003 alleging that, in policy decisions concerning the lower Colorado River, the department had breached its trust obligations to the nation. The complaint, pending before Judge Paul G. Rosenblatt in Phoenix, alleges that "[q]uantification of the Navajo Nation's rights to the waters of the Lower Basin of the Colorado River could result in a determination that the Navajo Nation's rights are superior to those subject to contracts with the Secretary, and thereby threatens the ability . . . to deliver Central Arizona Project water to the tribe and non-Indian contractors."[36]

Fort Hall Indian Water Rights Settlement

In 1985 the state of Idaho and the tribes entered into a government-to-government agreement to attempt to negotiate their differences over water rights. This negotiation ultimately led to the passage of the 1990 settlement act. It is one of the more creative settlements and relies on a number of innovative arrangements, including a tribal water bank, the use of federal storage space, and a recognition of the importance of maintaining instream flows for habitat preservation, recreation, and aesthetics. As with any settlement, it is not perfect, and there were detractors. But thus far the problems have been ironed out and the court decree is in place.

Daniel McCool, *Native Waters*

The Second Treaty of Fort Bridger established both the Wind River Reservation in Wyoming, discussed earlier in this chapter, and the Fort Hall Reservation in Idaho as permanent homelands for portions of the Shoshone Tribe. The Shoshone and Arapaho tribes share the Wind River Reservation, and the Shoshone and Bannock tribes share the Fort Hall Reservation. Both reservations are in fertile river valleys that attracted much non-Indian farming interest. Though the two reservations share history and important characteristics, each took a much different route to resolve its water claims.

The Fort Hall Indian Reservation was established by executive order in 1867 for various Shoshone and Bannock tribes, who later became parties to the Second Treaty of Fort Bridger. The reservation, initially intended to be 1.8 million acres but later reduced to approximately 544,000 acres, is located along the Snake River, near the city of Pocatello in southeastern Idaho (see map 9.4). The reservation is owned by the tribes collectively (47 percent) and by individual Indian allottees (43 percent), with individual non-Indians owning the remaining 10 percent. Originally a nomadic people, the Shoshone-Bannock tribes recognize the current Fort Hall Reservation as a part of their ancestral home.

Negotiations. In 1985, the state legislature directed the Idaho Department of Water Resources to seek a general stream adjudication in the Snake River basin. The legislature also passed a resolution, at the request of the Shoshone-Bannock tribes and the Idaho executive branch, authorizing negotiations to settle the tribes' water claims in the Snake River basin. Negotiations were viewed favorably by both the tribes and the state; both saw the advantages of crafting their own agreement rather than a solution dictated by the courts. The extended litigation involving the Wind River tribes in Wyoming made a strong impression on neighboring tribes and states, strengthening resolve to avoid similar litigation. In addition, the Fort Hall tribes have a history of settling disputes out of court and believed they would have more control over negotiations than in litigation, where Department of Justice attorneys would assume control of the process.

That same year, the tribes and the state entered into a memorandum of understanding that established a process for negotiating a settlement. The tribes obtained a special exemption from the Department of the Interior allowing them to hire their own technical experts and to pursue negotiations independently of the federal government. The United States and certain local water users were included in the negotiations later.

The strong will to settle shown by all involved major parties prompted good faith negotiations. The participants agreed at the outset to attempt to fashion an agreement that not only satisfied the tribes' water entitlements but also protected, to the extent pos-

MAP 9.4 Reservations in Idaho

sible, the rights of water users established under state law. They also agreed to share information openly so that decisions would be based on the best data available. In 1989, four years after negotiations began, an agreement was reached consistent with these goals. In late 1990, this agreement was ratified through congressional enactment.[37]

Settlement agreement. The settlement sets the tribes' entitlement to water from the Snake River basin at 581,031 acre-feet per year. The water supply is comprised of a combination of natural flow, groundwater, and federal contract storage water. This entitlement is in satisfaction of all claims to water that the tribes may have had under the *Winters* doctrine.

Crafting the settlement, which involved a highly developed reach of the Snake River, required creativity to identify water supplies that could fulfill the tribes' entitlement while minimizing the disruption to non-

Indian water rights holders. In addition, the tribes wanted flexibility in using their water entitlement. In examining alternative water sources, the environmental and economic costs of dam construction or modification were judged to be too high. The negotiating parties turned to federal storage rights, that were being held in trust for the benefit of the tribes, to provide a reliable source of water for the settlement. In the settlement, the tribes have access to the natural flow of the Snake River and its tributaries, when available, augmented in times of shortage with storage rights and pumped groundwater. Storage space will be available annually to the tribes from reservoirs on the Snake River system, with the associated water supplies delivered through the Fort Hall Indian Irrigation Project (FHIIP). Additional storage space will be provided to the tribes from the Blackfoot Reservoir and Grays Lake. The priority dates of these storage rights (1907 and 1919, respectively) coincide with the dates the Bureau of Reclamation acquired for the rights for the benefit of FHIIP water users.

The settlement relies on previously unallocated federal storage space to provide critical flexibility to meet diverse needs in the Snake River basin. In the settlement, tribal storage rights on the Snake River may be leased off reservation through a water bank run by the Idaho Department of Water Resources. Non-Indian water users in the FHIIP have the right of first refusal when any water is leased from the water bank. The flexibility of the storage rights and the agreement's marketing provisions furnish the tribes with a potential income source, important flexibility in managing their water entitlement, and a mechanism to make water in the upper Snake River basin available to maintain instream flows in the lower basin for steelhead and salmon production and other ecosystem protection.

Reflections. The settlement recognizes that the tribes may assume control and ownership of the FHIIP. Some consider this a major achievement, as it required overcoming objections of certain federal parties. The Bureau of Reclamation, for example, sought to protect existing supplies to meet its delivery obligations, and the local BIA endeavored to maintain control over the irrigation project. Prior to the settlement, all rights under the project were developed under state law with an 1891 priority date. Under the settlement, Indian

rights in the project were converted to *Winters* rights, with a priority of 1867, the date the reservation was established.

The settlement also recognizes traditional tribal values by allowing portions of the tribes' water entitlement to be used for fish, wildlife, and environmental values as well as for agriculture. In addition to water supplies and critical management flexibility, the settlement provides funds to the tribes for a tribal water-management system and other tribal development purposes.

Idaho initiated the Snake River adjudication for a variety of water-management purposes, but the litigation provided the impetus for the state and the Shoshone and Bannock tribes of the Fort Hall Reservation to forge an innovative and flexible agreement.

The Fort Hall Indian water settlement also illustrates how good faith negotiations, along with creativity and flexibility, can result in an agreement that meets the major goals of all parties, as illustrated by some of the key features of this settlement:

- Initiating negotiations prior to litigation provided the opportunity for the parties to establish relatively good working relationships.
- Participants have identified the openness of the negotiating process as the key to their success.
- Creative approaches to securing water supplies allowed tribal rights to be accommodated within a highly developed river system with minimal disruption to non-Indian water users.
- The administration of water rights was a key component of the settlement agreement, allowing for flexibility in managing and using tribal water entitlements for instream and other purposes.

As mentioned earlier in this chapter, the Shoshone and Arapaho tribes of the Wind River Reservation were unsuccessful in their efforts to transfer water quantified for irrigation purposes to instream uses. By contrast, the Fort Hall tribes were successful in securing the right to manage their water for fisheries. Also, their negotiated settlement gives them relative flexibility in using their entitlement to meet future tribal needs. The negotiation process resulted in an environment more conducive to resolving differences. Using a three-member intergovernmental board intended to mediate or otherwise resolve disputes arising under the agreement, this emphasis on collaboration is likely to continue during settlement implementation and ongoing water management.

Northern Cheyenne Compact

Barbara Cosens

On July 1, 1999, dedication of the restored Tongue River Dam took place, providing up to 20,000 acre-feet of new storage allocated to the Northern Cheyenne Reservation and making the Northern Cheyenne–Montana Indian Water Rights Settlement (Northern Cheyenne Compact) one of the few settlements with the major water infrastructure necessary to implement the agreement. The innovative design of the repaired and enlarged Tongue River Dam won numerous awards for the State of Montana and its consultants.[38] The following section describes the background of the Northern Cheyenne Compact and its implementation, and concludes with an analysis of the factors that facilitated rapid implementation and the pitfalls to be avoided.

Montana commenced a statewide general stream adjudication in the 1970s. To provide an alternative to the litigation, the legislature established a forum for resolving federal reserved water rights, the Reserved Water Rights Compact Commission (Compact Commission). The Northern Cheyenne Tribe initiated settlement negotiations with the Compact Commission in February 1980, making it among the first of the Montana reservations to begin the process.[39] The initiation of negotiations by the tribe came in the midst of their participation in cases before the U.S. Supreme Court, opposing federal district court dismissal of adjudication of Indian reserved water rights in favor of a state court forum.[40] Initiation of negotiations suspended formal adjudication under state law; however, serious negotiations did not begin until several years after the controversy between the state and federal forums was resolved in 1983.

The reservation and its water supply. The Northern Cheyenne Reservation spans approximately 445,000 acres between the Crow Reservation and the Tongue River in southeastern Montana. Over 4,000 of the 6,500 enrolled tribal members live on or near the reservation. Obtaining a firm supply of wet water was crucial to the tribe, which has 31.5 percent unemployment and a per capita income of $4,479.

The federally sanctioned presence of the Northern Cheyenne in the valleys of Rosebud Creek and the Tongue River began on October 1, 1881, when the U.S. Army settled eighty-six families there. This formal action by the federal government became the basis for the priority date agreed to in the Northern Cheyenne Compact. Formal establishment of the reservation took place in the vicinity of Rosebud Creek on November 26, 1884, by President Arthur's executive order, and in the vicinity of the Tongue River on March 19, 1900, by President McKinley's executive order.[41]

The Northern Cheyenne were not new to this part of Montana in 1881. Northern Cheyenne, Lakota Sioux, and Arapaho camped along the banks of the Little Bighorn River on what is now the Crow Reservation, defeated the 7th Cavalry, led by General George Armstrong Custer and guided by Crow and Arikara scouts, on June 25, 1876. Between 1876 and 1881, the Northern Cheyenne suffered both military defeat and malaria and ultimately surrendered to the U.S. military.[42] That Crow and Northern Cheyenne are now neighbors and share the heavily allocated Rosebud Creek underscores the fact that disputes over resources in this area cannot be settled outside the context of their rich history. The allocation of water to the Northern Cheyenne from Bighorn Lake, a reservoir located in part on the Crow Reservation, illustrates this point.

The two major drainages that supply water to the Northern Cheyenne Reservation are Rosebud Creek and the Tongue River. Rosebud Creek is basically a prairie stream with no significant snow pack in its headwaters on the Crow Reservation. Private irrigation development existing at the time of negotiation of the Northern Cheyenne Compact left little room for additional development.[43] In contrast, the Tongue River, with its headwaters in the Bighorn Mountains of Wyoming, carries significant spring runoff. The reservation lies roughly sixty miles downstream from the Montana–Wyoming border, and in that stretch of the Tongue River is located the state-owned Tongue River Dam. The Tongue River Reservoir was completed in 1940, with an approximate capacity of 69,000 acre-feet. Although the dam was designed to withstand a flood of 98,000 cubic feet per second (cfs), its spillway was damaged in a flood that passed 7,000 cubic feet per second over the spillway in 1978, and storage was reduced to a maximum of 40,000 acre-feet for safety.[44] The damaged dam lay upstream from sparsely populated farm and ranch land of the Tongue River valley and from the Northern Cheyenne Reservation. Among the communities that would require evacuation in the event of a dam break were several with little access to phone lines. Some of these communities include traditional tribal members who speak and understand only Northern Cheyenne.[45] The potential liability and prospect of great human tragedy drove the choice of water supply solutions.

The Northern Cheyenne Compact. The Northern Cheyenne–Montana Compact was finalized in 1991 and ratified by Congress in 1992.[46] Tribal council approval preceded action by Congress; however, final tribal approval required a referendum following congressional approval.[47] The Montana Water Court subsequently entered a decree approving the compact.

Because water sources on or near the reservation were almost fully developed, the negotiating parties turned to off-reservation sources. This approach, referred to as an exchange, resulted in a firmer tribal supply of water and protected existing use by private water users. The Northern Cheyenne Compact includes the following allocations from off-reservation sources to the tribe: (1) up to 20,000 acre-feet of water per year of new storage in a repaired and enlarged Tongue River Reservoir, and (2) up to 30,000 acre-feet of water per year in the Bureau of Reclamation's Bighorn Lake, a reservoir located in part on the Crow Reservation. Each source and the measures necessary to achieve compact allocations are described below.

Tongue River Reservoir. At the time of negotiations, the Tongue River Reservoir sat half full, posing high risk to downstream communities in the event of a flood and a potentially huge liability for its owner, the State of Montana. This hazard aside, the potential for storage of runoff from the Bighorn Mountains provided an untapped opportunity to supply water to the Northern Cheyenne Reservation. The answer: Repair and enlarge the spillway at Tongue River Dam, thus increasing the capacity of the reservoir. The enlarged capacity would then be granted to the tribe.

The primary hurdle to achieving this solution is the same one that had delayed state repair of the dam: cost. As part of settlement negotiations, Montana, the

United States, and the tribe negotiated a cost share for repair and enlargement of the dam of $31.5 million from the federal government and $16.5 million from the state, $11.5 million of which was to come from federal loans to the state and to be repaid by the state. When the agreement reached Congress, the cost-share agreement broke down over the state's insistence on a zero interest rate on the loan. In response, the tribe and state made a successful end-run around federal opposition by placing the $11.5 million into the Northern Cheyenne settlement fund and authorizing a loan of that money to the state with repayment to the tribe.[48]

Bighorn Lake. Bighorn Lake, impounded behind Yellowtail Dam, is located on the Bighorn River and lies partially within the Crow Reservation. The reservoir's unallocated capacity provided a ready source for settlement water. Since the Bighorn River does not flow through or adjacent to the Northern Cheyenne Reservation, use of the water will most likely be through marketing and hydropower generation.

The Crow Tribe opposed the Northern Cheyenne Settlement Act in Congress.[49] The Crow's opposition was based on a strong sense of their prior right to use water impounded on their reservation and on the long history of hostile relations with the Northern Cheyenne. Resolution of the dispute was achieved by making clear the subordination of the right to any Indian reserved water right by imposing a ten-year moratorium on any marketing of the water by the Northern Cheyenne Tribe without the agreement of the Crow Tribe, and by obtaining the agreement of the Northern Cheyenne to work with the Crow to resolve a long-standing dispute over the boundary between the two reservations.[50]

Implementation. Construction on the repair and enlargement of Tongue River Reservoir began in 1996, under the direction of the Montana Department of Natural Resources and Conservation (MDNRC), and was completed in 1999. Members of the Northern Cheyenne Tribe were provided hiring preferences. The total cost of the project was approximately $46.3 million, less than the $48 million allocated from state and federal sources.[51] In October 2001, the Northern Cheyenne Tribe obtained Department of the Interior approval of the tribal water code necessary for the tribe to take over allocation of its own water resource from Interior. Interior officials approved the water code despite a secretarial moratorium on the approval of such codes. The department maintained that approval was justified since Congress had approved compact language requiring the code.[52]

Although the tribe has not yet utilized its allocation of new storage in Tongue River Reservoir, it has marketed other water it holds (under a contract with the state from the reservoir) to the Tongue River Water Users Association.[53] Additional leasing potential exists both with local water users and with people interested in enhancing instream flow on the downstream Yellowstone River. In addition, although it has not marketed the water in Bighorn Lake, the ten-year moratorium requiring Crow approval is about to toll. Potential exists for both hydropower generation and instream flow purchases.

Tribes usually face many difficulties in achieving implementation of their settlements. The implementation of the Northern Cheyenne Compact provides a useful example of how settlements can be successfully implemented. Three major factors contributed to this success: strict deadlines with consequences; solution to a pending disaster with either financial or human costs to each party to the agreement; and personal commitment by representatives of the tribe, the State of Montana, and local federal representatives to seeing the agreement through to completion.

Strict deadlines. The Northern Cheyenne Compact provided that the agreement would become null and void if the Tongue River Dam repair and enlargement were not completed by December 31, 1997, or any extension agreed to by the parties. Although extension did become necessary, this timeline in the original agreement drove all subsequent actions, including the schedule of appropriations from Congress and the need for approval of the agreement by the Montana Water Court.

The pitfall of such a timeline was that although the consequences of missing deadlines fell primarily on the state as the responsible party for construction, meeting the deadlines required action by all three parties. In particular, the funding approach and implementing agreements required: appropriation of funds to the Bureau of Reclamation; disbursement from the Bureau of Reclamation to the tribe; and disbursement of funds from the tribe to the state. With the adverse consequences of delay falling primarily on

the state, the other parties were able to seek additional concessions in the agreement in exchange for extending deadlines. The December 31, 1997, deadline for completion of the dam project was ultimately extended to December 31, 2000.[54]

Additional delays were caused by the need to comply with the NEPA.[55] The congressional bill both chose and funded the specific project, yet the NEPA requires analysis of alternatives.[56] Funding for NEPA compliance itself required congressional authorization. In this Catch-22, review of alternatives was required despite the fact that the alternative to repairing and enlarging Tongue River Dam was already chosen and funded by Congress. Learning from this experience, the parties to a subsequent settlement (Fort Belknap–Montana) reached an initial agreement without choosing specific projects, then obtained funding for environmental review as part of the analysis of alternatives for the settlement.

Pending disaster. The urgency created by the real potential for dam failure in the event of a flood was a major factor in advancing implementation of the Northern Cheyenne Compact. While this draconian backdrop is unusual, solutions should be designed to give multiple parties an interest in their implementation. Parties to an agreement cannot go home content with state, tribal, and congressional approval of an agreement. Project authorization does not automatically lead to the appropriation of funds. Aggravating this reality is the fact that with balanced budget requirements and no separate fund for Indian water settlements, settlement appropriations reduce funding in other BIA programs. Implementation is more likely if the settlement provides reasons for state representatives and off-reservation interests to join tribes in seeking appropriations.

Personal commitment. The tribal council and its legal representatives, state representatives from the Compact Commission and MDNRC, and local federal representatives from the Department of the Interior office in Billings shared an important role in seeing the agreement through to completion. Tribal representatives fought hard for their rights. The MDNRC officials saw as personal challenges the completion of the dam in record time and under budget. Compact Commission representatives paid attention to when appropriations were needed in the state legislature and

Congress, and the federal representatives, always the scapegoat, persevered often at personal cost.[57]

Such personal efforts cannot always be replicated, but the time and effort necessary for Northern Cheyenne Compact implementation does provide practical guidance for other negotiations. Parties must provide for realistic timelines, budgets, and commitments of employee time. The Northern Cheyenne Compact took approximately three years to negotiate, one and one-half years to obtain congressional ratification, and seven years to implement dam construction. Construction of the dam itself required four contracts between the state and separate construction contractors. Tribal hiring preference, required by the congressional bill, faced hurdles due to the off-reservation location of the project. The Tribal Employment Rights Office missed deadlines in providing qualified workers, and ultimately contractors simply complied with the spirit of the law, hiring tribal liaisons to recruit tribal employees. Agreements were necessary for disbursement of funds to the tribe and the state. Issues vaguely addressed or not considered in the Northern Cheyenne Compact—such as whether the project, for purposes of meeting deadlines, included fish and wildlife enhancement—had to be negotiated during construction, often at the eleventh hour.[58]

Reflections. The Northern Cheyenne Compact was achieved as the result of an alternative decision-making process enacted by the Montana legislature. Water infrastructure required by the Northern Cheyenne Compact was completed in 1999, rendering the compact one of the few fully implemented. Although the settlement was unique in capitalizing on the opportunity to make safe an unsafe dam, other settlement elements can inform other negotiations. Specifically, solutions that generate broad support, the use of firm deadlines with consequences to all parties when they are missed, and realistic budgeting and provision for funding and employee time will facilitate the implementation and finalization of settlements.

The initial framework agreement for settlement of tribal water rights can rarely anticipate all the details of completing a project. Nor is it advisable that a document requiring congressional, legislative, and tribal member approval cast such details in stone. The main lesson is that the parties must anticipate that the initial agreement is merely a framework for more detailed efforts at implementation. The temptation is to celebrate and go home when Congress ratifies the settlement act. Celebrate—yes. Go home—no. The effort has only begun.

Tribal Settlement Initiatives

As we have seen, states may take actions, such as by commencing an adjudication, that focus attention and invite settlement discussions. Unless tribes become willing and active participants in negotiations, only litigation will result. Tribes themselves are sometimes the initial actor in exploring settlement. The following discussion of the Warm Spring Water Rights Settlement in Oregon is an excellent example of initial tribal leadership in inviting settlement discussions that received a positive and supportive response from the state. The Klamath tribes in southern Oregon also proposed an alternative dispute-resolution process to the state, and that effort is discussed later in a section concerning settlement efforts in the context of ESA issues.

Warm Springs Water Rights Settlement

Beth S. Wolfsong

> We worked for many years on this agreement. This agreement protects the fish that the Warm Springs people depend upon and enables both on- and off-reservation communities to grow and prosper.
>
> Olney Patt, Jr., chair, Warm Springs Tribal Council

In the early 1980s, the Confederated Tribes of the Warm Springs Indians (Warm Springs Nation), the State of Oregon, and the United States began the lengthy process to determine, quantify, and settle the reserved water rights of the Warm Springs Nation. Today, more than twenty years after the genesis of negotiations, the parties have achieved a comprehensive agreement to recognize and protect tribal, state, and private water rights holders both within the Warm Springs Reservation and in the Deschutes River basin at large.

In 1855, the Warm Springs Nation—comprised of the Wasco, Paiute, and Warm Springs bands—ceded 10 million acres of aboriginal territory to the United States government in the Treaty with the Tribes of Middle Oregon.[59] Of critical importance to the Warm

Springs people, particularly the Wasco and Warm Springs bands, was their relationship to the plentiful salmon thriving in the waters of the Columbia River and its many tributaries. In addition to acting as a valuable resource of food and trade, salmon represented a vital component of the cultural and religious identity of the tribal people. Therefore, despite immense pressure from increasing settlement and the imminent threat of force by the U.S. military, the Warm Springs Nation relinquished large tracts of land yet reserved their right to take fish, including in their "usual and accustomed places" off the reservation. Also, implied within the treaty is the right to enough water to fulfill the purpose of the reservation.[60]

Today, the Warm Springs Nation occupies a reservation of approximately 640,000 acres in what is now north-central Oregon and that is inhabited by 3,500 to 4,000 tribal members. The reservation lies between the Cascade Mountain range on the west and the Deschutes River on the east, and is cradled by the Metolius River, a tributary of the Deschutes, on the south. Within the reservation one finds a wealth of stunning natural beauty and plentiful resources. From the volcanic snow-capped peak of Mount Jefferson, rising to 10,497 feet above sea level, to the canyon lands and parched desert landscape to the east, the reservation is brimming with glacial-fed lakes, clear-running rivers, forests, and rangeland. The Deschutes River itself is a central feature on the reservation and an integral component in tribal life, both culturally and economically. The river originates in Little Lava Lake, nestled high in the Cascade Mountains, then embarks on a 250-mile path to its confluence with the Columbia River, being fed along the way by the Metolius and Crooked rivers.

Like other water users in the Deschutes River basin, the Warm Springs people depend on the Deschutes and its tributaries for commercial as well as domestic purposes. Salmon continue to play an integral role in tribal life, and the Warm Springs people co-manage a fish hatchery with the FWS along the Deschutes in order to supplement and sustain salmon populations. Among other endeavors, the reservation economy is also founded on such water-dependent industries as hydropower, timber and forest products, ranching, and recreation and tourism.

Negotiations. Aware that Indian nations all over the West were settling their water rights, the Warm Springs Nation, in an effort to avoid litigation, approached the State of Oregon in the early 1980s and offered to enter negotiations to determine, quantify, and settle their reserved water rights in an agreement that would later become part of the original Deschutes River Decree, issued February 10, 1928.[61] Before negotiations could ensue, however, the parties required time to assemble and authorize their negotiating teams. The state of Oregon enacted legislation authorizing the director of the Oregon Department of Water Resources (ODWR) to negotiate and settle any and all reserved water rights held by federally recognized tribes and requiring that the director facilitate public participation and input throughout the process.[62] The Warm Springs Nation adopted a tribal council resolution, pursuant to the tribal constitution, authorizing the tribal chair and the secretary-treasurer to negotiate on behalf of the tribe and its members.[63] Finally, the secretary of the Interior participated in his trust capacity for the tribes and allottees and the U.S. attorney general joined the negotiations pursuant to his authority to settle litigation.

On April 9, 1991, representatives from the Warm Springs Nation made the initial settlement proposal at the commencement of formal negotiations. Over the next six years, a total of fifteen negotiation sessions took place wherein the parties continued to counter and revise various proposals. Public notice was provided for each negotiation session, and although the public was not allowed to participate in the actual negotiation, they were encouraged to submit comments afterwards. The final agreement was signed and executed on November 17, 1997, and, pursuant to the authorizing legislation, remitted to the Deschutes County Circuit Court in 1999 for incorporation into a final court decree.[64]

Throughout the negotiations process, relations between the parties remained relatively amicable. In fact, the only significant difficulty in the process came after the final agreement was signed, when the parties sought to clarify a linguistic ambiguity in the agreement with potentially serious implications for the tribe's water rights.[65] In reaching the settlement, the parties had agreed *not* to use the PIA standard that has been typical of other water rights settlements. Instead, after studying seventy years of flow data from the Deschutes River, the parties felt that the region supplied enough water to satisfy all current and some future uses.[66] The Warm Springs Nation therefore felt that they could preserve their priority date and quantify their water rights by using a contemporary water use measurement. A date was selected (September 26, 1996), and the amount of water resources used, consumed, and reserved as of that date were deemed enough to satisfy their present and future water needs without subjecting other water users to a call by the tribe. Under the prior appropriation doctrine, putting a "call" on the river refers to when a senior water user, one who has first appropriated a share of water and put it to beneficial use, may require juniors, or subsequent users, to forego portions of their water appropriations so that the senior's appropriation may be filled. However, the State of Oregon itself has a rather large instream flow right, with a priority date of January 16, 1991. Tribal representatives feared that the state's earlier priority date, combined with the use of the phrase "Existing State Water Rights shall not be curtailed in favor of the Tribal Reserved Water Right" in the agreement, would subordinate the tribal right to the state's right and render it valueless. Therefore, two subsequent negotiation sessions were held in September and November of 2001, and the agreement was amended to include a new, earlier priority date of January 15, 1991, for the tribal water right.[67]

Settlement agreement. The settlement agreement exemplifies a productive working relationship between Indian and non-Indian communities, resulting in benefits to both. The agreement is also viewed as providing a desirable amount of certainty regarding water rights to protect water resources and water users on and off the reservation.

Because the parties agreed not to use the PIA standard for quantifying the tribe's water rights, and instead relied on the tribe's contemporary uses as of 1991, the tribe compiled technical data quantifying both the average streamflows and the tribe's existing uses, including consumptive uses and instream flow needs. In doing so, the Warm Springs Nation determined that their use of on-reservation streams amounted to 112.22 cfs, of which 56 was consumptive and 56.22 returned to surface flow. Their use of the streams bordering the reservation, the Metolius and Deschutes rivers, amounted to 48.12 cfs, of which 11 was consumptive and 37.12 returned to the surface flow. The on-reservation use is dominated primarily by the fish-

ery (50 cfs) and irrigation (46.7 cfs), followed by more minor uses for domestic, industrial, and cultural purposes (6.72, 8.13, and 0.67 cfs, respectively). By contrast, the water from bordering streams is used primarily for industry (21.18 cfs) and the fishery (20 cfs), followed by smaller amounts for irrigation and domestic use (2.22 cfs and 4.73 cfs, respectively).[68]

The agreement breaks the tribal water rights into five separate sections. First, the agreement reserves to the tribe all existing on-reservation uses as mentioned in the preceding paragraph.[69] Second, the Warm Springs people are entitled to the "entire natural flow" of all on-reservation streams and their tributaries for instream purposes "to sustain or enhance the aquatic ecosystem of the Reservation for the benefit of the fish and wildlife resources . . . which shall be protected and preserved for such purposes in perpetuity."[70] Third, as much as 250 cubic feet per second are reserved to the tribe from streams located on the reservation, for out-of-stream use on the reservation, as long as there is no "net degradation of the fishery." Fourth, as much as 200 cubic feet per second are reserved to the tribe from the Metolius and Deschutes rivers, for uses either on or off the reservation, essentially providing for marketable water rights. Finally, the Warm Springs people retain the instream flows from the Metolius and Deschutes rivers in such amounts as the parties have agreed are necessary to support the tribe's water rights and to benefit the aquatic ecosystems on the reservation.[71]

Supplemental adjudication. After the parties reached the final settlement agreement and amended the agreement to correct an apparent linguistic ambiguity, another issue surfaced. A look at the demographics of the reservation indicates that 93 percent of reservation lands are held in trust for the tribe, slightly less than 7 percent of the land is held by allottees, and approximately one-third of one percent is held in fee.[72] Therefore, the parties realized that there may be individual water users whose interests had not been represented in drafting the settlement agreement. Desiring to avoid future litigation by the individual water rights holders, the parties initiated a supplemental adjudication and provided notice to some 24,000 water users in the Deschutes River basin, notifying them of the settlement agreement and informing them that they were entitled by law to file claims and exceptions.[73] The supplemental adjudication was opened to "claims to the use of the waters of the streams and rivers of the Reservation, the use of which was initiated on or before February 24, 1909, and claims by individuals whose rights are derivative of the Treaty of June 25, 1855, between the United States and the Tribes and Bands of Middle Oregon."[74] Notice was mailed in early August 2002, with a filing deadline of September 25, 2002. Only fourteen exceptions were received, most of which were not expected to cause substantive legal repercussions.[75] The Deschutes County Circuit Court held hearings on the claims of the fourteen exceptors in 2002. The agreement has now been incorporated into the basin-wide Deschutes River Decree.

Although most settlement parties choose to take their agreement to Congress for congressional authorization and for appropriation of federal money to implement the settlement, the parties to the Warm Springs settlement have thus far elected not to go to Congress. Spokespersons for various parties offer several reasons for this choice. First, the participants noted that in other settlement processes, substantial changes to a locally negotiated settlement agreement had to be made in order to obtain congressional approval. Further, they observed several older Arizona settlements going back to Congress for amendments, indicating that congressional approval does not necessarily bring about finality. The parties have not ruled out the possibility of going to Congress in the future if the advantages of doing so seem to outweigh the disadvantages.

Reflections. The Warm Springs agreement illustrates how a tribe can initiate and pursue a negotiated settlement to fashion its water future. The agreement is also notable for the co-management regime in place among the three parties, but most conspicuously between the Warm Springs Nation and the State of Oregon. Seeking to respect and uphold the rights and powers of respective sovereigns, as well as acknowledge the complexity involved in managing a transboundary resource, the parties drafted a memorandum of understanding agreeing to "continue cooperative efforts to efficiently manage water, water quality, and other aquatic resources and to fairly resolve disputes arising under this Agreement without resorting to litigation."[76] Article IX of the agreement creates an intergovernmental board, comprising one representative from each party and operating by consensus, whose duty it is to help implement the agreement and mediate disputes.[77] The agreement seeks to circumvent future jurisdictional disputes by delineating which party will be responsible for administering and enforcing various individual water rights. Finally, the parties have determined, for the time being, that taking their settlement agreement to Congress presents more risk than benefits and have proceeded to a final decree without the usual step of congressional authorization.

Other Water Users' Settlement Initiatives

In some basins, other water users have initiated the Indian water rights settlement processes. Completed settlements and ongoing settlement efforts in Arizona provide the best example of this approach. Some of Arizona's settlements resulted from leadership by influential members of Congress. More recently, the SRP has led a group of utilities, municipalities, and commercial interests in pursuing settlements. Settlement discussions occur in the context of Arizona's adjudication of the state's two major river systems, the Gila River and the Little Colorado River. The negotiating process in Arizona is decidedly more ad hoc and private than in states like Montana. The process is productive, however; Arizona has achieved an impressive number of settlements.

Gila River Settlement and Little Colorado River Negotiations

> Indian tribes—America's first irrigators—were not always water destitute. Some tribes diverted and applied large amounts of water before encroaching settlement pilfered the water supply. A case in point is the Pima Indians of the Gila River Reservation in central Arizona. During the latter half of the nineteenth century the tribe grew prosperous from its large irrigated farms. Then the waters of the Gila were diverted upstream from the reservation, and the Pimas' fortunes declined precipitously.
>
> Daniel McCool, *Native Waters*

The Gila River and Little Colorado River adjudications trace their origins to proceedings initiated in the 1970s under the then-existing general adjudication procedures. Between 1974 and 1978, three major Arizona corporations (Salt River Valley Water Users' Association, Phelps Dodge Corporation, and ASARCO, Inc.) filed petitions with the Arizona Land Department to determine water rights along major state water sources in the Salt, Verde, Gila (Upper and Lower), Little Colorado, and San Pedro rivers and tributaries. In 1980, the Buckeye Irrigation Company filed a motion to intervene and a petition to enlarge the scope of the adjudication with respect to areas of the Gila River watershed not included in the previously filed petitions. Though this petition was granted, pending litigation in federal court relating to the Santa Cruz River watershed in Pima and Santa Cruz counties prevented initially including these waters in the state adjudication. The Santa Cruz River watershed was fully included in the state adjudication after federal litigation concluded in 1985.

In 1979, the legislature amended Arizona's general adjudication procedures. Under these amendments, the Salt River, Verde River, and Gila River adjudications were transferred from the Arizona Land Department to the Maricopa County Superior Court. The San Pedro River adjudication was transferred to the Cochise County Superior Court. In 1981, the Arizona Supreme Court consolidated these adjudications into one proceeding assigned to the Maricopa County Superior Court under the caption *In re the General Adjudication of All Rights to Use Water in the Gila River System and Source*, numbers W-1, W-2, W-3, and W-4 (Consolidated). The Little Colorado River adjudication was transferred to the Apache County Superior Court, where it is litigated under the caption *In re the General Adjudication of All Rights to Use Water in the Little Colorado River System and Source*, number 6417.

Maricopa and Apache County superior courts were assigned the cases because the largest number of potential claimants resided in these counties. Summons were issued in both adjudications and served on potential claimants in each watershed—a million summons in all. The summons required a claimant to file a statement with the ADWR if the person claimed a water use in the watershed. More than 83,500 statements of claimants were filed by more than 24,000 parties in the Gila River adjudication and over 3,100 parties filed more than 11,300 claims in the Little Colorado River adjudication.

Adjudication highlights. The general adjudication statutes went through substantial legislative changes in 1995; the constitutionality of these amendments were litigated before the Arizona Supreme Court, causing delay in adjudication proceedings until 1999. The court ruled some provisions of the 1995 legislation unconstitutional, upheld some, and required some provisions to be applied only prospectively.

Litigation relating to the jurisdiction of state courts to adjudicate Indian reserved rights began in 1979 and ended in an opinion by the U.S. Supreme Court in 1983, and a decision by the Arizona Supreme Court in January 1985.[78] The Arizona Supreme Court accepted six interlocutory appeals (developed in proceedings before the Maricopa County Superior Court) on substantial and long-standing legal issues. The supreme court has issued decisions on five of the appeals and, in 2002, vacated further proceedings with respect to the sixth.

Two of these decisions are especially relevant to the quantification of tribal water rights. In 1999, the supreme court held that federal reserved rights extend to groundwater to the extent groundwater is necessary to accomplish the purpose of a reservation.[79] In June 2000, the U.S. Supreme Court denied petitions filed by five parties for a writ of certiorari of this portion of the opinion. In 2001, the state supreme court held that the purpose of a federal Indian reservation is to serve as a "permanent home and abiding place" to the people living there; the primary-secondary purpose test for quantifying a federal reserved right does not apply to Indian reservations; the PIA standard is not the exclusive measure to quantify water rights on Indian lands; and quantifying an Indian reserved right is a fact-intensive, reservation-specific inquiry that must address numerous factors, such as a tribe's master land use plans, history, culture, geography, topography, natural resources, economic base, past water use, present and projected future population, and any others deemed relevant. Proposed uses must be reasonably feasible, however, and the amount of water adjudicated must be tailored to the reservation's minimal need.[80]

Major parties continue to engage in active efforts to resolve Indian and federal reserved rights by mutual settlement. To date, these efforts have resulted in the Maricopa County Superior Court's approval (following congressional approval) of four settlement agreements of Indian reserved rights. Negotiations to resolve the water right claims of several other Indian tribes actively continue after several years.

Little Colorado River settlement talks. As early as 1986, an attorney for the Hopi Tribe, Harry Sachse, suggested the establishment of a Settlement Committee to explore possibilities for a negotiated settlement. In 1987, Judge Allen G. Minker, the assigned superior court judge for the adjudication, issued Pretrial Order Number 1, which set forth the general framework of the adjudication, including a schedule for preparation of hydrographic survey reports (HSRs). Among the order's many provisions was the establishment of a Settlement Committee "to meet and explore the settlement potential of this litigation." The Settlement Committee initially comprised attorneys for the Hopi Tribe, Navajo Nation, United States, State of Arizona, Phelps Dodge Corporation, SRP, Seven Springs Ranch (and other claimants), Aztec Land and Cattle Company, Bar-T-Bar Ranch (and other claimants), and the ADWR. Harry Sachse was appointed chair of the Settlement Committee, a position held by no other person in all the years of the committee's existence. The parties involved in the settlement negotiations now include four tribes, multiple state and federal agencies, four large electric power utilities, and numerous water districts, water users, and municipal and county governments.

The ADWR filed the HSR for the Silver Creek watershed, part of the Little Colorado River adjudication, in 1990. At the conclusion of the 180-day objection period, more than 3,450 objections had been filed. More than 2,000 of the objections were filed by three tribes (Navajo, Hopi, and San Juan Southern Paiute) or the United States on the behalf of the tribes in an effort to protect Indian water rights.

In January 1992, Special Master John E. Thorson commenced proceedings to resolve objections to the Silver Creek HSR. Initially, objections were organized into contested cases involving many issues of broad legal significance concerning state law water rights. The complexity of this litigation soon convinced the parties and the court that a different approach was necessary.

In January 1994, Judge Minker modified previous orders concerning the schedule for HSRs, requesting the ADWR to proceed with an Indian lands HSR, to be filed within nine months. This change in focus was rooted in the excessive number of objections filed to the Silver Creek HSR, resulting in numerous pleadings, contentious hearings, and undue burdens on all parties, especially small claimants, and on the court. Judge Minker sought to curtail lengthy and costly litigation by focusing attention on claims of reserved rights of Indian lands and federal agencies.

During the first half of 1994, Judge Minker granted stays of the litigation schedule for the ongoing Silver Creek proceedings. This was done to enable the parties to concentrate on prospects for settlement, rather than expend time and resources at litigation. In September 1994, the ADWR filed the preliminary Indian lands HSR. Comments were solicited and considered, and Judge Minker ordered the ADWR to defer filing a final HSR until further order of the court. This accommodation was to permit parties the opportunity to pursue settlement negotiations without simultaneously preparing for litigation. As of 2004, a final Indian lands HSR has not been published.

After Judge Minker stayed litigation, the Settlement Committee met frequently and settlement negotiations have intensified. This was especially true after Judge Minker appointed a settlement judge to oversee and manage the negotiations. In November 1994, the Settlement Committee was ordered to meet at least one time with Michael C. Nelson, presiding judge of the Apache County Superior Court. The court directed that if, after the first meeting, any party wished to disqualify Judge Nelson, the court would consider such a request. No such request was made and, in fact, all parties have praised Judge Nelson's effectiveness and dedication to the settlement process.

Some of the issues. By all accounts, the first agreement among the parties was to seek protection of existing water uses while providing some means of developing wet water for Indian lands. As talks were getting under way, secretary of the Interior Bruce Babbitt suggested that any settlement should address issues surrounding the Black Mesa Mine. The Hopi Tribe and others, including some environmental groups, have opposed Peabody Western Coal Company's use of underground water from the N-Aquifer to slurry coal from Black Mesa Mine to the Mohave Generating Station in Laughlin, Nevada. Secretary Babbitt urged consideration of a pipeline from Lake Powell to the Black Mesa Mine and to the various Indian communities in the basin.

Under Judge Nelson's guidance, negotiations were split into north and south issues. On the north side, talks involved the proposed Lake Powell pipeline and sharing of water resources available to the Navajo Nation and the Hopi Tribe. The south issues are those affecting the vast majority of individual, non-Indian claimants in the watershed. Primary among the issues is grandfathering existing uses, some means of assuring future uses, and developing wet water for the Navajo Nation.

At the same time, the Zuni Pueblo and water users in the eastern portion of the watershed have engaged in fruitful talks, also with Judge Nelson's help. On a fourth front, state parties and federal agencies have conducted negotiations with respect to the non-Indian federal claims of the National Park Service, Forest Service, and Bureau of Land Management.

Current status of negotiations. Minute entries from various status conferences since settlement talks began in earnest in 1994 reveal disconcerting repetition. "We've reached agreement on most of the parties' water allocations, but the costs are problematic." "We are very close to settlement, and can submit a bill to Congress next month." "One or two issues are preventing final agreement." "All agree that settlement talks must continue, and litigation must remain in abeyance." In early 1998, in fact, Judge Minker expressed frustration about continuing to pursue a settlement that perpetually seems to be just beyond reach. Truth about actual settlement possibilities may lie in confidential documents not available for review.

What we do know is the Navajo Nation and Hopi Tribe agree on the need for and route of a pipeline from Lake Powell to the two reservations. Figures have not been released on how much it will cost or how it will be paid. Senator Jon Kyl (R-AZ) has commissioned a $1 million study, through the Bureau of Reclamation, to review existing reports concerning the feasibility and cost of the pipeline and other water development projects. That study was completed in 2004, but Senator Kyl has prevented its release, apparently because of some deficiencies. Discussions remain in abeyance on most areas of disagreement. Also, due to retirement, Judge Nelson no longer serves as mediator.

The tribes have agreed to forego any challenge to existing surface-water and groundwater uses (grandfathered uses) in exchange for limiting future surface diversions. The tribes have proposed methods to manage shared aquifers and the waters of five washes and arroyos that traverse both reservations. CAP water may be made available to supply the reservations, but there are significant questions about diversion of that water from Lake Powell.

There is a proposal to divert excess water in the southern portion of the watershed that flows north toward the reservations from the Mogollon Rim. Reservoirs would be constructed or enlarged in the Three Canyon area, including Chevelon Creek, Clear Creek, and Jacks Canyon. At various times, this proposal has involved transfer of Blue Ridge Reservoir from Phelps Dodge Corporation to the Navajo Nation, transfer of Show Low Lake from Phelps Dodge to the City of Show Low, and an exchange of water between Phelps Dodge and the Gila River Indian Community (as part of a possible settlement in the Gila River adjudication). Any of the new or expanded reservoirs could be affected by the ESA or other environmental laws.

Water marketing has been an important issue for the Navajo Nation. The ADWR has firmly opposed any possibility of marketing water, especially CAP water, outside of the watershed.

The attorney representing the Zuni Pueblo reported at a June 2002 status conference near completion of all issues relating to Zuni tribal lands in Arizona (Zuni Heaven). Although some parties initially opposed any settlement less than comprehensive, the Zuni issues were resolved independently. The settlement was submitted to Congress and approved in 2003. (See the later section in this chapter on the Zuni Heaven settlement.)

Federal non-Indian claims (National Park Service, Forest Service, Bureau of Land Management) have also taken an independent settlement track. During the second half of 2001, parties filed several stipulations as to water rights abstracts. The adjudication court has indicated it will approve the stipulations once minor technical changes are made.

Finally, Judge Eddward Ballinger, who replaced Judge Minker as the assigned judge for the adjudication, has requested that the ADWR proceed with the Hopi Tribe HSR. No due date has been established, pending the ADWR's available funding and personnel resources for adjudication-related work. In anticipation of returning to litigation, Judge Ballinger has ordered parties to submit disclosures concerning the claimed reserved rights of the Hopi Tribe, Navajo Nation, San Juan Southern Paiute Tribe, and the Zuni Pueblo. The Hopi Tribe and the United States were also invited to file new or amended statements of claimant.

To summarize, settlement negotiations remain active on some of the unresolved issues in the Little Colorado adjudication. The parties are waiting for feasibility studies (funded through Senator Kyl's efforts) and a Hopi HSR to be completed. However, it is not possible to predict whether a comprehensive settlement can be achieved and lengthy litigation averted.

Current status of the Gila River adjudication. In recent years, the principal activity in the Gila River adjudication has involved the water rights claims of the Gila River Indian Community. Two preliminary HSRs have been published by the ADWR, with the final HSR awaiting decisions concerning subflow and the applicability of factors other than PIA.

In 1995, Judge Susan Bolton, the superior court judge assigned to the adjudication, granted the Gila River community's motion to commence consideration of the community's water rights. Thereafter, in 1998, discovery and disclosure of documents began, followed by summary judgment motions relating to the preclusive effect of prior agreements and decrees, including the historic federal Globe Equity Decree, on Gila River Indian claims. The motions were briefed and argued before Special Master Thorson, who subsequently issued two reports to the trial court, recognizing that some tribal rights would be defined by earlier decrees. The parties filed objections to the special master's reports; those objections were briefed; and Judge Ballinger heard arguments and entered his decision.[81] The community and the United States have each filed petitions for interlocutory review of this decision. As of summer 2004, there has been no ruling from the Arizona Supreme Court on these petitions.

Simultaneously with the litigation track, the Gila River community and other parties eventually negotiated a framework for federal legislation. Senator Jon Kyl (R-AZ) introduced the Arizona Water Settlements Act in the 107th Congress and, on February 25, 2003, reintroduced the proposal as S. 437 in the 108th Congress.[82] After committee hearings, the Senate approved S. 437 on October 10, 2004. With rapidity rarely seen with Indian water settlements, the House of Representatives received the Senate's bill on November 16th and passed it the next day.

The final legislation links together many parties' interests, at a price of $445 million though 2014 (Congressional Budget Office). The legislation settles the water right claims of the Gila River Indian Community and the Tohono O'odham Nation using a combination of water and money. The legislation (Title I) also codifies Arizona's Central Arizona Project repayment obligation at $1.65 billion (instead of $3.2 billion), allowing more CAP water to be used for Indian settlements. Now, more than 650,000 acre-feet of CAP water (47 percent) will be assigned to Arizona tribes. Senate Bill 437 even enables New Mexico to utilize 18,000 acre-feet of Gila River water in partial satisfaction of its Colorado River basin entitlement.

Title II authorizes the Gila River Indian Community Water Rights Settlement. The Gila River community will receive a total water package of 655,000 acre-feet of water from the CAP and the Gila, Salt, and Verde rivers. The financial benefits to the community are estimated at $200 million.

Title III is designed to finalize the water right claims of the Tohono O'odham Nation, previously (but unsatisfactorily) addressed in the 1982 settlement. The nation will receive 37,800 acre-feet in CAP water for the San Xavier Reservation and Schuk Toak District. The federal government is financially obligated to construct the works necessary to deliver and distribute this water. An additional allocation of 28,200 acre-feet of CAP water, with lower priority, is also authorized. The San Xavier Reservation annually may pump up to 10,000 acre-feet of groundwater, and the Schuk Toak District may pump 3,200 acre-feet. Approximately $24 million is authorized to implement the settlement.

Both the Gila Indian Community and the Tohono O'odham Nation may sell or lease their water—but not out of state. Both Indian governments must adopt comprehensive water codes. Both settlements require Gila River adjudication court approval.

Title IV of the legislation assists other Arizona tribes in negotiating settlements. A total of $600,000 (fiscal year 2006) is authorized for legal and technical assistance to the San Carlos Apache Tribe, White

Mountain Apache Tribe, and other tribes. A separate section of the act retains 6,411 acre-feet of CAP water for a potential Navajo Nation settlement.

Reflections. The Arizona adjudications, for all their complexity, delay, and expense, have provided the context for a series of innovative and important Indian water rights settlements. One of these, the Salt River Pima–Maricopa Indian Community (SRPMIC) settlement (1991), was the first Indian water settlement to be successfully incorporated into a final general stream adjudication decree. In the following sections, we examine two settlements that have resulted from the Arizona adjudications: the Salt River settlement from the Gila River adjudication, and the Zuni Heaven settlement from the Little Colorado River adjudication.

Salt River Pima–Maricopa Indian Community

The Salt River Pima–Maricopa Indian Community water settlement was the first Arizona settlement negotiated in response to the Gila River adjudication and resolves water disputes that have existed between the Indian community and other water users in the Salt River Valley for more than 110 years. This agreement illustrates the increasing complexity of Arizona settlements. Only a few of the significant aspects of the settlement are discussed here.

- These disputes involved the water supplies and water delivery arrangements of two Indian communities, seven Phoenix area cities and towns, and three irrigation districts.
- The settlement relies on intricate arrangements for water transfers and exchanges, leasebacks, contract modifications and ratifications, and modified storage rights to satisfy the community's water entitlement.
- Determining an equitable measure of the local cost share posed a major obstacle in obtaining federal approval for the bill.

Pima and Maricopa Indians irrigated land along the Gila River in central Arizona prior to the arrival of Spanish explorers. During the mid-1800s, immigrants, miners, and the U.S. Army relied on these tribes for much of their food and hay supplies. In order to protect these lands from encroachment by non-Indians, the Gila River Indian Reservation was established in

1859. Beginning in 1868, upstream diversions by non-Indians depleted much of the water supply available to the reservation. During the 1870s, Pima and Maricopa Indians, in search of more dependable water supplies, began migrating from the Gila River Reservation to cultivate lands along the Salt River. By 1879, the Indians had brought about 3,400 acres under cultivation. In order to protect these Indians from further displacement by non-Indians, some of whom were attempting to homestead on the Indian's improved lands, the Salt River Pima–Maricopa Indian Reservation was created by executive order in 1879.

In 1905 a suit was filed in state court to determine the priority and ownership of water rights in the Salt River Valley in preparation for completion of the SRP. The federal government filed claims on behalf of the Salt River Pima–Maricopa Indian Community on the basis of its prior appropriation rights under state law. The United States filed no claims for reserved water rights, even after the Supreme Court's landmark *Winters* case had been decided in 1908. The resulting Kent Decree, issued by the court in 1910, awarded the Salt River Indian Community 18,766 acre-feet per year of the natural flow of the Salt and Verde rivers. The Indian community's repeated appeals to have the United States reopen the Kent Decree were unsuccessful.

The water supply problems of the Indian community were compounded when it was excluded from receiving storage water from the SRP. In 1935, the secretary of the Interior and the SRP agreed to build Bartlett Dam on the Verde River, in part to provide 20,000 acre-feet annually to the Salt River Reservation. The Bartlett Dam agreement provides a complex accounting system to allocate the storage rights behind the dam. When Bartlett Dam was operated with other SRP reservoirs, this accounting system worked to the disadvantage of the Indian community, effectively reducing its water storage credits.

For many years the Indian community protested the water entitlement it received under both the Kent Decree and the Bartlett Dam agreement. By the early 1980s the community had initiated a series of lawsuits against the federal government, the SRP, and local cities and irrigation districts. Concurrent efforts to negotiate failed to yield an acceptable compromise. In the 1980s, when the community was joined in the Gila River adjudication, the United States claimed a total of 202,000 acre-feet annually on behalf of the community.

Negotiations. Because these lawsuits threatened key water delivery arrangements for irrigators and for the Phoenix metropolitan area, non-Indians had a strong incentive to seek a negotiated settlement, rather than await the uncertain outcome of litigation. Negotiations resumed in 1985, with the added incentive of developing a cost-sharing plan to speed completion of CAP. The overall cost of the settlement and how it was to be distributed among the federal government, the Indian community, and local water users emerged as a critical issue that shaped the character of the final agreement. After more than two years of intensive negotiations, a local settlement was reached in 1988, and was ratified by Congress later that same year.[83]

Settlement agreement. The settlement entitles the Indian community to a maximum of 122,400 acre-feet annually (4.5 acre-feet per acre water duty applied to the 27,200 irrigable acres on the reservation). The water is to be provided from a combination of sources, including firming up existing rights under the Kent Decree and Bartlett Dam agreement; a series of exchanges involving CAP and non-CAP Colorado River water; Salt and Verde river water; and groundwater pumped from beneath the reservation. In addition, a trust fund was established to enable the community to rehabilitate, further develop, and maintain its irrigation systems and to put the settlement water to beneficial use.

The settlement relies upon complex transfers, leases, and exchanges to provide water for the Indian community and to protect existing non-Indian water users. For instance, the settlement requires the cities to provide the Indian community with 20,000 acre-feet annually of Salt and Verde river water available through the SRP. In exchange, the secretary of the Interior will provide the cities with 22,000 acre-feet per year of pre-CAP priority Colorado River water. The settlement provided that the Colorado River water could be made available from the Wellton-Mohawk Irrigation and Drainage District near Yuma, Arizona, although this district is not a party to the settlement. In exchange, the district received certain benefits from the federal government. Another provision of the act authorizes the community to lease its entire CAP allocation of 13,300 acre-feet per year to local cities for

ninety-nine years for $16 million.[84] This leasing provision is the only exception to the settlement's blanket prohibition on marketing or using the community's entitlement off reservation. Surrounding non-Indian water users are limited in their groundwater use by Arizona's Groundwater Management Act. The tribe may pump 38,000 acre-feet annually from groundwater wells, though groundwater use restrictions could become more stringent in the future if the east Salt River subbasin is no longer in "safe yield," as determined by the ADWR.

The overall goals of these arrangements were to satisfy the community's entitlement with native groundwater and surface flows; to minimize the impact of the settlement on existing non-Indian water users; and to provide the cities with renewable surface supplies. In addition to protecting existing water supplies, a major goal of local non-Indians in this settlement was to preserve and affirm existing water delivery agreements.

Local cities immediately negotiated lease contracts with the community for the CAP water. According to Bill Chase, the City of Phoenix water advisor, "the lease is going great." Phoenix contracted back in the late 1980s to begin taking their leased portion of the community's water in 2001. In exchange, the City of Phoenix provided the community a one-time lump-sum payment of approximately $1,200 per acre-foot. One of the important features of the lease is that the water retains its Indian priority and character. This means that when Phoenix orders the water, the city is not obliged to pay the CAP capital repayment cost it would if it were ordering the water as "the City." In addition, in times of shortage, the water retains its Indian priority date.

Congress has made necessary appropriations for settlement implementation. The settlement has been approved by the court presiding over the Gila River general stream adjudication, and will be incorporated in the final decree of that adjudication. Implementation of this settlement is proceeding smoothly.

Zuni Heaven Settlement

The Zuni Pueblo Reservation is located in northwestern New Mexico, near the Four Corners region where Arizona, New Mexico, Utah, and Colorado join. For time immemorial, the Zuni Tribe has made a pilgrimage to Kothluwala:wa, or Zuni Heaven. Zuni Heaven is a relatively flat and marshy riparian area of the Little Colorado River, approximately three miles downstream of the Zion Reservoir near Hunt Valley, Arizona. For many centuries selected members of the Zuni Tribe have trekked by foot or horseback over 110 miles to perform religious ceremonies for two days during the summer solstice period every four years.[85] In 1877, the land that comprised Zuni Heaven was lost to the tribe as a result of an executive order.[86] In 1984, Congress passed a law to reacquire lands around the religious site in northeastern Arizona, as well as permanent rights of ingress and egress.[87] Recently, the tribe purchased other lands needed for the restoration of the area in fee simple.

Though the Zuni reacquired the land, Zuni Heaven was much altered due to the construction of the Zion Dam in 1920.[88] The dam trapped sediment in the reservoir so that outflows scoured the channel of the Little Colorado River to the extent that the river abandoned its historical floodplain and caused rapid destruction of the surrounding wetland that supported watercress, cottonwoods, and willows. Groundwater pumping by nearby non-Indians exacerbated the destruction by draining the artesian springs. Finally, the introduction of nonnative plants like tamarisks, along with cattle grazing, further damaged the Zuni religious site.

Under the 1984 congressional act and subsequent 1990 legislation, the Zuni are funded to coordinate with the Bureau of Reclamation, the EPA, and the Arizona Water Protection Fund to develop a program to restore the wetland.[89] The legislation establishes the Zuni Indian Resource Development Trust Fund and provides an appropriation of $25 million to aid in the restoration plan. Further, the act declares certain private lands in Arizona to be Zuni Reservation. According to the legislative history, the lands were redesignated as reservation because "extensive damage to the trust lands within the Zuni Reservation have occurred, including severe land erosion, loss of timber and minerals, spoliation of archaeological sites, and loss of the use of water; . . . this damage occurred by acts and omissions of the United States in breach of its trust responsibility."[90]

Further, to successfully ensure proper habitat restoration, the Zuni acquired a couple of large ranches upstream from Zuni Heaven. Though few water rights were associated with the purchase of the ranches, the Zuni need this land to facilitate the volume of water delivery necessary to properly irrigate the critical restoration areas. Some parties to the settlement objected to the Zuni putting such fee lands into trust. Eventually, the talks focused on allowing a small corridor of land along the Little Colorado River to go into trust, with the rest remaining in fee unless Congress passed legislation authorizing the trust status.

Water quality was another important issue. Some parties to the negotiations wanted the tribe to waive water quality damages, that is, waive the right to sue for a certain quality of the tribe's entire decreed right. The tribe was willing to waive claims beyond a level of "natural water quality," or reasonable rises and falls of water quality due to currently practiced circumstances. The tribe was not willing to waive claims to damages that result from the introduction of a hazardous substance into the water supply.

In the later stages of the negotiation, the parties proposed to enable the tribe to purchase water rights surrounding the Zuni Heaven land in order to retire those rights from use. Though the tribe asserts a PIA-type claim for the fertile area, the dominant focus of the four-year settlement negotiation was for water to restore the religious spot as an oasis. Non-Indian reliance on groundwater pumping altered the natural hydrologic conditions so that springs no longer irrigate the area. The cornerstone of the negotiated settlement is a voluntary exchange of water rights so that the Zuni may use mostly surface water to irrigate the land to its original wetland habitat. The parties agreed to allow the Zuni Tribe, or the United States on its behalf, to purchase up to 3,600 acre-feet of rights from willing upstream sellers, in the Norviel Decree area, with the rights retaining the Norviel Decree priority date.[91] Once these rights are severed and transferred for the benefit of the tribe, state law will no longer apply, and the tribe may use the water in any way it deems appropriate on the reservation.

In addition, the parties agreed not to object to Zuni pumping of up to 1,500 acre-feet per year of groundwater on the reservation to supplement the surface-water irrigation. The groundwater will be used to ensure constant saturation of the most critical religious habitat, even in drought or shortage years. Further, two large utility companies with operations in the area developed noninterference groundwater compacts with the tribe. The SRP agreed not to pump groundwater south of a specified area, and Tucson Electric Power agreed not to move their groundwater-pumping operation any closer to the Little Colorado River than its current site is. Finally, smaller, private parties to the settlement, who are located within an area critical to the restoration habitat, agreed to limit their groundwater pumping to a rate below 500 gallons per minute. These agreements are "pumping protection agreements" that effectively create buffer zones surrounding the reservation and require limited or no use of groundwater by non-Indians in that area.[92]

Some parties in the settlement maintained that the Zuni Heaven deal had to be included in an overall Little Colorado River settlement. Though the Zuni Heaven portion of the Little Colorado River talks is minute compared to the claims, issues, and price tags of other interests, the Zuni lands represent a significant piece of leverage with which other American Indians would like to bargain, due to their close proximity to powerful utility interests. In addition, the federal government has multiple, and sometimes competing, trust obligations in the Little Colorado River negotiation and must make sure a binding and favorable agreement for one tribe does not unduly prejudice another trust beneficiary. Although there was some resistance to the Zuni Heaven settlement being introduced as a stand-alone piece of legislation, all local parties eventually signed off on the settlement agreement.[93]

Senator Kyl, accompanied by Senator McCain, introduced the Zuni Indian Tribe Water Rights Settlement Act of 2002 in July.[94] The bill is an agreement with the tribe, the United States, the State of Arizona, and major water users in the area of the tribe's religious lands in northeastern Arizona. The settlement provides the tribe with necessary resources to acquire lands around the religious site from willing sellers to restore the wetland environment that previously existed. In exchange for this settlement, the tribe waives its rights and claims it may have in the pending Little Colorado River adjudication. The bill was reported to the Senate in October 2002 from committee after changes were made over concern about the water quality waiver provisions and the United States' liability as sovereign and trustee, right-of-way access across tribal trust land, and sovereign immunity

and removal issues. The bill passed Congress and was signed into law by President Bush on June 23, 2003.[95]

Zuni Pueblo is developing plans for wetland restoration and use of water that will be acquired under the provisions of the settlement. The pueblo worked with the State of Arizona to achieve state legislation needed to facilitate water acquisitions. Arizona House Bill 2244, enacted in April 2004, clarifies state law on surface water transfers to pave the way for the water transfers necessary to implement the settlement.

Settlements Addressing Endangered Species Act Issues

The ESA prohibits any federal agency from engaging in activities that might jeopardize a listed species or adversely modify its critical habitat. Only limited exceptions apply to this mandate. Indian water rights settlements often occur in water-short basins where fish and riparian species are already under stress from prior water and land development, and federal agencies are always involved in these agreements. Thus, the goals of settlement efforts—to achieve additional water development—often conflict with the goals of the ESA—to recover threatened and endangered species. In basins having ESA-listed species, proposed tribal water projects receive special scrutiny, if not outright opposition, from the FWS. This dilemma has led to tribal complaints that Indian water rights settlements are unjustifiably burdened with the legacy of all past environmental abuses. ESA issues can be major hurdles for negotiators to overcome; but, as the profiles below indicate, there are workable strategies to do so. Still, the ESA has a major impact on water use throughout the West, and Indian water rights settlements are only one area of the ongoing controversy.

Colorado Ute Water Rights Settlement

Scott McElroy

> We need to look at Indian water rights in a basin-wide context alongside issues such as endangered species, drought, and water quality.
>
> Shaun McGrath, Western Governors' Association

In seeking to use their water rights for the benefit of tribal members, Indian tribes in the arid West face a gauntlet of complex federal environmental laws with the potential to limit much-needed water development on reservations. The construction of community water supply facilities, which is taken for granted in the rest of the country, is required in these water-short areas if Indian reservations are to function as permanent tribal homelands. Because water development has been so slowly advanced in Indian country, the rivers and streams that can satisfy these tribal water needs frequently provide the last remaining useful habitat for aquatic species on the brink of extinction. Sometimes, as at Pyramid Lake in Nevada, the tribal interest of preserving endangered species coincides with the values protected under federal environmental mandates. On other occasions, tribal interests conflict with the environmental concerns raised by the development of new water resources. On the Navajo Reservation, for example, approximately 40 percent of the population lacks a potable domestic water supply. Thus, while there is a widely perceived value to the Navajo Nation in conserving endangered species and maintaining the habitat on which those species depend, those benefits provide little comfort to tribal members who haul water to their homes. In short, despite the seniority of tribal reserved rights, Indian tribes may be limited in their use of water supplies now and in the future by the ESA and other applicable federal environmental laws.

These issues are most acute in the Southwest, where water is extremely limited. The states, along with non-Indian citizens, have aggressively sought to maximize the use of water within their boundaries. This has primarily benefited non-Indians without regard for the senior, but unquantified, tribal water rights in the rivers and aquifers being developed. Non-Indian water development has included the transportation of water over great distances or between basins and the construction of massive water storage projects. These activities have generally required extensive federal funding and have taken place with minimal attention to environmental consequences. Projects such as CAP, the SJCP, and CUP provide water to support large municipal populations and maintain economic growth throughout the regions that they serve.

As a result, Indian tribes that seek to resolve their outstanding water rights claims may be at odds with those who oppose the development of new water sup-plies in the West based on the theory that existing supplies should be reallocated to the most economically efficient uses, rather than to the construction of new water supply projects that have inevitable environmental consequences. Existing water supplies, on the other hand, are commonly committed to current non-Indian uses that are impractical, if not impossible, to dislodge in a negotiated setting.

The Southern Ute Indian Tribe and the Ute Mountain Ute Tribe (Colorado Ute tribes) were caught in this exact predicament in the settlement of their water rights in the eleven streams that cross their reservations in southwestern Colorado. The Colorado Ute tribes, the United States, the State of Colorado, and local water users sought to resolve the tribal claims in the 1986 Colorado Ute Indian Water Rights Final Settlement Agreement (Colorado Ute Settlement Agreement), which was endorsed by Congress in 1988.[96] In December 1991, final consent decrees were entered for all streams in which the two Colorado Ute tribes claimed water rights. Ultimately, since the ESA required the recovery of the populations of endangered fish found in the San Juan basin, the Colorado Ute tribes were forced to renegotiate the terms of the Colorado Ute Settlement Agreement, which included as its foundation the construction of the ALP. The various aspects of the ESA and the dilemma its application to the ALP caused for the Colorado Ute tribes, along with the solutions embraced by the parties to the Colorado Ute Settlement Agreement, are described below with the hope that these experiences will help to solve similar difficulties that other Indian tribes, states, and non-Indian water users may face.

As generally occurred elsewhere in the West, the United States paid little attention to the water rights reserved for the benefit of the Colorado Ute tribes. In 1930, the issues surrounding the Southern Ute Tribe's rights in Pine River were resolved in the *Morrison Ditch* case.[97] The final decree recognized the United States' "first and exclusive right, with a priority date [of] July 25, 1868" to divert water for use on over 16,000 acres of land on the reservation.[98] The other streams crossing the reservation were ignored, as were the streams that might serve the adjacent Ute Mountain Ute Reservation.

Despite the warning flags raised by the *Morrison Ditch* case, non-Indian farmers and ranchers, as well as local towns and communities, came to rely on the streams in the area of the Colorado Ute reservations for irrigation and domestic and municipal water supplies. Except for the Pine River, the tribal water rights were never quantified in any fashion. Nevertheless, the Southern Ute Tribe participated in the Florida Project, which stores and diverts water from the Florida River, and the Vallecito Project on the Pine River. In contrast, when the Jackson Gulch Project was developed on the Mancos River, the claims of the Ute Mountain Ute Tribe were ignored, and the benefits of the project were devoted to non-Indian farmers and ranchers.

With the confirmation of the reserved rights doctrine in *Arizona v. California*, and the increasing demands for water to meet growing populations and other new uses in the area, it soon became apparent that the question of tribal water rights could not be deferred forever.[99] The first question that was confronted was whether those rights should be addressed in state or in federal court. Ultimately, the U.S. Supreme Court determined that the federal courts should defer to the ongoing state adjudicatory process, so the issues were joined in the state water court.[100] In 1985, the leaders of the Colorado Ute tribes accepted the invitation of the governor and attorney general of Colorado to explore the possible settlement of the water rights litigation.

At the same time, the Colorado Ute tribes were active supporters of two federal water projects, the Dolores Project and the ALP, which had been authorized in 1968. The Dolores Project was under construction by the mid-1980s, but construction had not begun on the ALP, although a variety of significant preconstruction steps had been taken. The definite plan report for the ALP had been developed, a final environmental impact statement had been published, the project had received approval under section 7 of the ESA, and all necessary permits under the Federal Water Pollution Control Act, also known as the Clean Water Act, had been secured. In 1985, however, Congress added yet another requirement—that the ALP include local cost sharing in an amount acceptable to the secretary of the Interior.[101] The project had engendered considerable local opposition and, as the cost-sharing requirement indicated, was under attack from a national perspective due to its perceived environmental consequences and the federal funding provided for the delivery of irrigation water.

The underlying premise of the ALP as originally conceived was to store water from the Animas River, which has flows of over 500,000 acre-feet per year leaving the State of Colorado, and to deliver that water into La Plata basin, with its chronically short water supplies but abundant irrigable lands. Once delivered to La Plata basin, the water would be used for new irrigation on the lands of both tribes and to provide supplemental and new irrigation water for non-Indian lands in Colorado and New Mexico. The ALP also contemplated providing water for tribal and non-Indian municipal and industrial uses. The preeminent feature of the project was the Ridges Basin Reservoir, located off the Animas River near Durango, Colorado, where the water from the Animas River would be stored before being delivered by tunnel into La Plata basin.

Original settlement framework. The original settlement was comprehensive in nature, seeking to quantify the tribal rights on all of the streams in issue, as well as to resolve all anticipated issues related to the administration of the water rights in the future. It also provided state and federal economic-development funds for the tribes. The catalyst for the settlement was the provision of water to the Ute Mountain Ute Tribe from the Dolores Project, and to both tribes from the ALP. Although the settlement encompassed far more than the ALP, the project was at the heart of the agreement among the multitude of parties who were involved in the negotiations and underlying litigation. Not only did the project provide the two tribes with a firm water supply for irrigation and non-agricultural uses, it assured the non-Indian community that water would be available in the region to meet future needs in both New Mexico and Colorado. Thus, both the Colorado Ute tribes and the non-Indian water user communities viewed the ALP as a substantial benefit. On the other hand, the project remained controversial among local and national environmental groups who viewed its environmental impacts, federal funding, and benefits to irrigated agriculture as poor policies for the New West.

During consideration of the Colorado Ute Settlement Act, environmental groups lobbied against the settlement legislation, and the merits of the ALP were hotly debated in committee and on the House floor. Although the act ultimately passed Congress and was signed into law by the president, project opponents sought in subsequent years to halt the funding for the project and mounted an aggressive public relations campaign against its construction.

Role of the ALP in the settlement. The settlement of the tribal claims on the Animas and La Plata rivers was expressly contingent on the completion of Phase I of the ALP. Phase I included the construction of Ridges Basin Reservoir, the conduit to provide water to the reservoir, Long Hollow Tunnel to deliver water into La Plata basin, and certain irrigation facilities in La Plata basin that would provide irrigation water to Southern Ute (but not Ute Mountain Ute) and non-Indian lands. Municipal and industrial water would be stored in Ridges Basin Reservoir for the benefit of the Colorado Ute tribes as well as non-Indian users in New Mexico and Colorado. Although a wide variety of changes were made in the manner in which the two tribes would take their water, the fundamental configuration of the project and the amounts of water devoted to tribal purposes were not changed in order to remain consistent with the extensive environmental compliance work that had been done prior to the Colorado Ute Settlement Agreement.

Under the terms of the agreement, the two tribes could return to court to litigate their claims on the Animas and La Plata rivers if Phase I was not completed by January 1, 2000. The option to return to court would remain available until January 1, 2005.

New ESA concerns. Almost immediately after the Colorado Ute Settlement Agreement, new concerns were voiced about the ALP's compliance with the ESA. In 1979, the FWS had concluded that the population of the Colorado pikeminnow (then called the Colorado squawfish) in the San Juan River was not necessary to the recovery of the species due to continuing efforts in the upper Colorado River basin. There, a coalition of water users, states, federal agencies, and environmental groups were actively working toward recovery of the far more numerous populations of both the pikeminnow and the razorback sucker. The FWS, however, had required the Bureau of Reclamation to conduct ongoing surveys of the endangered fish in the San Juan River. Those surveys ultimately showed a more vital population in the San Juan River than originally anticipated. In addition, an oil spill on the Yampa River made the FWS leery of simply relying on the upper basin for recovery of the species. As a result, the FWS

concluded that the pikeminnow needed to be recovered in the San Juan basin as well as in the upper basin of the Colorado River. Recovery of the razorback sucker would also come to rely on the San Juan River.

After consultation was reinitiated under section 7, the FWS initially concluded that the ALP was likely to jeopardize the continued existence of the pikeminnow and that no "reasonable and prudent alternative" (RPA) existed. The pikeminnow did not reside in the Animas River, where the project would divert water, nor was it affected by any of the anticipated activities in La Plata basin. The impact that concerned the FWS was the downstream depletion of the San Juan River that would result from the project's diversion of water from the Animas River. The FWS acknowledged that the species was likely to be extirpated in the San Juan whether or not the ALP was constructed, due to the existing depletions to the system that totaled nearly 27 percent of the natural flow of the San Juan. According to the FWS, it was not clear that the species could be recovered with the additional depletions caused by the project, given the lack of knowledge of the factors limiting the pikeminnow. That, in the view of the FWS's biologists, constituted jeopardy under the ESA.

The San Juan was already a highly modified stream system. Navajo Dam, above Farmington, blocked the river and formed Navajo Reservoir, a huge multipurpose facility. The SJCP takes water from the San Juan River for diversion into the Rio Grande, where it is available for municipal uses in Albuquerque and elsewhere. The NIIP, though well behind schedule, was diverting substantial quantities of water from the San Juan River to allow the Navajo Nation to exercise a portion of its reserved water rights. Lake Powell altered the habitat in the lower reaches of the river, where it originally joined the Colorado River, eliminating backwaters and other areas that might be important to the various life stages of the fish.

From the FWS's point of view, the situation was so tenuous that no more harm to the ecosystem could be tolerated. From the Colorado Ute tribes' perspective, access to the water supplies, which they had been promised implicitly in 1868 and explicitly in 1988 to meet their present and future needs, was being denied because of the large-scale development that had been allowed in the past for the benefit of others. The draft jeopardy opinion also threatened the ability of the Jicarilla Apache Nation to use water secured for its benefit in its recent settlement. The Navajo Nation likewise feared that the NIIP was at risk.

Reasonable and prudent alternative. Determined that the tribal water rights settlement would be implemented, the local water users and the Colorado Ute tribes, along with the Navajo Nation, the Jicarilla Apache Nation, and the states of Colorado and New Mexico began discussions with the FWS and the Bureau of Reclamation over whether an RPA could be developed that would satisfy the FWS's concerns and allow the ALP to go forward. Ultimately, an RPA evolved that was acceptable to the project proponents, Bureau of Reclamation, and the FWS.[102] At the heart of the RPA were a series of activities that were intended to ascertain the problems that faced the endangered fish and to improve the conditions in the river for fish reproduction and survival. The RPA was the first significant effort to enhance environmental conditions on the San Juan River and certainly the most positive step that had been taken to restore the habitat affected by the prior water development.

The most momentous commitment was the Bureau of Reclamation's promise to operate Navajo Dam to mimic the natural hydrograph of the river. Since its completion in the early 1960s, the dam had been operated to maximize its water supply benefits. It stored water during high runoffs, principally in the spring, and released water when it would otherwise be in short supply. This modification of the natural flow had undoubtedly altered the habitat for the fish by curtailing the high spring flows and providing more steady summer flows, all of which changed the river in unspecified but significant ways. The return to a more natural regime was expected to significantly assist the recovery efforts.

The RPA further required that the bureau fund seven years of study to attempt to discover the factors that were limiting the endangered fish in the San Juan River and, as the action agency, to create a recovery implementation program for the San Juan River. Ultimately, the four tribes in the San Juan basin, the states of Colorado and New Mexico, the FWS, the Bureau of Reclamation, the BIA, and the water-development interests signed on to the program. The environmental interests in the basin refused to join, contending that the program only existed to further the construc-

tion of the ALP. The program has as its dual objectives the recovery of the endangered fish and water development, consistent with all applicable laws.

Finally, the RPA permitted only the Ridges Basin Reservoir, the diversion structure, and the inlet conduit to be built as an initial stage of the ALP. Moreover, the FWS approved only a first stage of the project, which was limited to 57,100 acre-feet of annual depletions for municipal and industrial purposes. Accordingly, there was no assurance that the irrigation facilities and depletions that were a part of Phase I, and that were needed for settlement of the tribal rights, would be built. The RPA, however, retained the possibility that additional facilities and depletions might be allowed in the future with the completion of the anticipated studies and the progress of the recovery program.

Revision of the settlement. Although not anticipated when the revised biological opinion was issued in 1991, the RPA required the existing environmental documentation for the ALP to be extensively supplemented. This included a new supplemental environmental impact statement and revised Clean Water Act compliance. In some cases, the need for new analysis was triggered by the revised schedule for the project, which contemplated a staging of the project with no guarantee that the future stages would be built. That brought into question whether Phase I, as required to settle the tribal rights, would be built, which altered the potential utility of the project. In other instances, new information was available or the governing regulations had changed. In any event, by 1996 it was clear that the ALP, as envisioned in the Colorado Ute Settlement Agreement, was not likely to be built.

An excruciating five years followed in which the ALP was eventually reconfigured to provide only municipal and industrial water and downsized so that its storage capacity was limited to provide the 57,100 acre-feet of annual depletions that the FWS had concluded in 1991 was consistent with recovery of the endangered fish. Nearly two-thirds of the water supply in the reduced project was to be devoted to the two Colorado Ute tribes and the Navajo Nation. The downsizing process began with two years of meetings, under the guidance of the State of Colorado. These meetings were between project opponents who almost unanimously refused to consider any storage project to meet the Colorado Ute tribes' needs, and the project supporters, who included the two Colorado Ute tribes, the Navajo Nation, the parties to the Colorado Ute Settlement Agreement, and representatives of the cities in northwestern New Mexico who would receive water from the project.

Under pressure from the State of Colorado, the Department of the Interior ultimately made a proposal in August 1998 for a greatly reduced project, which was sized to meet the FWS's depletion limits and would not be capable of expanding to supply irrigation water to either the Colorado Ute tribes or the non-Indian parties to the Colorado Ute Settlement Agreement. The department subsequently prepared a new environmental impact statement that studied both the downsized project and the various nonstructural alternatives proposed by the project opponents. Yet another biological opinion was prepared under section 7 of the ESA. In his record of decision, issued in September 2000, Secretary Babbitt—no fan of dams and reservoirs—concluded that the downsized project was the most environmentally responsible method for the United States to meet its commitments to the two Colorado Ute tribes. He also determined that the reduced project, as opposed to the nonstructural alternatives studied in the environmental impact statement, was in the best interests of the Jicarilla Apache Nation and the Navajo Nation, since it would provide the most flexibility in meeting their water needs in the San Juan basin.

Congress amended the 1988 settlement act in 2000 and provided $16 million towards the construction of the project for fiscal year 2002 (Omnibus Appropriations Act).[103] A formal construction start for the downsized project was announced on November 9, 2001. Despite the draconian changes to the ALP, its opponents from the local and regional environmental communities, as well as a few individuals with concerns over fiscal issues, staged a rally in Durango to protest the announcement and vowed to continue the fight against the project. They claimed, among other things, that the Colorado Ute tribes had no valid right to the quantity of water allocated to them from the project.

Reflections. The most difficult problem for the Colorado Ute tribes as they battled to build the ALP and fulfill the terms of the Colorado Ute Settlement Agreement, was that the opponents of the project were not parties to the water rights litigation and had no stake in resolving the tribal water rights claims. As a result, delay was the most formidable tactic invoked by the opponents. Delay inflated the costs of the project, rendered environmental studies stale, and stirred up doubts in the parties and other project supporters as to whether the ALP would ever be built. Because the opponents have generally refused to accept any storage facility using water from the Animas River, no matter how small or how minimal its environmental impact, they have had no incentive to find a compromise that involved construction of a reservoir that might meet the tribal needs in an environmentally responsible manner. The current version of the project has been reduced by 40 percent from the original and does not have an irrigation component, but it has been approved by the FWS under the ESA. Yet the vigor of many of the opponents has not diminished. Indeed, confronted with a project that principally supplies the Colorado Ute tribes and the Navajo Nation with municipal and industrial water, some of the opponents have vehemently attacked the merits of the underlying tribal claims, long after Congress approved the initial settlement in 1988 and the Colorado courts entered the consent decrees.

The issues related to the ESA's effect on the ALP were the major reason for the delay in moving forward with the project and a source of great frustration for the Colorado Ute tribes. The ESA-mandated reconfiguration of the project resulted in two supplemental environmental impact statements and a host of revisions and supplements to other environmental compliance documents. Although a solution was ultimately found that permitted the smaller project to move forward, that solution was the product of nearly fifteen years of negotiations. The last decade of those negotiations primarily involved disputes between federal agencies, such as the FWS and the EPA, and environmental groups that had no direct involvement in the water rights litigation. Although the final outcome treats the Colorado Ute tribes in an acceptable fashion, it deprives the non-Indian parties to the Colorado Ute Settlement Agreement of a substantial portion of the benefits they were originally promised. At the end of the day, those individuals and water districts were willing to make that sacrifice, because they thought it was important for the United States to keep its word to the Colorado Ute tribes, but that did not lessen the pain of their concession. Throughout the efforts to implement the settlement agreement, the tribes and the non-Indian parties treated each other with respect and honesty, recognizing that if the settlement did not work, the burden of the ensuing litigation would fall on them rather than on the project opponents or the federal agencies charged with the various environmental mandates.

Solving the project's problems related to the ESA required a tremendous amount of work and compromise by the Colorado Ute tribes, the other tribes in the San Juan basin, the non-Indian parties to the settlement, the states of Colorado and New Mexico, the BIA, and the Bureau of Reclamation. It was the commitment by those parties, occasionally given only begrudgingly, to provide the resources to recover the endangered fish that enabled the FWS to conclude that further depletions in the San Juan River would not adversely affect the ability to recover the endangered fish, and therefore that the smaller project could be built. Ultimately, it took strong leadership from the secretary of the Interior and his staff to compel the acceptance of the final compromises reflected in the Omnibus Appropriations Act. The secretary and his staff were the moving force behind the final reductions to the project in the period between 1998 and 2000. Having succeeded in persuading (beating?) the settlement parties into accepting a far smaller project, the secretary's advocacy of that project as an environmentally responsible way to meet the United States' commitments to the Colorado Ute tribes played a major role in convincing Congress to enact the Omnibus Appropriations Act. It took an environmentally credible advocate such as Secretary Babbitt to sort the facts from the emotion, as well as the settlement parties' concerted effort to address every legitimate environmental issue that was raised and to overcome the steadfast opposition from the environmental community.

To conclude, the Colorado Ute Settlement Agreement and the recent approval of the downsized ALP demonstrate that through perseverance, even difficult obstacles to tribal water settlements that depend on new water development can be overcome. Such successes require the settling parties to undertake an imposing amount of work and to show incredible dedication to resolving issues through the settlement process. Although Indian tribes have generally not benefited from the widespread existing water development in the West, the tribes nevertheless face the same formidable barriers to water development that confront any other water user. To overcome those obstacles, tribes must hire biologists, hydrologists, and lawyers, and be willing to accept a reasonable and practical solution that meets their water needs while complying with the ESA and other environmental laws.

The ALP Project is under active construction, with a dam, pipelines, and pumping plants under way. Endangered species issues continue to affect progress at specific construction sites, because federally protected bird species nest in the area. The project has incurred serious cost overruns and earned reprimands from even long-time project supporters in Congress.

Shivwits Band of the Paiute Indian Tribe of Utah

M. Evelyn Woods

We end up with a new community, a community integrated by working together to solve problems.

Lou Leonard, secretary of the Interior's Indian Water Rights Office (Shivwits negotiation team)

The Shivwits Band of the Paiute Indian Tribe of Utah, an agrarian people, has been in the Southern Utah area of the tribe's current reservation since before 1150 A.D.[104] Anglo explorers documented the Shivwits' irrigation systems along the Santa Clara River as early as 1826. Around 1850, Mormon settlers dislodged the band from the fertile Santa Clara River valley. Congress established the Shivwits Reservation approximately twelve miles northwest of the city of St. George, Utah, in 1891. The president confirmed the band's reservation boundaries and 26,880 total acres by executive order in 1916. Congress added lands in 1937 to bring the reservation to its current size of 28,160 acres. Of the currently enrolled three hundred tribal members, only a few can live on the reservation due to lack of housing and jobs.[105]

The Santa Clara River is part of the Virgin River adjudication, initiated by the State of Utah in 1980. The United States filed a claim in 1987 for 11,355 acre-feet for the benefit of the Shivwits Band. The waters of the Santa Clara River are fully appropriated, and have been since the early 1990s. Despite an average annual precipitation of only seven inches, flow rates of the river are highly variable. According to the Utah state engineer's testimony before Congress, the river's historic flow ranges from a high of 66,000 acre-feet per year to a low of 4,700 acre-feet per year—a true feast or famine situation.[106] The river is both impounded by the Gunlock Reservoir, upstream of the Shivwits Reservation, and diverted by an Ivins Irrigation Company canal. Most of the releases of non-Indians' irrigation water from Gunlock are diverted on the reservation stretch of the river through the canal, leading to another reservoir that partially trespasses reservation land. Until now, both structures have been limited to non-Indian use without compensation to the band. Lack of access to water has frustrated the band's efforts toward self-determination and economic self-sufficiency. Further, the band alleged that the United States failed in its trust relationship by allowing local governments and private irrigation companies to appropriate most of the water and to build water project works on the band's land without just compensation.

Settlement provisions. In the settlement of its federal reserved rights claims, passed by Congress in late 2000, the band acquired 4,000 acre-feet annually by three components.[107] First, the United States will appropriate $15 million on behalf of the band to cover the band's proportionate share of the construction and operating costs of the St. George Water Reuse Project. Pursuant to the agreement, the City of St. George will design, construct, own, and provide the operating costs for a water treatment facility, pipeline, and pumping and delivery facility that will make 2,000 acre-feet annually of "firm" water available to the band.[108] The band will have first priority to the project water.

Second, the Washington County Water Conservancy District (WCWCD) will design, construct, and provide the initial operating costs for the Santa Clara Project, which will run a pressurized pipeline from Gunlock Reservoir across the band's reservation to Ivins's reservoir. The water rights of all parties to the settlement have been pooled. The band will receive 1,900 acre-feet annually of Santa Clara River surface water with an 1890 priority date. That date is the most senior on the river, except that it is shared with the irri-

gation companies that are parties to the settlement.[109] If the pooled water rights cannot be met by surface flows, off-reservation groundwater will supplement each water right in pro rata shares. The band's chair estimates that groundwater pumping will account for 200 acre-feet in average flow years and up to 800 acre-feet in dry years. When the combination of both sources falls short, all pooling parties will take proportionate reductions in their delivered water.[110] To defray the band's operating costs, the federal government appropriated $1 million to the Shivwits Band trust fund.[111]

One component of the Santa Clara Project, the Habitat Acquisition Program, is unique among Indian water rights settlement components. This program permits the secretary of the Interior to establish a program in the Virgin River basin to benefit native wildlife and plant species that are, or are likely to be, listed under the ESA. To do so, the secretary may acquire water and water rights, with or without the appurtenant lands, and acquire shares in irrigation projects to assist the conservation and recovery of such endangered species. Congress appropriated $3 million as part of the settlement to accomplish the goals of the Habitat Acquisition Program.[112] In addition, the Santa Clara Project must provide a minimum instream flow of 3 cubic feet per second year-round in the river below Gunlock Reservoir to protect the virgin spinedace, a listed threatened fish species.

Third, the band will complete its right to 4,000 acre-feet per year with 100 acre-feet per year from groundwater pumped from beneath the reservation. This water will carry a 1916 priority date. In addition, the band may use water from springs and runoff located on the reservation but must report such amounts annually to the Utah state engineer to be credited against the band's 4,000 acre-feet per year. The band's right is not subject to loss, forfeiture, or abandonment due to nonuse. Further, the band may use or lease its water rights for any use on the reservation permitted by tribal and federal law, and any off-reservation beneficial use allowed under federal and state laws.[113] Finally, the band reached an agreement with the City of St. George to augment the reservation's potable water supply. The city agreed to sell the band 200 acre-feet per year of potable water at in-city rates. Also, the WCWCD and State of Utah agreed that the Shivwits Band will be given an equal opportunity to participate in certain water-development projects that are contemplated for the future.

Adequate federal appropriations were made in 2003 and the necessary steps required by various parties for waiver of tribal water rights were achieved, as documented in the *Federal Register* in November 2003.[114] The Shivwits water right was confirmed in the Virgin River adjudication by decree of the district court of the fifth judicial district in Washington County, Utah.

Reflections. Supporters of the Shivwits settlement state the agreement will help the band create new and meaningful employment opportunities, allow it to resume its historical agricultural practices, and promote the return of its members to the reservation. The settlement is also a good example of how parties can cooperate to identify and mitigate negative environmental consequences of proposed water-development projects prior to the ESA consultation process. Such cooperation during the settlement process may alleviate the kinds of problems and tensions that arise from the ESA's application to tribal water-development projects, as evidenced in the NIIP and the associated controversy surrounding the listed species of Colorado pikeminnow and razorback sucker.

What can others learn from the Shivwits settlement experience? From the perspective of the attorney representing the Shivwits Band in the settlement negotiations, these are some principal observations:

- With the leadership and experience of the federal negotiation team, the settlement parties attempted to identify all potential water-related conflicts and resolve them preemptively, using plain language in the underlying settlement contracts. So far, that approach has worked well to resolve the few bumps that have been encountered since the agreements were signed.
- The settlement act listed seven tasks that had to be completed before December 31, 2003, or the waivers of claim would not become effective. All but one task were accomplished by August 2003, including signing of the five settlement contracts by all twelve parties, obtaining a final state court decree, and obtaining state approval of the changes in place of use and point of diversion. The band also granted the right-of-way across the Shivwits Reser-

vation for the Santa Clara Pipeline and finished the environmental evaluations of that project. Subsequently, Congress appropriated the $24 million. On November 20, 2003, Secretary of the Interior Norton announced that all statutory requirements had been satisfied and the settlement was judged effective.

- Congress intended for this settlement to foster tribal self-determination and to create a new climate in the St. George area, with the band and its neighbors achieving and sustaining mutual respect and a cooperative relationship. For this to occur, the tribe must be able to participate on its own during the implementation process and beyond. This might be the most important lesson the Shivwits Band would share with other similarly situated tribes: Insist that money for implementation work be provided as a part of the settlement deal, rather than allowing the federal government as trustee to characterize it as a separate issue to be addressed at some later date. Otherwise, the tribe could end up still trying to achieve a meaningful role during implementation itself.

Klamath Water Crisis

Stephen E. Snyder

> With much more water given over to agriculture during this past summer drought and a particularly heavy chinook run this fall, tens of thousands of Klamath River fish, perhaps as many as thirty thousand so far, have died as chinook spawning gets underway. The fish did not have enough water to complete their full cycle of life. There are too many people, too many concerns, vying for too little water. . . . North coast Indian fishermen and tribes, among others, mourned the loss, expressing outrage at the calamity that threatens fish, industries and ways of life. . . . The issue is the right of the Salmon Nation to exist and thrive. . . . Our hearts ache for our lost relatives.
>
> "Grieving for the Salmon Nation," *Indian Country Today*

The Klamath River drains from its headwaters in the mountains of southern Oregon, through northern California, into the Pacific Ocean south of Crescent City. Tourists who come to the basin to fish, enjoy recreational boating, or visit the five national wildlife refuges are likely oblivious to the basin's water shortage problems. What tourists see are forests, mountains in the distance, fields under cultivation, and a few small towns. What they do not see is the hardship created by the basin's seasonal shortages of water.

The basin's water shortage results from competing demands for water in a semi-arid region. Irrigated agriculture demands water for hundreds of square miles of land under cultivation in southern Oregon and northern California. A network of dams demands water for hydroelectric power generation for residents of the Pacific Northwest. These and other human uses of water have significantly reduced the amount of water available to support what once was an incredible array of wildlife within the basin. In the thick of this competition for water are the Klamath tribes of southern Oregon, which are attempting to perfect their water rights claims to reestablish their once great fisheries.[115]

In 1996, the Klamath tribes took proactive steps to resolve their water rights claims by negotiation. The tribes proposed that the ODWR either replace or supplement the water rights adjudication in the basin with a negotiation process. The tribes' objective in making this proposal was to transform the win-lose struggle in the adjudication over water rights into a problem-solving process for creatively addressing the basin's water-management needs. The tribes' proposal was the catalyst for the ODWR's decision to sponsor an innovative process—known as the Klamath basin alternative dispute resolution (ADR) process—for negotiating all water rights claims in Oregon's portion of the basin.

The ADR process began in 1997 and continued until the summer of 2001, when it confronted a crisis. To protect three species of fish and their aquatic habitat, the Bureau of Reclamation terminated deliveries of irrigation water to over 200,000 acres of farmland in the Klamath basin. This decision significantly and adversely affected the economic well-being of over one thousand farm families and generated extreme hostility toward the federal water managers and those—such as the Klamath tribes—that supported the bureau's decision. Efforts to negotiate the tribes' water rights claims through the ADR process were abruptly terminated. As of this writing, it is not clear when, or if, those efforts will resume.

Just as the ESA disrupted existing water use patterns in the Klamath, the enforcement of senior Indian rights is likely to disrupt existing water use patterns elsewhere in the West. For this reason, the Klamath water crisis threatens to be a precursor of what might happen if steps are not taken to mitigate the impact of senior tribal claims in other fully appropriated basins.

Adjudication efforts. At the time the Klamath tribes proposed a negotiation process to the ODWR, they had been involved in litigation for over twenty-five years. In 1976, the tribes sought to protect their treaty rights by intervening in litigation the federal government had commenced to restrict water withdrawals that were adversely affecting forests and other federal lands in the upper Klamath basin. Seven years later, the ninth circuit court of appeals ruled in *United States v. Adair* that under the *Winters* doctrine, the tribes had rights, with a priority from "time immemorial," to sufficient water to support their fishing, hunting, and gathering needs.[116] The court, however, did not quantify the tribes' water rights. Instead the court retained jurisdiction to ensure that the tribes' interests were properly protected in any subsequent legal proceedings, such as a state-initiated water rights adjudication.

In 1990, Oregon took action to adjudicate all of the water rights in the Klamath basin, including the tribes' rights, by resuming the dormant Klamath basin water rights adjudication. Fearing that tribal and federal water rights claims would not be adequately protected, the tribes and the federal government challenged the state's jurisdiction to adjudicate their claims to water on several grounds, including Oregon's use of an administrative, rather than judicial, proceeding for the adjudication. The court rejected the challenge and, in so doing, ruled that the rights of the tribes and the federal government were sufficiently protected, since Oregon law authorized state court review of administrative rulings in adjudication.[117]

The jurisdictional litigation concluded in 1995. The ODWR then proceeded with the Klamath adjudication by establishing a three-year period for the filing of water rights claims, departmental review of claims, and challenges to claims by the ODWR and third parties. Hearings on the challenges were to commence immediately following this three-year period. Thus, when the tribes proposed that the ODWR negotiate their claims, both parties anticipated they had at least a three-year window for completing negotiations before litigation resumed.

Water allocation problems. In theory, water shortage problems are addressed through water rights enforcement. In times of shortage, users of senior water rights receive all of their water before those with junior rights. In the Klamath, rights are not enforced because their relative priority is uncertain and will not be known until the adjudication is completed. A serious water shortage, however, has produced conflicts that the existing system of water rights law is unable to address. The roots of the conflict can be traced to the federal government's decision at the turn of the twentieth century to promote agricultural development in the Klamath basin.

In 1905, at the behest of homesteaders who were having difficulty establishing viable farms in the basin, Congress authorized the construction of an irrigation and hydropower reclamation project known as the Klamath Project. Today, the project consists of six dams and an extensive network of tunnels, canals, and ditches that irrigate over 200,000 acres of cropland in southern Oregon and northern California.

As agricultural development proceeded in the basin, the project adversely affected the basin's aquatic environment and the wildlife dependent on that environment. Nevertheless, agricultural development continued without consideration for how the eventual enforcement of the tribes' senior water rights might affect the basin's agricultural economy. Today, agricultural development has proceeded to the point that there is insufficient water to meet the competing demands for irrigation water, instream flow for the aquatic environment, and water for the tribes' hunting, fishing, and gathering rights.

Two species of fish historically relied upon by the tribes for physical and spiritual sustenance have all but been eradicated by the diversion of irrigation waters from Upper Klamath Lake. These fish—known as the c'wam and quadpo to the tribes and as short nose suckers to non-Indians—were listed under the ESA in 1988.

Another species of fish—the coho salmon—has also been adversely affected by the project. The fish are no longer able to spawn upstream from the project, and their habitat downstream has deteriorated significantly as the result of agricultural diversions. Three

California-based tribes—the Yurok, Hoopa Valley, and Karuda—have historically relied on these fish for food and employment. Moreover, the fish are of spiritual importance to these tribes. The coho salmon in the Klamath were listed under the ESA in 1997.

Although neither the Klamath nor the California tribes have been able to protect their fisheries through enforcement of their water rights, their interest in restoring flows for the aquatic habitat is aided by the ESA. The tribes' interests are also aligned with those of environmental groups active in the basin. Both support protection of listed species and their aquatic habitat through the ESA.

The ESA requires that a federal project, such as the Klamath Project, not be operated in ways that adversely affect an endangered or threatened species or its habitat. For that reason, water deliveries to agricultural land from the Klamath Project can be curtailed to provide water for protected fish listed under the ESA. In fact, deliveries were somewhat curtailed in the summers of 1991 and 1994 to protect the endangered suckers in Upper Klamath Lake by maintaining the level of the lake. Arguably, these curtailments should have alerted the agricultural community to the risk that water deliveries might be completely curtailed in a critically dry year.

ADR process. The ODWR conceived of the ADR process as a forum for addressing two types of issues: (1) long-term water-management and watershed restoration needs; and (2) resolution of disputes over the nature and extent of water rights claims in the basin. Long-term water-management objectives were to be addressed through collaborative negotiations among stakeholders, leading to one or more agreements dealing with supply augmentation, demand reduction, and habitat-restoration measures. The ODWR hoped these agreements would also resolve water rights disputes in the adjudication by alleviating imbalances in the supply and demand for water.

The ADR process took the organizational form of two types of meetings—regularly scheduled monthly meetings and irregularly scheduled special meetings. The monthly meetings were open to the public, primarily as a vehicle for educating stakeholders about water-management problems, generating ideas for addressing those problems, and organizing caucuses and negotiating groups. The caucuses and negotiating groups met as they were needed to develop specific solutions to water-management problems. The caucuses consisted of stakeholders with similar interests (such as project irrigators or nonproject irrigators) and the negotiating groups consisted of stakeholders with conflicting interests (such as the Klamath tribes and irrigators). The ADR process was concurrent with the adjudication, and the ODWR anticipated that agreements reached in the ADR process would be incorporated into the final judicial decree. The ODWR had several roles in the ADR process: organizer and administrator of the process; provider of technical support; facilitator of the process; and representative of the state's interest in water rights and water-management matters.

The ADR process commenced in October 1997 with a series of monthly public meetings to develop an agreement among stakeholders on a vision for the basin's future, ground rules for how stakeholders would interact, and an organizational structure for administering the ADR. Work on these issues continued for ten months and culminated in a memorandum of understanding among the stakeholders about how the ADR process was to work. Thereafter, the monthly public meetings were primarily educational devices and forums for the ODWR's efforts to organize and facilitate negotiations over water-management and water rights issues.

The ODWR's efforts met with mixed results. The department's early attempt to negotiate what seemingly was an uncontroversial federal water rights claim failed. Some ADR participants asserted that the negotiations failed because other ADR participants intentionally undermined the negotiations. They also said that these other ADR participants have pursued a strategy to undermine the process.

Later in the ADR process, two different negotiating groups began meeting with the Klamath tribes in an effort to resolve their respective water rights claims. Several participants in those negotiations were hopeful that they might eventually reach agreement. The ODWR attempted to expedite such an agreement by organizing a week-long marathon negotiating session, tentatively scheduled for the spring of 2001. In early 2001, two events occurred that caused the parties to terminate negotiations and cast doubt on the viability of the ADR process.

Water crisis of 2001. The first event to disrupt negotiations was litigation initiated by the Klamath tribes and supported by the federal government. In the final days of the Clinton administration, the tribes and the federal government asked the federal court in the *Adair* case to exercise its retained jurisdiction and enter rulings that would have the practical effect of limiting the scope of Oregon's adjudication. Most, if not all, of the other ADR participants, including those who had been part of the two groups negotiating with the tribes, were enraged by this action. They asserted that it demonstrated the tribes' and federal government's lack of interest in working toward an agreement that promoted the interests of all stakeholder groups. Many ADR participants announced they would boycott the marathon negotiations should the ODWR attempt to proceed as planned.

Shortly after the tribes' action in the *Adair* litigation, a second event occurred that foreclosed any chance that negotiations might resume. On April 6, 2001, the Bureau of Reclamation announced it would not deliver irrigation water that summer. The bureau's decision was a response to its obligations under the ESA. In early spring of 2001, the federal agencies administering the ESA were officially informed that the 2001 irrigation season in the Klamath would be critically dry. Based on this information, the FWS concluded that the endangered suckers would be at risk unless the bureau maintained Upper Klamath Lake, the project's primary storage facility, at a minimum level. The National Marine Fisheries Service concluded that the threatened coho salmon would be put at risk unless the bureau also maintained a minimum flow of water in the Klamath River downstream of the project. The bureau concluded it could simultaneously maintain the level of Upper Klamath Lake and the flow of water below the project only if it made no deliveries of irrigation water that summer.

The bureau's decision not to deliver irrigation water created an economic and social crisis in the Klamath basin. Unless farmers had access to groundwater, farming was not possible without project water, and, as a consequence, 1,400 families were unable to grow crops. Farm equipment dealers and other farm-dependent businesses either closed or suffered severe financial hardship. Farmers confronted the prospect that they might lose their farms unless they received some form of economic relief. Social service agencies reported large increases in incidences of depression and domestic violence.

Rage at the bureau's action permeated the Klamath valley and expanded to include the Klamath tribes once they made clear their support for the bureau's action. Supporters of the farming community from within and outside the valley organized protests, including a boisterous tractor parade in downtown Klamath Falls. On four separate occasions, protesters used torches and crowbars to open irrigation headgates. Protesters camped on project land near the headgates. Three men from a local farming community were arrested for shooting at signs and buildings near the tribes' headquarters and for intimidating Indian schoolchildren headed to a basketball game. Local law enforcement officials (who, many assumed, sympathized with the farmers) refused to take action against protesters who trespassed on bureau property, citing concerns over their jurisdiction to do so. The bureau was forced to use federal law enforcement officials to guard the project.

Irrigation districts and their members sought to enjoin the bureau's action through litigation in Oregon's U.S. District Court. They also sought to reverse the bureau's action by seeking political support from their congressional delegation and the newly installed Bush administration. Vice President Richard Cheney and Secretary of the Interior Gale Norton met with farmers and water-management officials to attempt to work out a solution to the crisis. Although the farmers' plight had many sympathetic ears, the bureau's decision stood. With the exception of a small release in late August, no water was delivered to project irrigators in 2001.

Once the bureau announced its decision to withhold deliveries, the ODWR terminated its efforts to organize negotiations over the Klamath tribe's water rights. As the hostility in the community escalated, the ODWR temporarily suspended the monthly ADR meetings. The federal court ordered the parties to mediation, which was conducted by nationally prominent mediators. The federal court denied the farmers' request for an injunction, but urged that parties continue to negotiate.[118] The farmers refused, and the mediation terminated. Farmers and irrigation districts filed new litigation, seeking millions of dollars in damages from the federal government for injuries allegedly caused by the withholding of irrigation water.

After the irrigation season ended, efforts were made to deal with the consequences and underlying causes of the crisis. The National Academy of Sciences, at the request of Secretary Norton, appointed a panel of scientists to evaluate the scientific evidence supporting the decision to withhold irrigation deliveries. Members of Oregon's congressional delegation submitted various (and, to some extent, conflicting) proposals to amend the ESA, buy out farmland, build new dams, and provide economic relief to injured farmers.

The ADR process resumed monthly meetings to quell rumors and provide a forum for discussing actions that might prevent another crisis next irrigation season. Although questions have been raised about the utility of these meetings, they were well attended.

In January 2002, the National Academy of Sciences panel issued an interim report undermining the credibility of the federal government's environmental decision-making process.[119] The panel concluded that no "substantial scientific support" existed for either the decision to maintain higher water levels in Upper Klamath Lake or to maintain higher flows in the Klamath below the project. The implications of this conclusion were staggering. The federal government's decision to impose substantial economic and psychological hardship on the farmers of the Klamath basin served no useful purpose.

The next chapters of this sad story remain to be written. The academy panel did not conclude that a sufficient supply of water for environmental needs exists in the Klamath. In fact, the panel challenged recent proposals of the Bureau of Reclamation that would allow water levels in Upper Klamath Lake and in the main stem of the Klamath to fall below recent historical levels. This, the panel concluded, "cannot be justified," because it would present "an unknown risk" to suckers and salmon protected by the ESA. Thus, the stage is set for another water crisis in a particularly dry year. The panel's final report in 2004 concluded that cooperation between fish agencies and the Bureau of Reclamation was important, but recovery of threatened and endangered fish would depend on a set of actions broader than operation of the irrigation project.[120]

Reflections. The underlying factors in the Klamath

water crisis are present in many Indian water rights disputes throughout the West. As in the Klamath, water development proceeded in much of the West without regard to tribal claims of senior water rights. Likewise, only by reallocating significant amounts of water from existing uses can senior tribal claims in much of the West be satisfied. Further, the ESA exacerbates the water reallocation problem in many areas of the West by reducing the amount of water otherwise available to satisfy long-ignored senior tribal claims.

A primary objective of the Klamath ADR process was to mitigate the conflict associated with water reallocation problems by providing stakeholders with an opportunity to negotiate creative solutions to the basin's water supply problems. For a variety of reasons (many of which are yet to be understood), the Klamath stakeholders were not able to take advantage of this opportunity. Although some aspects of the design and implementation of the ADR process (such as the ODWR's conflicting roles as ADR facilitator, water manager, and adjudicator) may have been faulty, inadequacies in the process cannot fully explain why the process achieved such little success. Most likely, the intense and intractable nature of the Klamath conflict is attributable to the substantive issues underlying the conflict and the psychological forces unleashed by those issues.

The principal issue in the Klamath crisis frequently produces intense and intractable conflict—a high-stakes dispute over a scarce resource.[121] The conflict over termination of water deliveries to project irrigators was clearly high stakes. In fact, few resource-based disputes could have higher stakes. Irrigators depended on project water for their economic survival. This conflict was exacerbated by two other disputes frequently associated with intractable conflicts: (1) irreconcilable differences in personal and moral values, and (2) a struggle for power and political dominance among competing groups. In the Klamath, people who held a moral concern for the environment were pitted against farmers and their supporters, who valued an agricultural lifestyle. People who objected to governmental interference with their personal freedoms were in conflict with regulatory agencies and environmental groups that sought to impose constraints on the freedom to earn a living in a socially valued way.

As with all protracted conflicts, the psychological dynamics at work during the Klamath crisis overwhelmed the substantive issues as the conflict escalated. The tractor parade, the arrival of demonstrators from outside the basin, the forcible opening of the irrigation headgates, and the acts of intimidation directed toward the Klamath tribes were all overt manifestations of psychological forces that fueled and escalated the conflict. These psychological forces included stereotyping, misperceptions, selective perceptions, and dehumanization. These and other psychological states no doubt produced a cognitive rigidity and emotional intensity in many Klamath stakeholders that undermined all efforts to resolve the conflict.

Negotiation and mediation have not proved to be particularly effective tools for dealing with intractable conflicts. The high-stakes nature of the issues and their destructive psychological forces inevitably seem to produce negotiating deadlocks. For this reason, one can legitimately question whether negotiation and mediation are viable processes for resolving Indian water rights claims, at least in circumstances similar to those in the Klamath.

If mediation and negotiation are not viable processes, then what can be done to resolve Indian water claims in similar situations? One possibility is to recognize that Indian water rights disputes raise issues of social and personal change. If this proposition is true, recognition of Indian water rights claims is more likely to be achieved through a change-management strategy than through conventional dispute-resolution techniques.

A change-management strategy would lead to a subtle but significant shift in the types of interventions employed to resolve water rights claims. Mediators, negotiators, and others seeking to facilitate the resolution of tribal water rights would no longer engage in an extended search for win-win solutions to what may inherently be a win-lose dispute. Instead they would help stakeholders become aware of the complexity of the situation and the need for change. Mediators and other facilitators of change would help stakeholders explore their current situation, assess whether the situation was sustainable, and develop plans for responding to an unsustainable situation. Using agriculture as an example, mediators would help irrigators reflect on whether their current farming methods were sustainable, if alternative viable methods could be employed, and, if not, what actions irrigators might take to secure their economic futures.

A change-management strategy will not eliminate the intense conflict surrounding Indian water rights issues. As the events in the Klamath demonstrate, conflict is an invariable component of the process of change—conflict between those who seek change and those who resist it. Conflict cannot, and should not, be avoided, because it is often the catalyst to change. Conflict can provoke a reexamination of one's thoughts, feelings, attitudes, and beliefs. Conflict can unfreeze the mental processes that are barriers to change. Conflict, to the extent it performs these functions, is a constructive force.

Adopting a change-management perspective for dealing with Indian water rights issues transforms the goal of those who seek to resolve those issues. The goal is not to resolve the conflict. The goal, instead, is to prevent the destructive aspects of conflict from overwhelming the constructive aspects. This goal can be best achieved by recognizing that change creates fear and anxiety, which can be overcome only by creating conditions of safety for those who must change. What these conditions might be will depend on the situation. Identifying those conditions in a given situation will require much creativity, but the goal is clear. Those who seek to facilitate change in the context of a water rights negotiation must help stakeholders adapt to change. They must help stakeholders acquire the psychological, economic, and social resources needed to support healthy and adaptive change.

When Is a Settlement Settled?

As we have seen, achieving the settlement is not an end in itself but an important milepost on the way to settlement implementation. No settlement can anticipate all problems that will arise in the future. Since negotiators had little experience to guide them, some of the earlier pioneering agreements were incomplete or had deficiencies or problems that must be reconsidered. SAWRSA is one example. As states, tribes, and federal agencies have gained more experience in negotiating these agreements, some of the problems in earlier agreements have been avoided; however, time will disclose the unique, unanticipated problems of every agreement. Settlements should include procedures for addressing these future problems, and negotiators and their successors must monitor implementation and stay committed to the goals and processes of the agreement.

Southern Arizona Water Rights Settlement Act

The Tohono O'odham Nation, located near Tucson in Southern Arizona, has historically used groundwater to irrigate the crops of its agriculture-based culture. In the late 1970s, groundwater depletion began to make farming on the reservation increasingly expensive and difficult. To resolve the tense situation between thirsty Tucson and the tribes, the federal government promised a "firm delivery" of imported surface water and reclaimed municipal effluent in the SAWRSA.[122] As a condition to receiving their entitlement, the tribe agreed to limit groundwater pumping beneath the San Xavier Reservation to 10,000 acre-feet annually and to the existing pumped quantity below the Schuk Toak Reservation. The tribes have the right to off-reservation marketing of their groundwater entitlement, as long as it is marketed within the Tucson Active Management Area. In addition, the federal government is liable for damages in the amount of replacement costs if it fails to make its firm delivery quantity. The settlement also authorized the federal government to construct and operate delivery systems on and off the reservations to enable the nation to put their entitlements to beneficial use. Additionally, SAWRSA uses a three-way deal with the City of Tucson so that the secretary of the Interior can use the city's effluent to satisfy the nation's entitlement.

Amendments. Further amendments to SAWRSA are included in the 2004 Gila River basin settlement (see page 134). The SAWRSA amendments have many provisions. They would oblige the secretary of the Interior to deliver 37,800 acre-feet of agriculturally suitable water annually to the San Xavier and Schuk Toak districts of the nation, as well as another 28,200 acre-feet annually of non-Indian agricultural priority water from the main project works of CAP.[123] As a condition of its water delivery, the new amendments require that the Tohono O'odham limit the quantity of groundwater withdrawals by nonexempt wells beneath the reservation districts. The nation must also allocate as the "first right of beneficial consumptive use" a certain amount of its water to groundwater storage, instream flows, and riparian and vegetation habitat. The nation will enact and maintain a comprehensive water code to manage and establish permit requirements for the water resources of the tribe. Significantly, this code must be specifically sensitive to the nation's allottees and must include specific permitting and judicial review processes for allottee applications.

The 1982 SAWRSA provided that the City of Tucson would deliver about 22,000 acre-feet per year of effluent to the federal government to assist the United States in meeting its total obligation to the tribe. The nation has declined to use effluent for its agricultural needs, so the Department of the Interior looked for ways the federal government could recharge the effluent in exchange for state groundwater credits or CAP water delivery. The new SAWRSA amendments include a mechanism for the federal government to receive groundwater or CAP credits from the state for recharging Tucson's effluent, so the nation may use or save such credits. These amendments to SAWRSA will allow the nation to receive groundwater credits for certain recharge and storage acts, and for the retiring of their grandfathered well rights.[124] Like their non-Indian neighbors, the nation would like to develop these flex credits under the Arizona Groundwater Management Act to have the groundwater for its future use or value. A significant change in the new act allows the nation to market its waters within the three-county CAP service area, not just the Tucson Active Management Area.[125]

The SAWRSA amendments within the 2004 Gila River settlement also are designed to settle litigation by nation allottees that arose from the 1982 settlement, as well as adjust some of the old restrictions on the nation's water usage. Tribal allottees contend that they had only token representation in the 1982 negotiations and dispute some of SAWRSA's terms. The SAWRSA amendments will reallocate benefits between the nation and the allottees, as well as provide additional water to the nation.

We now have a quarter-century of experience in negotiating Indian water rights settlements. The experiences recounted in this chapter demonstrate the innovative approaches that governments and water users have employed both to settle past uncertainties and disputes and to plan for the future. Many lessons may be drawn from this rich body of experiences. Settlements take many years, and, even when finally approved, the settling parties must give sustained attention to implementation. Settlements may be slightly easier to achieve in water-abundant basins, but for agreements to have utility, they must include money to aid water development or, in some cases, environmental restoration. Money is always difficult to find, especially in a stagnant economy where state, federal, and tribal budgets are unbalanced.

More important, people make these agreements. Leaders have reached out to bring others into the process. Specialists have generated and compiled hydrologic, legal, engineering, and economic data. Negotiators have stayed at the table during exhausting, intense negotiations. Decision makers have approved the resulting accords and have appropriated money. Even after the excitement of successful legislation fades, people stay committed to the enterprise to ensure that water development occurs, watershed improvements are made, unanticipated problems are addressed, needed funds are appropriated, and future disagreements are expeditiously and fairly resolved. Fundamentally, Indian water right settlements are about people and creating durable interpersonal relationships in western watersheds.

PHOTO 10.1   1908 photo of a Navajo sweat house. Photo: Arizona State Museum, University of Arizona, S. Schwemberger

CHAPTER 10
Conclusion

In the aftermath of September 11th, the natural temptation is to believe that our daily lives and work aren't as
meaningful in the larger context and should somehow be
put on hold while the nation struggles with new realities,
new priorities. To the contrary, what I proposed to you....
is that this is the most meaningful and important time to
rededicate ourselves to our important work: how we can
share our most precious natural resource—water.... Use
this extraordinary time to push for civil discourse on these
contentious natural resource issues, to advocate reconciliation with our Native American neighbors.

Susan Cottingham, program manager, Montana Reserved
Water Rights Compact Commission

The year 2008 will mark the one hundredth anniver-
sary of the U.S. Supreme Court's *Winters* decision. The
implicit promise of the *Winters* case for most tribes was
sufficient water to transform nomadic tribal groups
into a pastoral people, to transform their remnant
lands into permanent, albeit diminished, homelands.
Will that promise have been achieved by the anniver-
sary of the *Winters* centennial? Do the settlement and
litigation processes discussed in these pages contribute
satisfactorily to that achievement?

The *Winters* Legacy

Twenty-five years ago, with the reemergence of tribal
sovereignty, tribes looked anew to their reserved water
rights as a principal vehicle for stabilizing cultural
values while improving the quality of life and economies on reservations. The realization of that promise
has been frustrated by the amount of time required
to settle or litigate their rights, the transaction costs
involved, constraints imposed by the ESA, state and
national political barriers and a shortage of funds to
develop and use water on reservations.

As of 2004, water rights have been completely quantified by litigation or settlement for only a fraction
of the tribal reservations in the American West. The
omissions are significant: the Navajo Nation, the country's largest reservation both in terms of land and
population; most of the Pueblos along the Rio Grande;
all Indian communities in Oklahoma; many California

tribal communities; most of the twenty-five tribal reservations in the Missouri River basin; and some of the
largest reservations in Oregon (Klamath), and Montana (Flathead and Blackfeet). On the other hand, substantial progress was made in 2004 with settlements
approved for the Gila River Indian Community, the
Tohono O'odham Nation and the Nez Perce Tribe.

Limited Benefits and Uneven Distribution

Over the last ninety-five years, the prosperity that
could be harnessed from *Winters* has been modestly
and unevenly achieved. Although the infrastructure
of reservations is affected by many factors other than
water availability, recent demographic information
underscores the weak impact *Winters* has had on improving the quality of life on reservations. Twenty percent of American Indian households on reservations
lack modern plumbing facilities. Eighteen percent of
these households use a means of sewage disposal other
than a public sewer, septic tank, or cesspool. The number of Navajos who live in crowded homes without
complete plumbing is twice the combined total of such
homes in New York and California. In all, in terms of
plumbing and sewage disposal, water and wastewater
facilities in these Indian households resemble conditions in American households prior to 1950.[1]

The tangible benefits of water settlements are unevenly distributed throughout the West. Completed
settlements are concentrated in Montana and Arizona,
two states that have taken very different approaches
to negotiating settlements. Some settlements, especially those involving tribes near major metropolitan
areas, include attractive financial components. Other
settlements, usually those in more rural areas, lack
large economic-development measures. Some tribes,
like the Salt River Pima–Maricopa Indian Community and Northern Cheyenne, have successfully ma-
neuvered beyond the process and are realizing the
benefit of their water for on-reservation uses and from
payments for off-reservation water leases.

Ironically, the frustrating water quantification process (whether evaluated from a starting point of 1908

or 1975) has produced fewer tangible benefits than those associated with the economic and social revolution ignited by Indian gaming, a phenomenon that was cover story news in a 2002 issue of *Time Magazine*.[2] Although Pojoaque Pueblo's recent water rights claims languished for decades in New Mexico's adjudications and associated settlement efforts, the pueblo built a profitable casino business on a major north-south interstate highway in the late 1990s, added a golf course, and is now the second largest nongovernmental employer in northern New Mexico.[3] Indian gaming brought western tribes around $13 billion in revenues in 2001 and provided thousands of jobs for tribal and nontribal members.[4] The economic benefits of gaming, however, are as unevenly distributed among western tribes as are the benefits of water quantification, primarily accruing to reservations near urban population centers or in popular tourism destinations.

Recent Success

This assessment is moderated, however, by the difficult but real progress that has been made in the last twenty-five years—especially when compared to the preceding seventy years following the *Winters* decision. Water rights have been painfully, but finally, quantified by litigation for the Yakima, Wind River, and Mescalero Apache reservations. Quantification has been achieved by the settlements discussed in these pages for nearly two dozen other reservations. Most of these settlements include provisions for economic development on the reservation and reservation water supplies. Indian leaders and attorneys have been more meaningfully involved in these processes—and hence in their tribes' destiny—than in the period of 1946 to 1978 when comparable Indian land claims were litigated before the Indian Claims Commission.

Factors Producing a Settlement

More than half of the settlements (especially those in Arizona and Montana) have been achieved in the context of pending general stream adjudications, but this litigation did not necessarily provide the specific motivation for the parties to reach agreement. With relatively abundant water supplies, the Montana settle-

ments have been the result of an active state program to secure agreements (the Reserved Water Rights Compact Commission) and the possibility of mutual state–tribal advantages such as joint water-marketing possibilities (Fort Peck), improved reservoir storage and dam safety (Northern Cheyenne), and improved domestic water supplies (Rocky Boy's). In Arizona, urban interests have worked toward settlement as a means to enhance long-term water supplies by gaining access to Indian water. The availability of CAP water from the Colorado River has augmented the supplies that may be used for settlement and allowed for creative water exchanges to deliver water to where it is needed. In Florida, regional water-management issues were linked with a successful effort to settle tribal land claims.

Preexisting, ongoing water rights conflicts between upstream non-Indian users and downstream reservations, or between Indian and non-Indian groundwater pumpers, have been settled in Arizona (Ak-Chin), Nevada (Truckee-Carson–Pyramid Lake and Fallon Paiute-Shoshone), California (San Luis Rey), and Florida (Seminole). The 2000 congressional amendments that finally resolved the ALP in Colorado resulted from a deadline that would have allowed the Southern Ute and Ute Mountain Ute tribes to recommence their water rights litigation. Some settlements (Idaho–Fort Hall) appear to have resulted simply from efforts to avoid the expense and conflict of litigation, rather than from deadlines, adjudications, or long-term conflicts.

How Final Is Final?

When local parties finally reach a settlement agreement, they frequently are frustrated to learn that their work is not done, and the settlement is not final. Even after full congressional approval and the president's signature is secured, many states require that water quantifications in settlements be entered as a final decree by an adjudication court. In addition, settlement agreements usually must be approved through tribal referendum, by the state legislature, and perhaps by irrigation district boards and city councils.

Problems typically arise in the course of settlement implementation that may threaten the integrity of the agreement. Potential issues involve court dismissal of current and future tribal claims, disputes over management jurisdiction, congressional appropriations, drought, and water quality problems. Implementing settlements involves going back to address issues that were set aside during negotiations and encountering new, unforeseen problems. Addressing these concerns may entail fine-tuning the settlements or may require major new negotiations. The following examples illustrate settlement modifications.[5]

- The Ak-Chin settlement, authorized by Congress in 1976, was amended in 1984 (to address water supply problems) and again in 1992 (to provide for limited off-reservation water marketing).
- SAWRSA, authorized by Congress in 1982, required technical amendments in 1992. The Arizona Water Settlements Act of 2004 further modified the agreement. Title III of the Act waives the water rights claims of the Tohono O'odham Nation and obligates the federal government to construct the works necessary to deliver CAP water to the reservation.
- The Colorado Ute settlement, first ratified by Congress in 1988, was stalled and in serious jeopardy for over ten years due to concerns with the impact of the ALP on endangered species. A new bill approved by Congress in 2001 provides for settlement implementation to move forward.
- Negotiations between Montana and the Assiniboine and Sioux tribes of the Fort Peck Indian Reservation were concluded in 1985. The Fort Peck compact is still awaiting congressional approval.
- The compact among the Crow Tribe, the United States, and Montana passed the state legislature in 1999. Negotiations on a streamflow-management plan for the Bighorn River and section 2 of the Crow Allotment Act still must be completed before the compact is submitted to Congress.[6]
- The Northern Ute settlement, ratified by Congress in 1992, has yet to be approved by the tribal council.
- A permanent water supply has not yet been identified to satisfy the water entitlements for various Southern Californian Indian bands that are parties to the San Luis Rey settlement, ratified in 1988.
- Full implementation of the Pyramid Lake settlement, ratified in 1990, is still elusive. Litigation continues with an irrigation district that is a key party

in basin-wide water-management conflict. In addition, the federal government is expected to be working on endangered fish recovery plans (an essential component of this settlement) for another decade.

Delays and revisions do not mean that a particular settlement was unsuccessful. These examples do raise the question, however, of whether a settlement is ever really final. Ideally, tribal water settlements need to identify an ongoing dispute resolution mechanism to address potential conflicts. This may be a formal mechanism, as in the Fort Peck and Fort Hall settlements, or ongoing problem solving that relies on improved working relationships among historically suspicious and hostile parties.

Observations and Recommendations

In retrospect, we can see that a golden opportunity was missed during the 1990s to make substantial progress in resolving Indian water rights claims through settlements. In the 1980s, tribal and non-Indian water users developed personal and professional relationships and pioneered workable procedures and substantive approaches. The U.S. economy improved, and the federal budget went into surplus. The impressive momentum of the late 1980s, with settlements like Salt River Pima, Fort Hall, Fort McDowell, Northern Cheyenne, and others, was interrupted by several false starts in the Clinton administration's first term and increasingly chilly relationships between Congress and the administration and its Department of the Interior. Only late in the 1990s did the intensive efforts by senior Interior Department officials lead to significant progress in the Gila River Indian Community, San Luis Rey, and ALP settlements.

From these experiences, whether successful, unsuccessful, or still under way, we offer these observations and recommendations:

Congress can do more to promote progress and equity. We have discussed the uneven progress in settlement efforts over the last two decades and the uneven distribution of settlement benefits, influenced in large part by changing administrations and congressional priorities. Congress would do well to establish a dedicated flow of revenues, such as the measure proposed by Senator Pete Domenici (R-NM), to fund settlements, as well as a timetable, perhaps by each biennial session, of when particular settlements will be taken up. In turn, this approach would systematically prioritize the resources of the Interior and Justice departments. It would also impose a deadline, motivating parties toward dispute resolution. Parties not utilizing their two-year window would fall to the bottom of the schedule.

The federal McCarran Amendment's insistence on comprehensive adjudications warrants reconsideration. One aspect of comprehensiveness, the call for all water users on large river systems to be brought before the court, needs to be deemphasized. The original federal argument that one large lawsuit avoids repeated trips to western courts by federal agencies is no longer a meaningful rationale. The federal government will remain perpetually involved in these watersheds. The accompanying federal argument that a comprehensive joinder of water users is necessary for final, binding decrees is only slightly more convincing. Despite the desire for certainty, western water rights decrees are never going to be final and permanent due to the hybrid public-private nature of the rights, changing uses, and the overlay of federal and state environmental regulation. Litigation can be simplified and decrees made more durable by a careful selection, based on principles of hydrologically based risk assessment, of those major water users who should be bound by litigation.

The second aspect of comprehensiveness, hydrologic comprehensiveness, actually deserves more attention in water rights litigation and negotiations. Settlements or court decrees ignoring groundwater only invite future problems from the pumping of groundwater tributary to surface streams, as well as from reduced groundwater recharge from surface-water uses. Groundwater and the major users of this source should be fully integrated into both litigation and settlement processes.

Settlements require consistent leadership. State and tribal leaders can labor diligently for years toward settlement and ultimately fail because federal officials are disorganized, have other priorities, or have insufficient funds to engage in the negotiation processes or fund any resulting settlement. Similarly, federal officials may prioritize settlements and Congress may be prepared to appropriate the money, but if water users,

state and local governments, and tribes have not done the local political and technical work, they will not have the trust, confidence, or capacity to engage in meaningful negotiations.

Inconsistent political leadership has been a principal barrier to the settlement process, and it is a problem that is not easily addressed. Given the many challenges facing federal, state, and tribal leaders, it is difficult to keep even well-intentioned decision makers engaged for the long haul. An ongoing institution of influential officials and private citizens, similar to the U.S. Commission on Civil Rights, which had significant influence in the 1960s and 1970s, could be created to provide more leadership and continuity in securing settlements.

Mediation has been too infrequently used in Indian water rights settlement processes. Most parties and their attorneys seem to prefer it that way. The reason seems to be a combination of polite disdain for a third party who has not mastered the nuances of western water and Indian law, resistance to ceding to someone else any more control over the process than is absolutely necessary, and the desire not to increase already high transaction costs. Where mediators have been used, they have been respected members of Congress, judicial officials, or persons selected by a court. Mediators can help provide the continuity that is often lacking and help keep the parties accountable. Mediation efforts are under way concerning tribal rights in selected basins in Arizona, Idaho, Nevada, and New Mexico. Because of the complexity of these cases, the settlement of one or more of them would be a major success.

Professional mediators, however, would do well to systematically examine why their services have not been in more demand. Also, negotiating parties might do themselves a favor by hiring a mediator or facilitator and seeing if their concerns are valid. Certainly, foundation or governmental funds could be sought to conduct a pilot program to explore the advantages and disadvantages of using trained, neutral facilitators and mediators in Indian water rights settlement efforts.

The quantification standard is changing; parties need to adapt. In a long history of neglect, the PIA standard has remained a principled statement by the U.S. Supreme Court that large amounts of water with senior priority dates ultimately will be available to western tribes. The Court's original confidence that PIA would serve as a stable, objective rule for determining tribal rights is now obscured by evidence that PIA results are quite susceptible to different economic and technical assumptions. In litigation, PIA has been used in only two major cases, Wyoming's *Bighorn River* and New Mexico's *Lewis* adjudications. Those PIA awards did not guarantee any money to develop the water. In most instances, differing assessments of PIA are the opening bargaining positions of states, tribes, and the federal government and are gradually superceded by more individually tailored, interest-based negotiations. The resulting settlement will likely have a water rights award based on a complex reservation-specific calculus of water availability, water needs for a range of tribal uses, water necessary for existing users, ESA considerations, and money available for water development and other purposes.

The Arizona Supreme Court's recent reaffirmation of the "permanent homeland" purpose of reservations in the Gila River adjudication, and its rejection of PIA as the sole quantification tool to attain that purpose, is an important conceptual leap forward. Other courts are likely to reach similar results if presented the opportunity. The decision has introduced both uncertainty and a more realistic appraisal of tribal water needs into litigation and settlement efforts. The decision, with its emphasis on linking realistic reservation development plans with water needs, probably speaks more helpfully to settlement negotiators than to trial courts faced with adjudicating tribal claims. For negotiators, the Arizona Supreme Court's decision validates the interest-based processes that are under way. For a trial judge, the "permanent homeland" objective provides little methodological guidance. The new standard, however, is probably no more amorphous than other legal standards, such as "reasonable care" and "due process," that courts have wrestled with in the past and defined through a progression of cases.

The dance between litigation and negotiation may be essential. A few settlements have been relatively easily achieved, with little or no litigation, through the ready availability of water, money, or a combination thereof. Most of these easier settlements are behind us, and we are left with situations of insufficient water, money, or both. For the challenges ahead, we must better appreciate the difficult but necessary relationship between litigation and negotiation.

Litigation is often favored by parties for several reasons. First, one or more parties may genuinely desire a court ruling that will set a precedent or clarify a specific legal issue. A negotiated solution may not satisfy the desire for a clear legal precedent. Second, in disputes that are expected to have multiple rounds, a party may seek a court ruling that benefits them in future rounds *more than* they want to resolve the current issues being disputed. They believe a favorable ruling will give them a stronger position for bargaining in future rounds. Litigation is pursued to enhance bargaining power, to provide a credible threat at the negotiating table. Finally, litigation may be pursued because those with the deepest pockets believe they have the advantage in a courtroom setting due to superior staying power in an expensive process.

Although litigation may have desirable features for some disputants, it evokes a sense of antagonism among those whose interests are at stake—to the detriment of future cooperative water-management efforts. Furthermore, the parties generally know the characteristics of their basin and their respective demands for water more thoroughly than a judge can absorb this information, even in an extended trial. Litigation is characterized by the use of technical information as a weapon and persuasive device, rather than by a collective search for the best data on the watershed and on competing water needs. In addition, courts generally do not specify how compliance with their rulings is to be accomplished, leaving the litigants with the task of interpreting and working out implementation details themselves.

In a consensus-oriented process, the parties can address practical matters of water management as they forge mutually acceptable agreements. Settlement negotiations have greater potential than litigation to build trust and functional working relationships among the protagonists. This can be viewed as analogous to building social infrastructure. Just as investments in building dams and canals pay off in terms of improved water storage and conveyance, investment in settlement processes can build regional problem-solving capability and pay off in cost savings over the long run, as the parties learn to solve water problems more quickly and cost effectively than they could in litigation.

We have learned that litigation may be a necessary

tool even when most parties want to settle. Without any litigation pressure, the involved parties may meet initially in an expression of goodwill, but they are unlikely to progress once difficult issues emerge. Without litigation pressure, settlement talks may soon disband. If they continue, settlement talks may consume as much time and resources as litigation. Some parties benefit from the status quo and may encourage neverending settlement processes. The real, increasingly intensified pressure of litigation may force the parties to finally make a cold assessment of the risks and costs of litigation versus settlement, leading to incentives for the parties to reach agreement. As litigation pressure intensifies, with expert reports due and lengthy discovery, the parties' focus and resources are increasingly directed toward trial. On the eve of trial and even into the trial itself, the prospects of settlement may increase with the risks of litigation so immediate. By that time, however, the advantage of reduced transaction costs that a settlement process could offer may have been lost to all.

Litigation commonly serves as the catalyst to settlement, but other deadlines can provide needed pressure as well: legislative deadlines that are not easily extended, mutual agreements to suspend negotiations, funding and budgetary deadlines, the impending release of fact-finding reports, or the results of advisory arbitration. Negotiations are a voluntary and nonviolent conflict-resolution process, but they are far from painless. The parties may need to experience lots of present and prospective pain to forge concessions and agreement, but we hope that settlements result in less pain and more benefits than litigation or other imposed solutions.

Environmental mitigation must be shared by all. Most western watersheds are both overappropriated and beset with a host of environmental problems from past use of water and adjoining lands. As tribes attempt to secure their water rights, they are caught on the horns of a dilemma. If they proceed to establish senior rights by litigation, tribes may be theoretically in a better position than juniors when water use is curtailed for environmental purposes. But the tribes need new projects to use their decreed water, and these projects may be frustrated or vetoed because they threaten to cause significant adverse environmental effects. If tribes proceed by settlement, their position is often more vulnerable to environmental regulation. To safeguard existing users, they may accept more junior priority dates; but they still must navigate complicated environmental laws and meet environmental groups' concerns to secure project approval.

Tribes should not be penalized for being later participants in water infrastructure development. A century of disregard should not result in tribes bearing a disproportionate burden in addressing the environmental needs of these watersheds. Tribes, for their part, should realistically project their future water needs. State and federal environmental agencies need to definitively identify their priorities early in the negotiation process, with environmental protection requirements based on the best available science. The resulting settlement should include an equitable allocation of environmental costs. Congress would do well to adopt a principle of not approving settlements unless these costs are fairly allocated among all major water users, or unless sufficient funds are also appropriated for environmental purposes.

Follow-through is indispensable. The work of quantifying tribal rights, bringing water to reservations, and managing those water resources is an ongoing process. Whether by litigation or settlement, a sustained effort will be required to quantify the water rights of western tribes. After settlements or decrees are achieved, equally diligent efforts will be necessary to secure their implementation. A steady flow of funding will be necessary to assist tribes in using their water. Countless implementation and water administration issues, often involving issues of relative state-tribal jurisdiction, will need to be resolved. We expect that multifaceted relationships between state and tribal parties will develop, and these relationships will be characterized by episodes of friction and mutual readjustment. Rather than providing finality, the original compacts or agreements will be modified over time to meet unexpected circumstances and changing needs.

Negotiations build relationships. Although final settlements often elude us, the negotiating process itself remains important and should be encouraged. Even though settlement discussions may continue for many years, a settlement or lack thereof may be somewhat beside the point. In those cases where years of effort still have not produced a settlement, multiple parties have been engaged in uneasy dialogue, exchanging information and perspectives, learning more about the physical and social characteristics of the basin, developing new information, influencing one another, and mutually changing behaviors in ways that would not have happened otherwise. Yes, a settlement is desirable, but perhaps what is almost as important is productive dialogue and preventing one or more of the parties from walking away from the process to file a lawsuit or take some other destabilizing action.

At the end of the day, maybe the settlement process itself is the real meaning of the last twenty-five years. There is no silver bullet, no perfectly crafted treaty or compact that ensures permanent peace or a certain water supply. The promise of *Winters*, treaties, water rights settlements, and even our governmental constitutions all must be attended to on a daily basis. These hard-wrought documents disclose their true value in the ongoing relationships they make possible among different communities and constituencies. These foundational documents, and the relationships and institutions they have forged, must be continuously and perpetually renewed.

To Celebrate or Not to Celebrate?

We return to the opening question of this chapter: Will the promise of *Winters* be achieved by the case's centennial? *Winters* itself was a reaffirmation of the promises this nation made in its treaties and laws to Indian communities dispossessed by westward expansion. We have a long way to go before today's Indian communities become full participants in our political, educational, and economic systems. This is a social obligation that is too burdensome for water rights policy to carry alone and must be addressed in multifarious ways.

Yet, the Indian water rights settlements studied in the preceding pages are remarkable—perhaps astounding—in three important respects. Through these settlements, tribes have begun to exercise real authority and management over their natural re-

sources; indeed, these challenges have helped tribal governments to come into their own. Through these settlements, tribal senior rights to large amounts of what the West values most highly—water—have been permanently recognized. This asset, or reserve, can be the means for a tribe to return to more traditional ways or to participate strategically in the growing western economy. And through these settlements, Indians and non-Indians have found a reason to talk to one another. The hydrology of these river basins ensures that the dialogue continues.

But lest we forget: We're only halfway done. If we continue the settlement initiatives of the last twenty-five years, history likely will look kindly on all who contributed. If we stumble and falter now, we will leave a legacy of intertribal and Indian–non-Indian inequities, dashed expectations, contentious and divisive litigation, and resource degradation. No doubt, the remaining settlements will be difficult to achieve in terms of marshalling sufficient money and water, and they will have to be negotiated at a time when we are distracted by other pressing national and international matters. No doubt, these settlements will be more creatively prepared than the large quantifications of the past. We are confident, however, that these settlements will be achieved. The American West continues to grow and needs water for cities, farms, recreation, and the environment. Tribes continue to have strong, senior legal claims to that water. They have those claims because the justices writing an obscure U.S. Supreme Court decision in 1908 committed this nation to deal more justly with its first residents.

> On what road am I?
> The white man's road,
> Or the Indian's?
> There are no sign posts.
> The road is uphill,
> And the wind in my face.
> Still I go on.
>
> *Yellow Bird, Sioux Leader*

NOTES

Foreword

1. 207 U.S. 564 (1908).

2. See John Shurts, *Indian Reserved Water Rights: The Winters Doctrine in Its Social and Legal Context, 1880s–1930s.* Legal History of North America, vol. 8 (Norman: University of Oklahoma Press, 2000).

3. 373 U.S. 546 (1963). Another Indian water rights case that reached the Supreme Court after *Winters* was *United States v. Powers*, 305 U.S. 527 (1939), affirming that purchasers of Indian reservation allotments are entitled to a share of the tribe's irrigation water.

4. See, e.g., *United States v. Ahtanum Irrigation District*, 236 F.2d 321 (9th Cir. 1956), *cert. denied*, 352 U.S. 988 (1957).

5. *Pyramid Lake Paiute Tribe v. Morton*, 354 F. Supp. 252 (D.D.C. 1972); see Reid P. Chambers, "Judicial Enforcement of the Federal Trust Responsibility to Indians," *Stanford Law Review* 27 (1975): 1213.

6. *In re General Adjudication of All Rights to Use Water in the Big Horn River System*, 753 P.2d 76, (Wyo. 1988), *affirmed sub. nom., Wyoming v. United States*, 492 U.S. 406 (1989) *[Big Horn I]*.

Chapter 1

1. See Frederick E. Hoxie, ed., *Encyclopedia of North American Indians: Native American History, Culture, and Life From Paleo-Indians to the Present* (New York: Houghton Mifflin, 1996).

2. See Alvin M. Josephy, *America in 1492: The World of the Indian Peoples Before the Arrival of Columbus* (New York: Knopf, 1992).

3. Arrell Morgan Gibson, *The American Indian: Prehistory to the Present* (Lexington, Mass.: D.C. Heath, 1980), 236.

4. Myra Ellen Jenkins, "Spanish Land Grants in the Tewa Area," *New Mexico Historical Review* 47 (April 1972): 113–34.

5. See Francis Paul Prucha, *American Indian Treaties: The History of a Political Anomaly* (Berkeley: University of California Press, 1994).

6. See F.P. Prucha, ed., *Documents of United States Indian Policy* (Lincoln: University of Nebraska Press, 2000) for a comprehensive compilation of documents and legislation.

7. 25 U.S.C. §§ 331-334, 339, 341, 342, 348, 349, 354, 381 (1983).

8. See Daniel C. McCool, *Command of the Waters: Iron Triangles, Federal Water Development, and Indian Water* (Tucson: University of Arizona Press, 1994) for examination of federal water-development programs in their political framework from the turn of the century.

9. Gibson, *The American Indian*, 551.

Chapter 2

1. 16 U.S.C. § 1531 (1973); 33 U.S.C. § 1251-1387 (1988).

2. 43 U.S.C. § 666(a) (1952).

3. *Colorado River Water Conservation District v. United States*, 424 U.S. 800 (1976). Federal courts must defer to state court proceedings.

4. See *Arizona v. San Carlos Apache Tribe*, 463 U.S. 545 (1983).

5. See, e.g., *United States v. Winans*, 198 U.S. 371 (1905); Felix S. Cohen and Rennard Strickland, *Felix S. Cohen's Handbook of Federal Indian Law* (Charlottesville, Va.: Michie Bobbs-Merrill, 1982).

6. *Winters*, 207 U.S. 564 (1908).

7. In some instances, these rights go back to time immemorial. See *United States v. Adair*, 723 F.2d 1394 (9th Cir. 1983), *cert. denied*, 467 U.S. 1252 (1984).

8. *Arizona v. California*, 373 U.S. 546 (1963), *decreed in final form*, 376 U.S. 340 (1964), *decree amended*, 383 U.S. 268 (1966), *supplemental decree entered*, 439 U.S. 419 (1979), *supplemental opinion*, 460 U.S. 605 (1983) *[Arizona II], second supplemental decree entered*, 466 U.S. 144 (1984). The report by Special Master Tuttle contains a detailed discussion of the rationale for the rule adopted by the Court rejecting open-ended decrees.

9. The five reservations were Chemehuevi, Cocopah, Yuma, Colorado River, and Fort Mojave. Other Indian tribes in the region with potential claims to the Colorado River were not included in the adjudication.

10. See, e.g., Ann E. Amundson and American Indian Resources Institute, *Tribal Water Management Handbook* (Oakland, Calif.: AIRI, 1988), 144.

11. See *Colville Confederated Tribes v. Walton*, 752 F.2d 397 (9th Cir. 1985), *cert. denied*, 454 U.S. 1092 (1981); *Adair*, 723 F.2d 1394, 1412–14 (9th Cir. 1983), *cert. denied*, 467 U.S. 1252 (1984); *Muckleshoot Indian Tribe v. Trans-Canada Enterprises, Ltd.*, 713 F.2d 455 (9th Cir. 1983), *cert. denied*, 465 U.S. 1049 (1984); *Confederated Salish and Kootenai v. Flathead Irr. Dist.*, 616 F. Supp. 1292 (D. Mont. 1985); *Board of Control v. United States*, 646 F. Supp. 410 (D. Mont. 1986), 832 F. 2d 1127 (9th Cir. 1987), 862 F.2d 195 (9th Cir. 1988).

12. See *In re Rights to Use Water in the Big Horn River*, 753 P.2d 76 (Wyo. 1988), *affirmed sub. nom., Wyoming v. United States*, 492 U.S. 406 (1989) *[Big Horn I]*; see also *Nevada v. United States*, 463 U.S. 110, 113 (1983).

13. See *United States v. Washington*, 384 F. Supp. 312 (W.D. Wash. 1974), *aff'd*, 520 F.2d 676 (9th Cir. 1975), *cert. denied*, 423 U.S. 1086 (1976); *United States v. Washington*, Phase II, No. 9213 (W.D. Wash., September 26, 1980).

14. See generally Charles T. DuMars, Marilyn O'Leary, and Albert E. Utton, *Pueblo Indian Water Rights: Struggle for a Precious Resource* (Tucson: University of Arizona Press, 1984).

15. *United States v. Mazurie*, 419 U.S. 544 (1975), citations omitted.

16. See, e.g., *Brendale v. Confederated Tribes and Bands of the Yakima Indian Nation*, 492 U.S. 408 (1989).

17. This began in 1970 when the Nixon administration announced the policy of self-determination without termination and Congress passed the Indian Self-Determination and Educational Assistance Act of 1975, 25 U.S.C. §§ 450-450n, 455-458e (1982).

18. See, e.g., *Colville Tribes v. Walton*, 752 F.2d 397 (9th Cir. 1985).

19. See *Rice v. Rehner*, 463 U.S. 713 (1983); see also *Washington v. Confederated Tribes*, 447 U.S. 134 (1980); *Puyallup Tribe, Inc., v. Department of Game*, 443 U.S. 165 (1977); *Brendale v. Confederated Tribes and Bands of the Yakima Indian Nation*, 492 U.S. 408 (1989).

20. *Cherokee Nation v. Georgia*, 30 U.S. 1 (1831).

21. See *Seminole Nation v. United States*, 316 U.S. 286, 297 (1942); *Navajo Tribe of Indians v. United States*, 364 F.2d 320 (Cl. Ct. 1966); *United States v. Mitchell*, 463 U.S. 206 (1983).

22. See *Pyramid Lake Paiute Tribe v. Morton*, 354 F. Supp. 252 (D.D.C. 1972); *Pyramid Lake Paiute Tribe v. U.S. Department of Navy*, 898 F.2d 1410 (9th Cir. 1990); *Northern Arapahoe Tribe v. Hodel*, 808 F.2d 741 (10th Cir. 1987).

23. *Morton v. Mancari*, 417 U.S. 535 (1974).

24. *United States v. Eberhardt*, 789 F.2d 1354 (9th Cir. 1986).

25. See, e.g., *United States v. Winnebago Tribe*, 542 F.2d 1002 (8th Cir. 1976); *United States v. Southern Pacific Trans. Co.*, 543 F.2d 676 (9th Cir. 1976). But see *Seneca Nation of Indians v. United States*, 338 F.2d 55 (2nd Cir. 1964), *cert. denied*, 380 U.S. 952 (1965); *Seneca Nation of Indians v. Brucker*, 262 F.2d 27 (D.C. Cir.1958), *cert. denied*, 360 U.S. 909 (1959).

26. 463 U.S. 129 (1983).

27. 32 Stat. 388, 43 U.S.C. 391 (1902).

28. U.S. National Water Commission, *Water Policies for the Future*. (Port Washington, N.Y.: Water Information Center, 1973), 474–75.

Chapter 3

1. See http://yosemite.epa.gov/oar/globalwarming.nsf/content/index.html (visited July 3, 2004).

2. IPCC, *Water: The Potential Consequences of Climate Variability and Change for the Water Resources of the United States* (National Assessment of the Potential Consequences of Climate Variability and Change, 2000).

3. Ibid.

Chapter 4

1. Michael B. Gerrard, ed., *The Law of Environmental Justice: Theories and Procedures to Address Disproportionate Risks* (Chicago: ABA Section of Environment, Energy, and Resources, 1999), xxix.

2. See *Federal Register* 55 (1990), 9223.

Chapter 5

1. 463 U.S. 545 (1983).

2. 492 U.S. 406 (1989).

3. *New Mexico ex rel. State Engineer v. Abeyta*, no. 69CV7896BB and 69CV7939BB, consolidated (D.N.M. 1969).

4. *New Mexico ex rel. State Engineer v. Aamodt*, no. 66CV6639 MV (D.N.M. 1966).

5. Ariz. Rev. Stat. § 45-401 *et seq.* (1980).

6. 42 U.S.C. § 9601 *et seq.* (2003).

7. *In re General Adjudication of All Rights to Use Water in the Gila River System and Source*, 35 P.3d 68 (Ariz. 2001) *[Gila V]*.

Chapter 6

1. 42 U.S.C. §§ 4321 to 4370e (2003).

2. 532 U.S. 1 (2001).

3. Eddie F. Brown, Assistant Secretary for Indian Affairs, Department of the Interior, remarks made at the Settlement of Indian Reserved Water Rights Claims symposium (Native American Rights Fund and the Western States Water Council, Albuquerque, New Mexico, September 1–3, 1992).

4. The settlement authorized by the Reclamation Projects Authorization and Adjustment Act of 1992, Public Law 102-575, 106 Stat. 4600, is designed as direct compensation for the federal government's failure to fulfill promises made to the Utes in the 1965 deferral agreement.

5. See, generally, Joseph R. Membrino, "Indian Water Rights and Water Resources Management Goals and Objectives of the Affected Parties: A Federal Perspective," *Sourcebook on Indian Water Settlements*, ed. American Indian Lawyer Training Program (Oakland, Calif.: AIRI, 1989).

6. 107th Cong., 1st sess., S. 1186 (2001).

7. Title XIII, Public Law 101-508, 104 Stat. 1388 (1990).

8. Ad Hoc Group on Indian Water Rights for the Western Governors' Association, *Questions and Answers Regarding the Domenici Amendment to the Budget Act* (April 24, 2001).

9. Ibid.

10. Ibid.

11. Michael Connor, majority staff, U.S. Senate Energy and Natural Resources Committee, remarks made at the Indian Water Rights Settlement Conference, sponsored by the Native American Rights Fund and Western States Water Council Conference (St. George, Utah, October 10–12, 2001).

12. Patricia Zell, majority staff director and counsel, U.S. Senate Committee on Indian Affairs, remarks made at the Indian Water Rights Settlement Conference (St. George, Utah, October 10–12, 2001).

13. The cases are Fort Belknap, in Montana; the Arizona Gila River system settlement; Idaho's Snake River adjudication; the Zuni Heaven settlement in Arizona's Little Colorado River adjudication; and the settlement of the *Aamodt* case in New Mexico, concerning four Pueblo tribes.

14. Pam Williams, head of the Interior Office of Indian Water Rights, remarks made at the Indian Water Rights Settlement Conference (St. George, Utah, October 10–12, 2001).

15. 107th Cong., 1st sess., S. 1186, § 2(a).

Chapter 7

1. Public Law 108-34, 117 Stat. 782 (2003).

2. See Bruce Driver, *Western Water: Tuning the System* (Denver: Western Governors' Association, 1986) and Teresa A. Rice and Lawrence J. MacDonnell, *Agricultural to Urban Water Transfers: An Assessment of the Issues and Options* (Fort Collins: Colorado Water Resources Research Institute, Colorado State University, 1993) for an overview of policies in the 1970s, 1980s, and early 1990s.

3. David H. Getches, "The Metamorphosis of Western Water Policy: Have Federal Laws and Local Decisions Eclipsed the States' Role?" *Stanford Environmental Law Journal* 20, no. 1 (2000): 3–72.

4. Charles W. Howe et al., *Urban Water Supply Reliability: Preferences of Managers, Elected Officials and Water Users in Boulder, Colorado* (Fort Collins: Colorado Water Resources Research Institute, Colorado State University, 1990); Elizabeth Checchio and University of Arizona Department of Hydrology and Water Resources, *Water Farming: The Promise and Problems of Water Transfers in Arizona* (Tucson: Department of Hydrology and Water Resources, University of Arizona, 1988).

5. Howe, *Urban Water Supply Reliability*.

6. Portions of this discussion are adapted from a presentation by Susan Williams, "Big Horn Adjudication," at the Settlement of Indian Reserved Water Rights symposium (Native American Rights Fund and Western States Water Council, Albuquerque, New Mexico, September 1–3, 1992).

7. 25 U.S.C. § 177 (2003). Some Indian law scholars disagree on this point, arguing that congressional approval of off-reservation water leases is not required.

8. 25 U.S.C. § 415 (2003), an act of August 9, 1955, that has been amended many times.

9. *An act to authorize the secretary of the Interior to construct, operate, and maintain the Navajo Indian Irrigation Project and the initial stage of the San Juan–Chama Project as participating projects of the Colorado River storage project, and for other purposes,* (hereafter *Act of June 13, 1962*), Public Law 87-483, 76 Stat. 96 (codified as amended in 43 U.S.C. 620), June 13, 1962. The agreement was not renewed.

10. For more details on the history of the Northern Ute settlement, see, generally, Daniel McCool, "The Northern Utes' Long Water Ordeal," *High Country News*, July 15, 1991, p. 8.

11. Daniel McCool, "Intergovernmental Conflict and Indian Water Rights: An Assessment of Negotiated Settlements," *Publius* 23, no. 1 (1993).

12. *High Country News*, August 17, 1990.

13. Teno Roncalio, special master, in appendix H of *Wyoming's Petition for a Writ of Certiorari to the Supreme Court of Wyoming* (August 19, 1988).

14. Mont. Code Ann. § 85-20-1001 (2003).

15. Mont. Code Ann. § 85-20-201, art. IX (2003).

Chapter 8

1. Water does not always need to be physically conveyed to an area to accomplish the broader purpose of economic development. Revenues earned from leasing water for non-Indian use away from the reservation can still support a tribe's overall economic objectives.

2. The Chippewa Cree Tribe obtained rights to 10,000 acre-feet per year of stored water in Tiber Reservoir, which is outside the local watershed and would be otherwise unavailable for use in the local area. The Jicarilla Apache Nation obtained rights to 6,500 acre-feet per year of water from the SJCP, which transports water across the continental divide, and 33,500 acre-feet per year diverted from Navajo Reservoir, which is located downstream from the Jicarilla Apache Reservation.

3. Although two examples of additional river development to support water rights settlements are cited in the text, further development is likely to be rare. The best dam sites have already been developed, making additional development much more expensive. Increasing awareness of the environmental impacts from altering or depleting river flows makes it much more difficult to find politically acceptable new developments.

4. *Reclamation Projects Authorization and Adjustment Act*, Public Law 102-575, 106 Stat. 4600 (1992).

5. *Truckee-Carson–Pyramid Lake Water Rights Settlement Act*, Public Law 101-618, 104 Stat. 3289, 3206(c) (1990).

6. Water consumption refers both to ET and to water not used for ET but unavailable for reuse in irrigation, such as runoff or percolation to a saline water body.

7. Deep percolation and surface runoff, however, may be degraded in quality from having higher levels of dissolved solids or other chemical constituents than the original water source. In addition, the delay in rejoining a useable water body may decrease its usefulness for timely irrigation.

8. Central Valley Water Use Study Committee, *Irrigation Water Use in the Central Valley of California*. (Division of Agriculture and Natural Resources, University of California and California Department of Water Resources, 1987), 22.

9. Although water flowing to a saline water body may be unavailable for reuse in irrigation, it may have environmental benefits. Irrigation return flows and subsurface drainage have long supported brackish estuaries such as California's Sacramento River delta and the Colorado River delta as well as the saline Salton Sea.

10. The Salton Sea's importance as a rest stop for migrating birds on the Pacific Flyway has lately focused attention on the role of agricultural drainage water in maintaining the water level and salinity concentration of the sea.

Chapter 9

1. For detailed legal analyses, see Peg Rogers, "*In re Rights to Use Water in the Big Horn River*, 753 P.2d 76 (Wyo. 1988)," *Natural Resources Journal* 30 (1990): 439; and Susan Williams, "The *Winters* Doctrine on Water Administration," *Rocky Mountain Mineral Law Institute* 36 (1990): 24–1.

2. T. Roncalio, special master, *Report Concerning Reserved Rights Claims by and on Behalf of the Wind River Indian Reservation, In re Rights to Use Water in the Big Horn River* (Wyo. 5th Dist., December 15, 1982).

3. See *In re Rights to Use Water in the Big Horn River*, 753 P.2d 76 (Wyo. 1988), *affirmed sub. nom., Wyoming v. United States*, 492 U.S. 406 (1989), *[Big Horn I]*.

4. *In re Rights to Use Water in the Big Horn River*, 492 U.S. 406 (1989).

5. *In re Rights to Use Water in the Big Horn River*, 803 P.2d 61 (Wyo. 1990) *[Big Horn II]*.

6. *In re Rights to Use Water in the Big Horn River*, 835 P.2d 273 (Wyo. 1992) *[Big Horn III]*.

7. *Big Horn II* held that all parties who have appeared in the case, at least to the extent of filing an answer, were entitled to the application of any rule that was the law of the case, including the rule adopted in *Big Horn I* that recognized that *Walton* rights existed. This determination prompted the district court to set up a process to include all possible *Walton* rights claims, and increased the number of claims from ten to over four hundred.

8. *Homestead Act*, 43 U.S.C. § 161 *et seq.* (repealed 1976); *Cash Entry Act*, 3 Stat. 566 (1820); *Desert Land Act*, 43 U.S.C. § 321 *et seq.* (2003).

9. Wyoming Supreme Court Opinion No. 93-49, slip op. (October 26, 1993).

10. *In re Rights to Use Water in the Big Horn River*, 899 P.2d 848 (Wyo. 1995) *[Big Horn V]*.

11. *In re Rights to Use Water in the Big Horn River*, 48 P.3d 1040 (Wyo. 2002) *[Big Horn VI]*.

12. "Big Horn Adjudication," Settlement of Indian Water Rights, symposium sponsored by the Native American Rights Fund and the Western States Water Council (Albuquerque, New Mexico, September 1–3, 1992).

13. See *Settlement of Ak-Chin Water Rights Claims*, Public Law 95-328, 92 Stat. 409, and H. Rep. 95-954, 95th Cong., 2d sess. (1978). For a detailed analysis of the Ak-Chin settlement negotiation process, see Susana Eden, "Negotiation and the Resolution of Water Allocation Disputes" (master's thesis, University of Arizona, 1988).

14. The Yuma Mesa Division includes three Yuma area irrigation districts: the North Gila Valley Irrigation District, the Yuma Irrigation District, and the Yuma Mesa Irrigation and Drainage District.

15. Public Law 70-642, 45 Stat. 1057 (1928).

16. This water was allocated to the Ak-Chin Indian Community pursuant to the secretarial decision of March 24, 1983, *Federal Register* 48 (1983): 12446, which established an Indian CAP pool.

17. Arizona's agricultural community argues that they were promised any excess water. This proved to be a contentious issue in the San Carlos Apache Tribe settlement, which relies on this source of water to satisfy tribal entitlements. Agricultural interests attempted unsuccessfully to get relief from Reclamation Reform Act requirements in return for the use of this water in the San Carlos settlement.

18. *Ak-Chin Water Use Amendments Act of 1992*, Public Law 102-497, 106 Stat. 3255 (1992).

19. "Assured Water Supply Requirement–Legal Availability of Central Arizona Project Water or Colorado River Water Leased from an Indian Community," R 12-15-703.01, *Ariz. Admin. Reg.* 7, no. 28 (July 13, 2001): 3038.

20. The authors thank Gregg Houtz for much of this information.

21. See Title I, the *Fallon Paiute-Shoshone Indian Tribes Water Rights Settlement Act of 1990*, and Title II, the *Truckee-Carson–Pyramid Lake Water Rights Settlement Act*, Public Law 101-618, 104 Stat. 3289 (1990). For a detailed discussion of this settlement, see also David Yardes, "Restoring Endangered Ecosystems: The Truckee-Carson Water Rights Settlement," *Natural Resource Law Notes* (January 1992); Joe Ely, "Pyramid Lake Negotiated Settlement: Overview and Perspectives" (paper presented at the Innovations in Western Water Law and Management Conference, Natural Resources Law Center, University of Colorado, Boulder, 1991).

22. See, generally, Martha C. Knack and Omer Call Stewart, *As Long as the River Shall Run: An Ethnohistory of Pyramid Lake Indian Reservation* (Berkeley: University of California Press, 1984).

23. *United States v. Orr Ditch Co.*, Final Decree No. A-3 (D. Nev. 1944).

24. *Nevada v. United States*, 463 U.S. 110, 113 (1983). The Court determined that the tribe's reserved water rights to appropriated water had been previously quantified in the Orr Ditch Decree and could not be relitigated.

25. *Carson-Truckee Water Conservancy District v. Clark*, 741 F.2d 257 (9th Cir. 1984), *cert. denied*, 470 U.S. 1083 (1985).

26. See, e.g., John E. Thorson, "Resolving Conflicts through Intergovernmental Agreements: The Pros and Cons of Negotiated Settlements," *Indian Water 1985*, ed. Christine L. Miklas and Steven J. Shupe (Oakland, Calif.: American Indian Lawyer Training Program, 1986).

27. Wyo. Stat. 41-12-401 (2003).

28. *Act of June 13, 1962*, Public Law 87-483, 76 Stat. 96 (1962).

29. Shea Anderson, "Navajo Farm Is a Federal Money Pit," *New Mexico Business Weekly*, January 14, 2002.

30. New Mexico Office of the State Engineer, "Navajo Irrigation Project Can Go Forward," *Water Line* (March 2000).

31. Anderson, "Navajo Farm."

32. Ibid., quoting an Environmental Working Group report.

33. See Charles T. DuMars and Helen Ingram, "Congressional Quantification of Indian Reserved Water Rights: A Definitive Solution or a Mirage?" *Natural Resources Journal* 20 (1980): 17.

34. *New Mexico ex rel. Reynolds v. United States*, No. 75-184 (11th Jud. Dist., San Juan County, N.M., filed March 13, 1975).

35. Judith Jacobson, "A Promise Made: The Navajo Indian Irrigation Project" (Cooperative Thesis 119, University of Colorado and National Center for Atmospheric Research, 1989).

36. Complaint, *Navajo Nation v. U.S. Department of Interior*, no. CIV030507PCTPER (D. Ariz., filed March 14, 2003).

37. *Fort Hall Indian Water Rights Act of 1990*, Public Law 101-602, 104 Stat. 3059 (1990). See also Committee Report 101-831 to accompany H. Rep. 5308, 101st Cong., 2d sess. (1990).

38. Susan Cottingham, Anne Yates, and Faye Bergan, staff of the Montana Reserved Water Rights Compact Commission, telephone interview with author, October 18, 2002. The author wishes to thank them for their assistance.

39. Montana Reserved Water Rights Compact Commission, *Historical Report for the Northern Cheyenne–Montana Compact* (Commission Staff Historical Report, Compact Commission, Missoula, Montana, December 1990).

40. *Arizona v. San Carlos Apache Tribe*, 463 U.S. 545 (1983), deciding that dismissal was appropriate and also reversing the ninth circuit ruling in favor of a federal forum in *Northern Cheyenne v. Adsit*, 668 F.2d 1080 (9th Cir. 1982).

41. Montana Reserved Water Rights Compact Commission, *Historical Report for the Northern Cheyenne–Montana Compact*.

42. Ibid.

43. Montana Reserved Water Rights Compact Commission, *Land and Water Resources of the Northern Cheyenne Indian Reservation* (Commission Staff Technical Report, Compact Commission, Missoula, Montana, July 1990).

44. Ibid.

45. Richard K. Aldrich, field solicitor, Department of the Interior, Billings, telephone interview with author, October 16, 2002.

46. Mont. Code Ann. § 85-20-301 (2002); *Northern Cheyenne Indian Reserved Water Rights Settlement Act of 1992*, Public Law 102-374, 106 Stat. 1186. Changes to the agreement by Congress resulted in re-ratification by the Montana legislature in 1992 (1993 Mont. Laws, Nov. Sp. sess., ch. 7, § 1).

47. Tribal chair Edwin Dahl passed away during the congressional process. Rather than stop the process, the new leader, Cowboy Fisher, sought amendment to the congressional bill to provide for a tribal referendum to gauge tribal support for the compact. The referendum supported the agreement.

48. *Northern Cheyenne Settlement Act*, Public Law 102-374, 106 Stat. 1186 (1992). Although this change in the original agreement gave the state an interest-free loan and increased the ultimate settlement fund held by the tribe, it cost Montana substantially in its credibility for ongoing negotiations with the United States concerning other reservations.

49. Telephone interview with Aldrich.

50. *Northern Cheyenne Settlement Act*, Public Law 102-374, 106 Stat. 1186 (1992). When agreement was achieved, representatives of the Crow and Northern Cheyenne tribes gathered in Representative Pat Williams's (D-MT) office. Momentarily forgetting his history, Williams indicated the historic nature of the agreement because it

was the first time the two tribes had worked together on anything since Custer's Last Stand. Edwin Dahl, chair of the Northern Cheyenne Tribe, the tribe who, among others, defeated General Custer, who was led by Crow scouts, did not miss the opportunity and replied, "You could say we worked together. They brought him in, and we took him out." And so a fragile truce on at least one issue between the tribes was achieved. The boundary dispute over the surveyed location of the 107th meridian was subsequently resolved between the tribes. Telephone interview with Cottingham et al.

51. Jim Domino, Water Resources Division, MDNRC, interview with author, October 16, 2002.

52. Telephone interview with Aldrich.

53. Ibid. The decision to use contract water rather than settlement water for marketing is due primarily to the requirement in the Northern Cheyenne Compact of a 180-day notice for marketing settlement water. The parties had not anticipated the short time frame involved in water marketing during drought. Telephone interviews with Cottingham et al. and Aldrich.

54. Telephone interview with Cottingham et al.

55. 42 U.S.C. §§ 4321 to 4370e (2003).

56. 42 U.S.C. § 4332(2)(C)(iii).

57. Interviews indicated disagreement among the parties over whether the federal representatives provided a positive addition to the effort to complete the project. The views expressed are those of the author after both observing the process and interviewing state and federal representatives.

58. Interview with Cottingham et al.

59. *Treaty with the Tribes of Middle Oregon*, 12 Stat. 963 (June 25, 1855).

60. *Winters*, 207 U.S. 564 (1908).

61. *Findings of Fact and Order of Determination, In re the Relative Rights to the Use of Waters of the Streams and Rivers of the Warm Springs Indian Reservation* (Deschutes County Cir. Ct. 2002); Reed Marbut, ODWR, telephone interview with author, November 7, 2002.

62. Or. Rev. Stat. §§ 539.310(1)-(2) (2001).

63. *The Confederated Tribes of the Warm Springs Reservation Water Rights Settlement Agreement* (November 17, 1997).

64. Or. Rev. Stat. §§ 539.320 and 539.340.

65. Telephone interview with Marbut.

66. James Noteboom, Warm Springs tribal attorney, telephone interview with author, November 6, 2002.

67. Deschutes County Circuit Court, *Findings of Fact and Order of Determination*; telephone interview with Marbut.

68. Exhibit A, *Warms Springs Settlement Agreement*.

69. *Warms Springs Settlement Agreement*.

70. Ibid.

71. Ibid. The agreed-on instream flows amount to between 3,000 and 3,500 cubic feet per second per month on the Deschutes River and between 1,080 and 1,240 cubic feet per second per month on the Metolius.

72. Telephone interview with Noteboom.

73. Ibid. *Findings of Fact and Order of Determination*.

74. Ibid.

75. Telephone interview with Marbut.

76. *Warms Springs Settlement Agreement*.

77. Ibid.

78. *Arizona v. San Carlos Apache Tribe*, 463 U.S. 545 (1983); *United States v. Superior Court*, 697 P.2d 658 (Ariz. 1985).

79. *In re All Rights to Water in the Gila River*, 989 P.2d 739 (Ariz. 1999), *cert. denied sub nom., Phelps Dodge Corp. v. United States* and *Salt River Valley Water Users' Association v. United States*, 530 U.S. 1250 (2000).

80. *In re All Rights to Water in the Gila River*, 35 P.3d 68 (Ariz. 2001).

81. Order of February 20, 2002, amended *nunc pro tunc* March 7, 2002, *In re All Rights to Water in the Gila River*, No. W-1 (Maricopa County Super. Ct.).

82. *Arizona Water Settlements Act of 2002*, S. 2992, 107th Cong., 2d sess. (2002); reintroduced as S. 437, 108th Cong., 1st sess. (2003). Introduced in House as HR 885 by John D. Hayworth (R-AZ); signed by the president December 10, 2004 P.L., 108–451.

83. See *Salt River Pima–Maricopa Indian Community Water Rights Settlement Act of 1988*, Public Law 100-512, 102 Stat. 2549; S. Rep. 1495, 100th Cong., 2d sess. (1988); H. Rep. 100-868, 100th Cong., 2d sess. (1988).

84. The lease proceeds are intended to provide additional capital for the community trust fund for investing in water facilities and related economic development.

85. The first European documentation of Zuni cultural use of this specific area dates to 1540 A.D. *Zuni Tribe v. Platt*, 730 F. Supp. 318 (D. Ariz. 1990).

86. Ibid.

87. *Act to Convey Certain Lands to the Zuni Indian Tribe for Religious Purposes*, Public Law 98-408, 98 Stat. 1533 (1984).

88. "The Zuni Experience: Floodplains, Wetlands, and Intertwined Spiritual Traditions," *Arizona Flood Management Association Newsletter* (July 2000), 8.

89. *Zuni Land Conservation Act of 1990*, Public Law 101-486, 104 Stat. 1174 (1990).

90. HR 4143, H. Rep. 101-727, 101st Cong., 2d sess. (1990).

91. Susan Williams, "Acquiring Water for Tribes" (paper presented at Two Decades of Water Law Policy and Reform: A Retrospective and Agenda for the Future, Natural Resources Law Center, University of Colorado, Boulder, June 13–15, 2001).

92. Ibid.

93. Gregg Houtz, telephone interview with author, December 13, 2002.

94. S. 2743, 107th Cong., 2d sess. (2002).

95. *Zuni Indian Tribe Water Rights Settlement Act of 2003*, Public Law 108-34, 117 Stat. 782 (2003).

96. *Colorado Ute Indian Water Rights Settlement Act of 1988*, Public Law 100-585, 102 Stat. 2973 (1988).

97. *United States v. Morrison Consolidated Ditch Co.*, No. 7736 (D. Colo. February 14, 1931).

98. Ibid. at ¶ 3.

99. 373 U.S. 546 (1963).

100. *Colorado River Water Conservation District*, 424 U.S. 800 (1976).

101. *Supplemental Appropriations Act*, Public Law 99-88, 99 Stat. 293 (1985).

102. See U.S. Fish and Wildlife Service, *Final Biological Opinion for the Animas–La Plata Project, Colorado and New Mexico*, October 25, 1991.

103. *Omnibus Appropriations Act of 2000*, Public Law 106-544, 114 Stat. 2763, *Conf. Report* 106-1033 at Div. B, ch. 14, tit. 3.

104. *Shivwits Band of the Paiute Indian Tribe of Utah Water Rights Settlement Act*, Public Law 106-263, 114 Stat. 737 (2000).

105. Statement by David J. Hayes, deputy secretary of the Interior, hearing on S. 2351, *Shivwits Band Settlement Act*, May 2, 2000; testimony of Glenn Rogers, chair of the Shivwits Band, hearing on HR 3291, *To Provide for the Settlement of the Water Rights Claims of the Shivwits Band of the Paiute Indian Tribe of Utah, and for Other Purposes*, April 4, 2000.

106. Testimony of Robert L. Morgan, P.E., Utah state engineer, Department of Natural Resources, hearing on HR 3291, April 4, 2000.

107. *Shivwits Band Settlement Act*, Public Law 106-263, 114, Stat. 737.

108. Ibid. §§ 5(a), 11(b)(2).

109. Ibid. § 6(a).

110. Testimony of Ronald W. Thompson, district manager, WCWCD, hearing on HR 3291, April 4, 2000.

111. *Shivwits Band Settlement Act*, Public Law 106-263, § 11(c), 114 Stat. 737. Deputy Secretary Hayes expressed the concern of the Department of the Interior whether the $1 million appropriation would cover all of the band's operating costs for the project. Hayes stated that Interior has a policy that opposes paying the full costs associated with tribal water use secured in settlements, because tribal contribution is a means to ensure settlement projects are economically viable and efficient.

112. Ibid. §§ 10, 10(f).

113. Ibid. §§ 7(a)(3), 7(e).

114. See *Federal Register* 68 (2003): 66473–66474.

115. The present-day Klamath tribes consist of three Indian groups: the Klamath and Modoc tribes and the Yahooskin Band of Snake Indians.

116. *Adair*, 723 F.2d 1394 (9th Cir. 1983), *cert. denied*, 467 U.S. 1252 (1984).

117. *United States v. Oregon*, 44 F 3d. 758 (9th Cir. 1994), *cert. denied*, 516 U.S. 934 (1995).

118. *Kandra v. United States*, 145 F. Supp. 2d 1192 (D. Ore. 2001).

119. National Academy of Sciences, *Scientific Evaluation of Biological Opinions on Endangered and Threatened Fishes in the Klamath River Basin: Interim Report* (Washington, D.C.: 2002).

120. National Academy of Sciences, *Endangered and Threatened Fishes in the Klamath River Basin: Causes of Decline and Strategies of Recovery* (Washington D.C.: 2004).

121. The characteristics, causes, and consequences of intractable conflict are described in Peter T. Coleman, "Intractable Conflict," *The Handbook of Conflict Resolution: Theory and Practice*, ed. Morton Deutsch and Peter T. Coleman (San Francisco, Calif.: Jossey-Bass, 2000): 428–50.

122. Public Law 97-293, 96 Stat. 1261 (1982); amended by Public Law 102-497, 106 Stat. 3255 (1992); amended by Public Law 108-451 (2004).

123. *Arizona Water Settlements Act of 2002*, S. 2992, 107th Cong., 2d sess. tit. III, §§ 304 & 306 (2002), reintroduced as S. 437, 108th Cong., 1st sess. (2003); signed by the president on December 10, 2004, P.L. 108-451 (2004).

124. Ibid. § 308.

125. Ibid. § 310; Houtz interview.

Chapter 10

1. U.S. Department of Commerce, Bureau of the Census, *Statistical Brief: Housing of American Indians on Reservations* (Washington, D.C., 1995).

2. "Look Who's Cashing in at Indian Casinos," *Time*, December 16, 2002.

3. Pojoaque Pueblo website (visited December 12, 2003): www.citiesofgold.com.

4. National Indian Gaming Commission, "Tribal Gaming Revenues (1997–2001)" (visited December 12, 2003): www.nigc.gov/pr revenuechart.htm.

5. See also Montana Reserved Water Compact Commission website, "Compacts" (visited February 24, 2003): www.dnrc.state.mt.us/rwrcc/; Daniel McCool, "Indian Water Settlements: Negotiating Tribal Claims to Water" (visited July 2, 2004): www.ucowr.siu.edu/updates/pdf/v107_A5.pdf

6. 41 Stat. 751 (June 4, 1920).

Sidebar 1.1

1. See Charles F. Wilkinson and Christine L. Miklas, *Indian Tribes as Sovereign Governments: A Sourcebook on Federal-Tribal History, Law, and Policy* (Oakland, Calif.: AIRI Press, 1988).

2. See *Colville Confederated Tribes v. Walton*, 460 F. Supp. 1320 (E.D. Wash. 1978) *[Walton I]*; *Colville Confederated Tribes v. Walton*, 647 F.2d 42 (9th Cir.), *cert. denied*, 454 U.S. 1092 (1981) *[Walton II]*; and *Colville Confederated Tribes v. Walton*, 752 F.2d 397 (1985).

3. For more comprehensive discussions of allotments and their associated water rights, see David H. Getches, "Water Rights on Indian Allotments," *South Dakota Law Review* 26 (1981): 405; Richard B. Collins, "Indian Allotment Water Rights," *Land and Water Law Review* 20 (1985): 421; *Grey v. United States*, 21 Cl. Ct. 285 (1990), *aff'd without opp.*, 935 F.2d 281 (Fed. Cir. 1991), *cert. denied*, 112 S. Ct. 934 (1992); and *Salt River Pima–Maricopa Indian Community v. United States*, 26 Cl. Ct. 201 (1992).

Sidebar 3.1

1. Consumptive use of water (water going to evaporation, transpiration, and plant growth) is the most direct measure of water lost to regional watersheds.

2. National Agricultural Statistical Service, *1998 Farm and Ranch Irrigation Survey*, AC97 SP-1 (Washington, D.C.: U.S. Department of Agriculture, 1999).

3. Public Law 104-127, 110 Stat. 888 (1996).

4. M. Vesterby, "Land Use," *Agricultural Resources and Environmental Indicators*, Agricultural Handbook No. 722 (Washington, D.C.: Economic Research Service, U.S. Department of Agriculture, 2001).

5. R. Howitt, "Water Policy Effects on Crop Production and Vice Versa: An Empirical Approach," *Commodity and Resource Policies in Agricultural Systems*, ed. R. Just and N. Bockstael (Berlin: Springer-Verlag, 1991): 234–53.

6. G. Horner et al., "Impacts of San Joaquin Valley Drainage-Related Policies on State and National Agricultural Production," *The Economics and Management of Water and Drainage in Agriculture*, ed. A. Dinar and D. Zilberman (Boston: Kluwer Academic Publishers, 1991): 557–74.

7. R. Just et al. "Effects of the Feed Grain and Wheat Programs on Irrigation and Groundwater Depletion in Nebraska," *Commodity and Resource Policies in Agricultural Systems*, ed. R. Just and N. Bockstael (Berlin: Springer-Verlag, 1991): 215–33.

8. K. Konyar and K. Knapp, "Dynamic Regional Analysis of the

California Alfalfa Market with Government Policy Impacts," *Western Journal of Agricultural Economics* 15, no. 1 (1990): 22–32.

9. M. Moore et al., "Cropland Allocation Decisions: The Role of Agricultural Commodity Programs and the Reclamation Program," *The Economics and Management of Water and Drainages in Agriculture*, ed. A. Dinar and D. Zilberman (Boston: Kluwer Academic Publishers, 1991): 575–96.

10. Andrea Cattaneo, "EQIP: Conserving While Farming," *Agricultural Outlook* AGO-284 (September 2001): 26–27.

11. M. Smith, "Conservation Reserve Enhancement Program: Early Results from a Federal-State Partnership," *Agricultural Outlook* AO-277 (November 2000): 16–20.

12. Timothy Searchinger, *Suggestions to States Interested in Developing Conservation Reserve Enhancement Programs* (Washington, D.C.: Environmental Defense, 1997). Present value captures the notion that a dollar received today is generally worth more to people than a dollar received some time in the (distant) future. Economists and businesses use present-value formulas to convert payments over multiple years to a common unit of measure.

13. Farmers are still prohibited from growing fruits or vegetables on acreage used to compute their payment levels. For a discussion of the effect of legislative changes on crop-planting decisions, see C. Jaggers and J. Harwood, "Ms. Farmer's Wheat Program Adventures—Before and after the 1996 Farm Bill: A Case Study for the Classroom," *Review of Agricultural Economics* 20 (1998): 259–72.

Sidebar 3.2

1. Alan F. Hamlet et al., "Preparing for Climate Change in the Pacific Northwest: A Discussion of Water Resources Adaptation Pathways" (preparatory White Paper for Climate and Water Policy Meeting, Skamania, Washington, July 2001. Climate Impacts Group, University of Washington, Seattle.)

2. Peter H. Gleick, "Vulnerability of Water Systems," *Climate Change and U.S. Water Resources*, ed. P.E. Waggoner (New York: John Wiley and Sons, 1990).

3. A.F. Hamlet and D.P. Lettenmaier, "Long-Range Climate Forecasting and its Use for Water Management in the Pacific North-

west Region of North America," *Journal of Hydroinformatics* 2, no. 3 (2000): 163–82.

4. Edward L. Miles et al., "Pacific Northwest Regional Assessment: The Impacts of Climate Variability and Climate Change on the Water Resources of the Columbia River Basin," *Journal of the American Water Resources Association* 36, no. 2 (2000): 399–420.

Sidebar 4.1

1. *Safe Drinking Water Act*, 42 U.S.C. § 300f *et seq.* (1991).

2. See discussion of the Clean Water Act's legislative history at *Federal Register* 56 (1991): 64,876.

3. 42 U.S.C. § 300j-11 (1998).

4. *City of Albuquerque v. Browner*, 865 F. Supp. 733 (D.N.M. 1993).

Sidebar 6.2

1. 5 U.S.C. § 552 (2004).

2. *Department of the Interior v. Klamath Water Users Protective Association*, 532 U.S. 1 (2001).

Sidebar 6.6

1. Art. I, § 9, cl. 7.

2. *Balanced Budget and Emergency Deficit Control Act*, Public Law 99-177, 99 Stat. 1037 (1985); *Balanced Budget and Emergency Deficit Control Reaffirmation Act*, Public Law 100-119, 101 Stat. 754 (1987).

Sidebar 7.1

1. Although the U.S. Supreme Court in 1980 awarded $122.5 million to the Sioux Nation for abrogation of treaties and loss of lands (including South Dakota's Black Hills), many Sioux concluded that money was not land, and that they wanted the land. See Patricia N. Limerick, *The Legacy of Conquest* (New York: W.W. Norton & Co., 1987): 334.

2. See Helen Ingram and Lee Brown, *Water and Poverty in the Southwest* (Tucson: University of Arizona Press, 1987).

APPENDIX

TABLE A.1 Indian water rights settlements and quantification cases (chronological)

Settlement or court case	Indian tribe(s)	State	Quantity of entitlement (afa)*	Year of settlement/ case	References	Comments
Ak-Chin Indian Water Rights Settlement Act	Ak-Chin Indian Community	AZ	85,000	1978 1984 1992	P.L. 95-328, 92 Stat. 409 (1978) P.L. 95-530, 98 Stat. 2698 (1984) P.L. 102-497, 106 Stat. 3255 (1992) P.L. 106-285, 114 Stat. 878 (2000)	▪ Original legislation modified due to impractical water supply plans ▪ No local cost share; fully federally funded
Southern Arizona Water Rights Settlement Act (SAWRSA)	San Xavier and Schuk Toak districts, Tohono O'odham Nation	AZ	66,000	1982 1992 2004	P.L. 97-293, 96 Stat. 1274 (1982) P.L. 102-497, 106 Stat. 3255 (1992)	▪ Allows limited off-reservation leasing ▪ Provides federal project water for tribe ▪ Title III of Arizona Water Settlements Act of 2004 (Kyl/McCain, R-AZ) settles Tohono O'odham's litigation concerning implementation of 1982 settlement
Fort Peck– Montana Compact	Assiniboine and Sioux tribes	MT	1,050,472	1985	Mont. Code Ann. § 85-20-201 *et seq.* (1987 Supp.)	▪ Established permanent compact board to oversee implementation and to resolve disputes ▪ Allows limited off-reservation leasing ▪ Settlement never ratified by Congress
Salt River Pima– Maricopa Indian Community Water Rights Settlement Act	Salt River Pima– Maricopa Indian Community	AZ	122,400	1988	P.L. 100-512, 102 Stat. 2549 (1988)	▪ Complex multiparty water exchanges ▪ Significant local cost sharing at insistence of federal government

TABLE A.1 Continued

Settlement or court case	Indian tribe(s)	State	Quantity of entitlement (afa)*	Year of settlement/ case	References	Comments
Colorado Ute Indian Water Rights Settlement Act	Southern Ute and Ute Mountain Ute tribes	CO	70,000	1988	P.L. 100-585, 102 Stat. 2973 (1988) P.L. 106-554, 114 Stat. 2763 (2000)	▪ Implementation delayed due to controversy over Animas–La Plata Project ▪ Off-reservation water-leasing provisions ▪ Colorado Ute Settlement Act Amendments of 2000 downsized reservoir (120,000 af)
San Luis Rey Indian Water Rights Settlement Act	La Jolla, Rincon, San Pasquale, Pauma, and Pala bands of Mission Indians	CA		1988	P.L. 100-675, 102 Stat. 4000 (1988)	▪ No firm source of settlement water identified ▪ Envisions conservation measures to provide water for entitlement
Wind River adjudication	Eastern Shoshone and Northern Arapaho	WY	490,000 divided into historic and future water uses	1989	Fully litigated, decreed water right; *In re General Adjudication of All Rights to Use Water in the Big Horn River System*, 753 P.2d 76 (Wyo. 1988)	▪ Tribes disallowed use of water for instream flow purposes ▪ Continuing litigation concerning different aspects of the settlement and implementation
Truckee-Carson–Pyramid Lake Water Rights Settlement Act	Pyramid Lake Paiute Tribes	NV	520,000	1990	P.L. 101-618, 104 Stat. 3289 (1990)	▪ Environmental concerns played major role in shaping settlement ▪ Revised criteria for reservoir operation a key component
Fallon Paiute-Shoshone Tribes Water Rights Settlement Act	Fallon Paiute and Shoshone tribes	NV	10,588	1990	P.L. 101-618, 104 Stat. 3289 (1990)	▪ Designed primarily to settle tribal claims against federal government for failure to construct a long-promised irrigation system ▪ Not initially intended to settle reserved water rights claims

TABLE A.1 Continued

Settlement or court case	Indian tribe(s)	State	Quantity of entitle-ment (afa)*	Year of settle-ment/case	References	Comments
Fort Hall Indian Water Rights Act	Shoshone and Bannock tribes	ID	581,331	1990	P.L. 101-602, 104 Stat. 3059 (1990)	▪ Relies on unallocated federal water supplies ▪ Authorizes establishment of a water bank ▪ Established intergovernmental board to resolve settlement-related disputes
Fort McDowell Indian Community Water Rights Settlement Act	Fort McDowell Indian Community	AZ	36,350	1990	P.L. 101-628, 104 Stat. 4480 (1990)	▪ Considerable controversy over water supply ▪ Secretary left to identify water source ▪ Allows limited off-reservation leasing
Northern Cheyenne Indian Reserved Water Rights Settlement Act	Northern Cheyenne Tribe	MT	91,330	1992	P.L. 102-374, 106 Stat. 1186 (1992)	▪ Addresses issues of tribal and state jurisdiction and water rights administration ▪ Most off-reservation leases subject to state law
San Carlos Apache Tribe Water Rights Settlement Act	San Carlos Apache Tribe	AZ	77,435	1992	P.L. 102-575, 106 Stat. 4600 (1992)	▪ Entitlement primarily comprises CAP water ▪ Allows limited off-reservation leasing ▪ Portion of water source strongly opposed by Arizona's non-Indian agricultural community
Reclamation Projects Authorization and Adjustment Act	Northern Ute Tribe	UT	481,000	1992	P.L. 102-575, 106 Stat. 4600 (1992)	▪ Designed primarily to resolve tribal claims against the federal government

TABLE A.1 Continued

Settlement or court case	Indian tribe(s)	State	Quantity of entitlement (afa)*	Year of settlement/ case	References	Comments
Jicarilla Apache Tribe Water Rights Settlement Act	Jicarilla Apache Tribe	NM	40,000	1992	P.L. 102-441, 106 Stat. 2237 (1992)	▪ Tribe received off-reservation water-marketing rights ▪ Extensive endangered species recovery and conservation program coordination ▪ Federal court approval in 1998 ▪ 1,560 afa historic uses plus 40,000 afa future uses
Yakima basin adjudication	Yakima Indian Nation	WA	Instream and irrigation rights	1993	*State of Wash. v. Yakima Reservation Irrigation Dist.*, 850 P.2d 1306 (Wash. 1993)	▪ State supreme court affirms general adjudication court of instream flow right limited to "minimum flow" and irrigation rights substantially less than claimed
Yavapai-Prescott Indian Tribe Water Rights Settlement Act	Yavapai-Prescott Tribe	AZ	Up to 16,000	1994	P.L. 103-434, 108 Stat. 4526 (1994)	▪ Tribe has the right to pump groundwater within the boundaries of the reservation ▪ Water contract with the City of Prescott ▪ May divert water from nearby creek currently diverted by local irrigation district
Las Vegas Artesian Basin	Las Vegas Paiute Tribe	NV	2,000	1996	*In re Rights to Waters of the Las Vegas Artesian Basin* (Clark Co., Sept. 30, 1996)	▪ Stipulated settlement among tribe, United States, Nevada, and Las Vegas Valley Water District ▪ Settles litigation over tribal rights ▪ Recognizes permanent groundwater rights
Warm Springs	Confederated Tribes of Warm Springs	OR	Up to 450 cfs** diverted	1997	Confederated Tribes of the Warm Springs Reservation Water Rights Settlement Agreement (1997)	▪ Recognizes instream flows in Metolius and Deschutes rivers ▪ 200 cfs may be marketed off-reservation ▪ Tribal rights recognized as most senior; can be used for any on-reservation purpose, and may be satisfied with groundwater ▪ Congressional approval not anticipated

TABLE A.1   Continued

Settlement or court case	Indian tribe(s)	State	Quantity of entitlement (afa)*	Year of settlement/ case	References	Comments
Chippewa Cree Tribe of the Rocky Boy's Reservation Indian Reserved Water Rights Settlement and Water Supply Enhancement Act	Chippewa Cree Tribe	MT	20,000	1999	P.L. 106-163, 113 Stat. 1778 (1999)	▪ Court order approving the Chippewa Cree Tribe–Montana compact filed on 5/22/02 ▪ Federal funding for a water treatment plant and piping to the reservation ▪ Bush administration opposes $200 million authorization necessary to build pipe from Tiber Reservoir
Crow Tribe–Montana Compact	Crow Tribe	MT	500,000 plus 300,000 storage	1999	Mont. Code Ann. § 85-20-901 (2003)	▪ 500,000 afa from Bighorn River; tribe entitled to 300,000 afa of water stored in Bighorn Lake ▪ Closes certain basins to new appropriations under state law ▪ Negotiations on streamflow management plan for Bighorn River and allotment issues must be completed before settlement is submitted to Congress and ratified by tribal referendum
Shivwits Band of the Paiute Indian Tribe of Utah Water Rights Settlement Act	Shivwits Paiute Band	UT	4,000	2000	P.L. 106-263, 114 Stat. 737 (2000)	▪ Cost sharing for operating costs for a water treatment facility to provide 2,000 afa of "firm" water to the band ▪ Pooling of water in Gunlock Reservoir to be provided to band by local water conservation district, with supplements in dry years through groundwater pumping ▪ Some instream flow rights, and a habitat acquisition program ▪ $24 million federal appropriation ▪ State court has approved

TABLE A.1 Continued

Settlement or court case	Indian tribe(s)	State	Quantity of entitlement (afa)*	Year of settlement/ case	References	Comments
Fort Belknap–Montana Compact	Gros Ventre and Assiniboine tribes	MT	650 cfs plus other diversions	2001	Mont. Code Ann. § 85-20-1001 (2003)	▪ Right to divert 645 cfs from Milk River plus other amounts for specific lands; tribes may divert hydrologically connected groundwater within quantification limits ▪ Negotiations continue on bill that must go to Congress; issues concern damages for past federal takings of land and water
Zuni Indian Tribe Water Rights Settlement Act	Zuni Pueblo	AZ	1,500 afa groundwater; up to 3,500 afa surface water may be purchased	2003	P.L. 108-34, 117 Stat. 782 (2003)	▪ Settlement addresses Zuni Pueblo's land in Arizona, known as Zuni Heaven ▪ $26.5 million would be used to acquire water and settle claims, implement the agreement, and restore Zuni Reservation land. Of that sum, $19.25 million will come from federal government.
Arizona Water Settlements Act	Gila River Indian Community	AZ	655,000	2004	P.L. 108-451 (2004)	▪ Water from CAP, Gila, Salt and Verde Rivers used for the settlement ▪ Allows off-reservation sale or leasing, but not out of state ▪ Sets Arizona's CAP repayment obligation at $1.65 billion ▪ $24 million authorized for implementation of the settlement
Snake River Water Rights Act	Nez Perce	ID	50,000	2004	P.L. 108-447, 118 Stat. 2809 (2004)	▪ Gives the tribe access and use rights for the Nez Perce Springs ▪ Waives future tribal and allottee water rights claims and claims for injuries to the tribe's treaty fishing rights ▪ Allows leasing of tribal water

*acre-feet annually, unless otherwise indicated
**cubic feet per second

BIBLIOGRAPHY

Legislation

Act to Convey Certain Lands to the Zuni Indian Tribe for Religious Purposes. Public Law 98-408, 98 Stat. 1533 (1984).

Act of June 13, 1962. Public Law 87-483, 76 Stat. 96 (codified as amended in 43 U.S.C. § 620).

Ak-Chin Water Use Amendments Act of 1992. Public Law 102-497, 106 Stat. 3255 (1992).

Arizona Water Settlements Act of 2004, S. 2992, 107th Cong., 2d sess. tit. III, §§ 304 & 306 (2002), reintroduced as S. 437 and HR 885, 108th Cong., 1st sess. (2003), signed by president December 10, 2004, P.L. 108-451.

Balanced Budget and Emergency Deficit Control Act. Public Law 99-177, 99 Stat. 1037 (1985).

Balanced Budget and Emergency Deficit Control Reaffirmation Act. Public Law 100-119, 101 Stat. 754 (1987).

Budget Enforcement Act of 1990. Public Law 101-508, 104 Stat. 1388 (1990).

Chippewa Cree Tribe of the Rocky Boy's Reservation Indian Reserved Water Rights Settlement and Water Supply Enhancement Act of 1999. Public Law 106-163, 113 Stat. 1778 (December 9, 1999).

Clean Water Act. 33 U.S.C. § 1251–1387 (1988).

Colorado Ute Indian Water Rights Settlement Act of 1988. Public Law 100-585, 102 Stat. 2973 (November 3, 1988).

Comprehensive Environmental Response and Liability Act. 42 U.S.C. § 9601 et seq. (2003).

Endangered Species Act of 1973. 16 U.S.C. § 1531 (1973).

Fallon Paiute-Shoshone Indian Tribes Water Rights Settlement Act of 1990. Public Law 101-618, 104 Stat. 3289 (1990).

Federal Agricultural Improvement and Reform Act. Public Law 104-127, 110 Stat. 888 (1996).

Fort Hall Indian Water Rights Act of 1990. Public Law 101-602, 104 Stat. 3059 (November 16, 1990).

Freedom of Information Act. 5 U.S.C. § 552 (2004).

General Allotment Act. 25 U.S.C. §§ 331-334, 339, 341, 342, 348, 349, 354, 381 (1983).

Indian Nonintercourse Act. 25 U.S.C. § 177 (2003).

Indian Reorganization Act. 25 U.S.C. § 461 et seq. (1934).

Indian Self-Determination and Educational Assistance Act of 1975. 25 U.S.C. §§ 450-450n, 455-458e (1982).

Jicarilla Apache Tribe Water Rights Settlement Act. Public Law 102-441, 106 Stat. 2237 (October 23, 1992).

McCarran Amendment. 43 U.S.C. § 666(a) (1952).

National Environmental Policy Act. 42 U.S.C. §§ 4321 to 4370e (2003).

Northern Cheyenne Indian Reserved Water Rights Settlement Act of 1992. Public Law 102-374, 106 Stat. 1186 (September 30, 1992).

Northern Cheyenne–Montana Compact. Mont. Code Ann. § 85-20-301 (2002).

Omnibus Appropriations Act of 2000. Public Law 106-544, 114 Stat. 2763 (2000).

Reclamation Act of 1902. 32 Stat. 388, 43 U.S.C. § 391 (June 17, 1902).

Reclamation Projects Authorization and Adjustment Act of 1992. Public Law 102-575, 106 Stat. 4600 (1992).

Safe Drinking Water Act. 42 U.S.C. § 300f et seq. (1991).

Salt River Pima–Maricopa Indian Community Water Rights Settlement Act of 1988. Public Law 100-512, 102 Stat. 2549 (1988).

Settlement of Ak-Chin Water Rights Claims. Public Law 95-328, 92 Stat. 409 (1978).

Shivwits Band of the Paiute Indian Tribe of Utah Water Rights Settlement Act. Public Law 106-263, 114 Stat. 737. August 18, 2000.

Snake River Water Rights Act. Public Law 108-447, 118 Stat. 2809 (December 8, 2004).

Southern Arizona Water Rights Settlement Act. Public Law 97-293, 96 Stat. 1261 (1982); amended by Public Law 102-497, 106 Stat. 3255 (1992); amended by Public Law 108-451 (2004).

Supplemental Appropriations Act. Public Law 99-88, 99 Stat. 293 (1985).

Treaty with the Tribes of Middle Oregon. 12 Stat. 963 (June 25, 1855).

Truckee-Carson–Pyramid Lake Water Rights Settlement Act. Public Law 101-618, 104 Stat. 3289 (1990).

U.S. Senate. *Fiscal Integrity of Indian Settlements Protection Act of 2001.* 107th Cong., 1st sess., S. 1186.

Zuni Indian Tribe Water Rights Settlement Act of 2003. Public Law 108-34, 117 Stat. 782 (June 23, 2003).

Zuni Land Conservation Act of 1990, Public Law 101-486, 104 Stat. 1174 (1990).

Cases

Arizona v. California. 373 U.S. 546 (1963), *decreed in final form*, 376 U.S. 340 (1964), *decree amended*, 383 U.S. 268 (1966), *supplemental decree entered*, 439 U.S. 419 (1979), *supplemental opinion*, 460 U.S. 605 (1983) *[Arizona II], second supplemental decree entered*, 466 U.S. 144 (1984).

Arizona v. San Carlos Apache Tribe. 463 U.S. 545 (1983).

Board of Control v. United States, 646 F. Supp. 410 (D. Mont. 1986), 832 F.2d 1127 (9th Cir. 1987), 862 F.2d 195 (9th Cir. 1988).

Brendale v. Confederated Tribes and Bands of the Yakima Indian Nation, 492 U.S. 408 (1989).

Carson-Truckee Water Conservancy District v. Clark. 741 F.2d 257 (9th Cir. 1984), *cert. denied*, 470 U.S. 1083 (1985).

Cherokee Nation v. Georgia. 30 U.S. 1 (1831).

City of Albuquerque v. Browner. 865 F. Supp. 733 (D.N.M. 1993).

Colville Confederated Tribes v. Walton. 460 F. Supp. 1320 (E.D. Wash. 1978).

Colville Confederated Tribes v. Walton. 752 F.2d 397 (9th Cir. 1985), *cert. denied*, 454 U.S. 1092 (1981).

Colville Confederated Tribes v. Walton. 647 F.2d 42 (9th Cir.), *cert. denied*, 454 U.S. 1092 (1981).

Confederated Salish and Kootenai v. Flathead Irr. Dist. 616 F. Supp. 1292 (D. Mont. 1985).

Department of the Interior v. Klamath Water Users Protective Association, 532 U.S. 1 (2001).

Findings of Fact and Order of Determination, In re the Relative Rights to the Use of Waters of the Streams and Rivers of the Warm Springs Indian Reservation. (Deschutes County Cir. Ct. 2002)

Grey v. United States. 21 Cl. Ct. 285 (1990), *aff'd without opp.*, 935 F.2d 281 (Fed. Cir. 1991), *cert. denied*, 112 S. Ct. 934 (1992).

In re General Adjudication of All Rights to Use Water in the Big Horn River System, 753 P.2d 76, (Wyo. 1988), *affirmed sub. nom.*, *Wyoming v. United States*, 492 U.S. 406 (1989) *[Big Horn I]*; 803 P.2d 61 (Wyo. 1990) *[Big Horn II]*; 835 P.2d 273 (Wyo. 1992) *[Big Horn III]*; Wyoming Supreme Court Opinion No. 93-49, slip op. (October 26, 1993) *[Big Horn IV]*; 899 P.2d 848 (Wyo. 1995) *[Big Horn V]*; 48 P.3d 1040 (Wyo. 2002) *[Big Horn VI]*.

In re General Adjudication of All Rights to Use Water in the Gila River System and Source, 989 P.2d 739 (Ariz. 1999), *cert. denied sub. nom.*, *Phelps Dodge Corp. v. United States* and *Salt River Valley Water Users' Association v. United States*, 530 U.S. 1250 (2000); 35 P.3d 68 (Ariz. 2001); Order of February 20, 2002, amended *nunc pro tunc* March 7, 2002, *In re All Rights to Water in the Gila River*, No. W-1 (Maricopa County Super. Ct.).

Kandra v. United States, 145 F. Supp. 2d 1192 (D. Ore. 2001).

Morton v. Mancari, 417 U.S. 535 (1974).

Muckleshoot Indian Tribe v. Trans-Canada Enterprises, Ltd., 713 F.2d 455 (9th Cir. 1983), *cert. denied*, 465 U.S. 1049 (1984).

Navajo Tribe of Indians v. United States, 364 F.2d 320 (Cl. Ct. 1966).

Nevada v. United States, 463 U.S. 110 (1983).

New Mexico ex rel. Reynolds v. United States, No. 75-184 (11th Jud. Dist., San Juan County, N.M., filed March 13, 1975).

New Mexico ex rel. State Engineer v. Aamodt, No. 66CV6639MV (D.N.M. 1966).

New Mexico ex rel. State Engineer v. Abeyta, No. 69CV7896BB and 69CV7939BB, consolidated (D.N.M. 1969).

Northern Arapahoe Tribe v. Hodel, 808 F.2d 741 (10th Cir. 1987).

Northern Cheyenne v. Adsit, 668 F.2d 1080 (9th Cir. 1982).

Puyallup Tribe, Inc., v. Department of Game, 443 U.S. 165 (1977).

Pyramid Lake Paiute Tribe v. Morton, 354 F. Supp. 252 (D.D.C. 1972).

Pyramid Lake Paiute Tribe v. U.S. Department of Navy, 898 F.2d 1410 (9th Cir. 1990).

Rice v. Rehner, 463 U.S. 713 (1983).

Salt River Pima–Maricopa Indian Community v. United States, 26 Cl. Ct. 201 (1992).

San Carlos Apache Tribe v. Superior Court, 972 P.2d 179 (Ariz. 1999).

Seminole Nation v. United States, 316 U.S. 286 (1942).

Seneca Nation of Indians v. Brucker, 262 F.2d 27 (D.C. Cir. 1958), *cert. denied*, 360 U.S. 909 (1959).

Seneca Nation of Indians v. United States, 338 F.2d 55 (2nd Cir. 1964), *cert. denied*, 380 U.S. 952 (1965).

United States v. Adair, 723 F.2d 1394 (9th Cir. 1983), *cert. denied*, 467 U.S. 1252 (1984).

United States v. Ahtanum Irrigation District, 236 F.2d 321 (9th Cir. 1956), *cert. denied*, 352 U.S. 988 (1957).

United States v. Eberhardt, 789 F.2d 1354 (9th Cir. 1986).

United States v. Mazurie, 419 U.S. 544 (1975).

United States v. Mitchell, 463 U.S. 206 (1983).

United States v. Morrison Consolidated Ditch Co., No. 7736 (D. Colo. February 14, 1931).

United States v. Oregon, 44 F.3d 758 (9th Cir. 1994), *cert. denied*, 516 U.S. 934 (1995).

United States v. Orr Ditch Co., Final Decree No. A-3 (D. Nev. 1944).

United States v. Powers, 305 U.S. 527 (1939).

United States v. Southern Pacific Trans. Co., 543 F.2d 676 (9th Cir. 1976).

United States v. Superior Court, 697 P.2d 658 (Ariz. 1985).

United States v. Washington, 384 F. Supp. 312 (W.D. Wash. 1974) *aff'd*, 520 F.2d 676 (9th Cir. 1975), *cert. denied*, 423 U.S. 1086 (1976).

United States v. Washington, Phase II, No. 9213 (W.D. Wash., September 26, 1980).

United States v. Winans, 198 U.S. 371 (1905).

United States v. Winnebago Tribe, 542 F.2d 1002 (8th Cir. 1976).

Washington v. Confederated Tribes, 447 U.S. 134 (1980).

Winters v. United States, 207 U.S. 564 (1908).

Wyoming v. United States, 492 U.S. 406 (1989).

Zuni Tribe v. Platt, 730 F. Supp. 318 (D. Ariz. 1990).

Books

Amundson, Ann E., and American Indian Resources Institute [AIRI]. *Tribal Water Management Handbook*. Oakland, Calif.: AIRI, 1988.

Burton, Lloyd. *American Indian Water Rights and the Limits of Law*. Lawrence: University Press of Kansas, 1991.

Cather, Willa. *My Antonia*. Boston: Houghton Mifflin, 1949.

Checchio, Elizabeth, and Bonnie·G. Colby. *Indian Water Rights: Negotiating the Future*. Tucson: Water Resources Research Center, College of Agriculture, University of Arizona, 1993.

Checchio, Elizabeth, and the University of Arizona Department of Hydrology and Water Resources. *Water Farming: The Promise and Problems of Water Transfers in Arizona*. Tucson: Dept. of Hydrology and Water Resources, University of Arizona, 1988.

Cohen, Felix S. *Handbook of Federal Indian Law*. Albuquerque: University of New Mexico Press, 1971.

Cohen, Felix S., and Rennard Strickland. *Felix S. Cohen's Handbook of Federal Indian Law*. Charlottesville, Va.: Michie Bobbs-Merrill, 1982.

Cohen, Felix S., and U.S. Department of the Interior. Office of the Solicitor. *Handbook of Federal Indian Law with Reference Tables and Index*. Washington: U.S. G.P.O., 1942. Microform.

Coleman, Peter T. "Intractable Conflict." In *The Handbook of Conflict Resolution: Theory and Practice*, edited by Morton Deutsch and Peter T. Coleman, 428–50. San Francisco, Calif.: Jossey-Bass, 2000.

Crawford, Stanley G. *Mayordomo: Chronicle of an Acequia in Northern New Mexico*. 1st ed. Albuquerque: University of New Mexico Press, 1988.

DuMars, Charles T., Marilyn O'Leary, and Albert E. Utton. *Pueblo Indian Water Rights: Struggle for a Precious Resource*. Tucson: University of Arizona Press, 1984.

Folk-Williams, John A., and Lucy Hilgendorf. *What Indian Water Means to the West: A Sourcebook*. Edited by John A. Folk-Williams. Water in the West, vol. 1. Santa Fe, N.Mex.: Western Network, 1982.

Foreman, Richard L. *Indian Water Rights: A Public Policy and Administrative Mess*. Danville, Ill.: Interstate Printers and Publishers, 1981.

Gerrard, Michael B., ed. *The Law of Environmental Justice: Theories and Procedures to Address Disproportionate Risks*. Chicago: ABA Section of Environment, Energy, and Resources, 1999.

Getches, David H. *Water Law in a Nutshell*. 3rd ed. St. Paul, Minn.: West Publishing, 1997.

Getches, David H., Charles F. Wilkinson, and Robert A. Williams. *Cases and Materials on Federal Indian Law*. 4th ed. St. Paul, Minn.: West Group, 1998.

Gibson, Arrell Morgan. *The American Indian: Prehistory to the Present*. Lexington, Mass.: D.C. Heath, 1980.

Gleick, Peter H. "Vulnerability of Water Systems." In *Climate*

Change and U.S. Water Resources, edited by P.E. Waggoner, 223–40. New York: John Wiley and Sons, 1990.

Grey, Zane. *Riders of the Purple Sage*. New York: Harper and Brothers, 1912.

Hare, Jon C. *Indian Water Rights: An Analysis of Current and Pending Indian Water Rights Settlements*. Washington, D.C.: Office of Trust Responsibilities, Bureau of Indian Affairs; Oakville, Wash.: Confederated Tribes of the Chehalis Reservation, 1996.

Heizer, Robert Fleming, and Albert B. Elsasser. *The Natural World of the California Indians*. Berkeley: University of California Press, 1980.

Horner, G., S. Hatchett, R. House, and R. Howitt. "Impacts of San Joaquin Valley Drainage-Related Policies on State and National Agricultural Production." In *The Economics and Management of Water and Drainage in Agriculture*, edited by A. Dinar and D. Zilberman, 557–74. Boston: Kluwer Academic Publishers, 1991.

Howe, Charles W., Colorado Water Resources Research Institute, and U.S. Geological Survey. *Urban Water Supply Reliability: Preferences of Managers, Elected Officials and Water Users in Boulder, Colorado*. Fort Collins: Colorado Water Resources Research Institute, Colorado State University, 1990.

Howitt, R. "Water Policy Effects on Crop Production and Vice Versa: An Empirical Approach." In *Commodity and Resource Policies in Agricultural Systems*, edited by R. Just and N. Bockstael, 234–53. Berlin: Springer-Verlag, 1991.

Hoxie, Frederick E. *A Final Promise: The Campaign to Assimilate the Indians, 1880–1920*. Bison Books ed. Lincoln: University of Nebraska Press, 2001.

———, ed. *Encyclopedia of North American Indians: Native American History, Culture, and Life From Paleo-Indians to the Present*. New York: Houghton Mifflin, 1996.

Hoxie, Frederick E., Peter C. Mancall, and James Hart Merrell. *American Nations: Encounters in Indian Country, 1850 to the Present*. New York; London: Routledge, 2001.

Ingram, Helen, and Lee Brown. *Water and Poverty in the Southwest*. Tucson: University of Arizona Press, 1987.

Institute for the Development of Indian Law. *Indian Water Rights*. Washington, D.C.: Institute for the Development of Indian Law, 1984.

Josephy, Alvin M. *America in 1492: The World of the Indian Peoples Before the Arrival of Columbus*. New York: Knopf, 1992.

Just, R., E. Lichtenberg, and D. Zilberman. "Effects of the Feed Grain and Wheat Programs on Irrigation and Groundwater Depletion in Nebraska." In *Commodity and Resource Policies in Agricultural Systems*, edited by R. Just and N. Bockstael, 215–33. Berlin: Springer-Verlag, 1991.

Kemmis, Daniel. *This Sovereign Land: A New Vision for Governing the West*. Washington, D.C.: Island Press, 2001.

Knack, Martha C., and Omer Call Stewart. *As Long as the River Shall Run: An Ethnohistory of Pyramid Lake Indian Reservation*. Berkeley: University of California Press, 1984.

Limerick, Patricia Nelson. *The Legacy of Conquest: The Unbroken Past of the American West*. 1st ed. New York: Norton, 1987.

Maass, Arthur, and Raymond Lloyd Anderson. *. . . And the Desert Shall Rejoice: Conflict, Growth, and Justice in Arid Environments*. Cambridge, Mass.: MIT Press, 1978.

McCool, Daniel. *Command of the Waters: Iron Triangles, Federal Water Development, and Indian Water*. Tucson: University of Arizona Press, 1994.

———. *Native Waters: Contemporary Indian Water Settlements and the Second Treaty Era*. Tucson: University of Arizona Press, 2002.

McGuire, Thomas R., William B. Lord, and Mary G. Wallace. *Indian Water in the New West*. Tucson: University of Arizona Press, 1993.

Membrino, Joseph R. "Indian Water Rights and Water Resources Management Goals and Objectives of the Affected Parties: A Federal Perspective." In *Sourcebook on Indian Water Settlements*, edited by American Indian Lawyer Training Program. Oakland, Calif.: AIRI, 1989.

Momaday, N. Scott. *The Way to Rainy Mountain*. 1st ed. Albuquerque: University of New Mexico Press, 1969.

Moore, M., D. Negri, and J. Miranowski. "Cropland Allocation Decisions: The Role of Agricultural Commodity Programs and the Reclamation Program." In *The Economics and Management of Water and Drainages in Agriculture*, edited by A. Dinar and D. Zilberman, 575–96. Boston: Kluwer Academic Publishers, 1991.

O'Gara, Geoffrey. *What You See in Clear Water: Life on the Wind River Reservation*. New York: Alfred Knopf, 2000.

Otis, D.S., Francis Paul Prucha, and U.S. Congress, Committee on Indian Affairs. *The Dawes Act and the Allotment of Indian Lands*. Norman: University of Oklahoma Press, 1973.

Prucha, Francis Paul. *American Indian Policy in Crisis: Christian Reformers and the Indian, 1865–1900*. 1st ed. Norman: University of Oklahoma Press, 1976.

———. *American Indian Policy in the Formative Years: The Indian Trade and Intercourse Acts, 1780–1834*. Cambridge: Harvard University Press, 1962.

———. *American Indian Treaties: The History of a Political Anomaly*. Berkeley: University of California Press, 1994.

———, ed. *Documents of United States Indian Policy*. Lincoln: University of Nebraska Press, 2000.

———. *The Great Father: The United States Government and the American Indians*. Abridged ed. Lincoln: University of Nebraska Press, 1986.

Rassier, Phillip J. *Indian Water Rights: A Study of the Historical and Legal Factors Affecting the Water Rights of the Indians of the State of Idaho*. Prepared for State of Idaho, Department of Water Resources. Boise: Idaho Department of Water Resources, 1978.

Reisner, Marc. *Cadillac Desert: The American West and Its Disappearing Water*. Rev. ed. New York: Penguin Books, 1993.

Rice, Teresa A., and Lawrence J. MacDonnell. *Agricultural to Urban Water Transfers: An Assessment of the Issues and Options*. Fort Collins: Colorado Water Resources Research Institute, Colorado State University, 1993.

Shaake, John C. "From Climate to Flow." In *Climate Change and U.S. Water Resources*, edited by P.E. Waggoner. New York: John Wiley and Sons, 1990.

Shurts, John. *Indian Reserved Water Rights: The Winters Doctrine in Its Social and Legal Context, 1880s–1930s*. Legal History of North America, vol. 8. Norman: University of Oklahoma Press, 2000.

Sly, Peter W. *Reserved Water Rights Settlement Manual*. Washington, D.C.: Island Press, 1988.

Thorson, John E. "Resolving Conflicts through Intergovernmental Agreements: The Pros and Cons of Negotiated Settlements." In *Indian Water 1985*, edited by Christine L. Miklas and Steven J. Shupe, 25–47. Oakland, Calif.: American Indian Lawyer Training Program, 1986.

U.S. Department of the Interior, Bureau of Indian Affairs. *Indian*

Water Rights: A Fact Book. Washington, D.C.: Department of the Interior, Bureau of Indian Affairs, 1978.

Veeder, William H. *Indian Water Rights in the Concluding Years of the Twentieth Century.* Chicago, Ill.: Newberry Library, 1982.

Vesterby, M. "Land Use." In *Agricultural Resources and Environmental Indicators.* Agricultural Handbook No. 722. Washington, D.C.: Economic Research Service, U.S. Department of Agriculture, 2001.

Weatherford, Gary D., and F. Lee Brown. *New Courses for the Colorado River: Major Issues for the Next Century.* 1st ed. Albuquerque: University of New Mexico Press, 1986.

Weatherford, Gary D., Mary Wallace, and Lee Herold Storey. *Leasing Indian Water: Choices in the Colorado River Basin.* Washington, D.C.: Conservation Foundation; Napa, Calif.: John Muir Institute, 1988.

Wilkinson, Charles F. *American Indians, Time and the Law: Native Societies in a Modern Constitutional Democracy.* New Haven, Conn.; London: Yale University Press, 1987.

———. *The Eagle Bird: Mapping a New West.* 1st ed. New York: Pantheon Books, 1992.

Wilkinson, Charles F., Christine L. Miklas, American Indian Lawyer Training Program, and Indian Resources Institute (U.S.). *Indian Tribes as Sovereign Governments: A Sourcebook on Federal-Tribal History, Law, and Policy.* Oakland, Calif.: AIRI Press, 1988.

Williams, Terry Tempest. "A Soft Wind Blowing Through the American West." In *A Society to Match the Scenery: Personal Visions of the Future of the American West,* edited by Gary Holthaus, Patricia Nelson Limerick, Charles F. Wilkinson, and Eve Stryker Munson, 51–60. Boulder: University Press of Colorado, 1991.

Periodicals

Anderson, Shea. "Navajo Farm Is a Federal Money Pit." *New Mexico Business Weekly,* January 14, 2002.

Cattaneo, Andrea. "EQIP: Conserving While Farming." *Agricultural Outlook,* AGO-284 (September 2001): 26–27.

Chambers, Reid P. "Judicial Enforcement of the Federal Trust Responsibility to Indians." *Stanford Law Journal* 27 (1975): 1213.

Colby, Bonnie G., Mark McGinnis, and Kent Rait. "Mitigating Environmental Externalities through Voluntary and Involuntary Water Reallocation." *Natural Resources Journal* 30 (1991): 757.

Collins, Richard B. "Indian Allotment Water Rights." *Land and Water Law Review* 20 (1985): 421.

Cosens, Barbara A. "The 1997 Water Rights Settlement between the State of Montana and the Chippewa Cree Tribe of the Rocky Boy's Reservation: The Role of Community and of the Trustee." *UCLA Journal of Environmental Law and Policy* (1997/1998): 255.

———. "Water Dispute Resolution in the West: Process Elements for the Modern Era in Basin-Wide Problem Solving." *Environmental Law* 33 (2003): 949.

DuMars, Charles T., and Helen Ingram. "Congressional Quantification of Indian Reserved Water Rights: A Definitive Solution or a Mirage?" *Natural Resources Journal* 20 (1980): 17.

Folk-Williams, John A. "The Use of Negotiated Agreements to Resolve Water Disputes Involving Indian Water Rights." *Natural Resources Journal* 28 (1988): 1.

Getches, David H. "The Metamorphosis of Western Water Policy: Have Federal Laws and Local Decisions Eclipsed the States' Role?" *Stanford Environmental Law Journal* 20, no. 1 (2000): 3–72.

———. "Water Rights on Indian Allotments." *South Dakota Law Review* 26 (1981): 405.

"Grieving for the Salmon Nation." *Indian Country Today.* Editorial. October 4, 2002. Available at www.indiancountry.com/?103374 0362 (visited July 6, 2004).

Hamlet, Alan F., and Dennis P. Lettenmaier, "Long-Range Climate Forecasting and its Use for Water Management in the Pacific Northwest Region of North America." *Journal of Hydroinformatics* 2, no. 3 (2000): 163–82.

Hobbs, Gregory J., Jr. *Manchu Picchu* book review. *University of Denver Water Law Review* 6, no. 1 (Fall 2002): 137, 140.

Jaggers, C., and J. Harwood. "Ms. Farmer's Wheat Program Adventures—Before and after the 1996 Farm Bill: A Case Study for the Classroom." *Review of Agricultural Economics* 20 (1998): 259–72.

Jenkins, Myra Ellen. "Spanish Land Grants in the Tewa Area." *New Mexico Historical Review* 47 (April 1972): 113–34.

Konyar, K., and K. Knapp. "Dynamic Regional Analysis of the California Alfalfa Market with Government Policy Impacts." *Western Journal of Agricultural Economics* 15, no. 1 (1990): 22–32.

"Look Who's Cashing in at Indian Casinos." *Time,* December 16, 2002, p. 48+.

McCool, Daniel. "Intergovernmental Conflict and Indian Water Rights: An Assessment of Negotiated Settlements." *Publius* 23, no. 1 (1993): 85–102.

———. "The Northern Utes' Long Water Ordeal." *High Country News,* July 15, 1991, 8.

Miles, E.L., A.K. Snover, A. Hamlet, B. Callahan, and D. Fluharty. "Pacific Northwest Regional Assessment: The Impacts of Climate Variability and Climate Change on the Water Resources of the Columbia River Basin." *Journal of the American Water Resources Association* 36, no. 2 (2000): 399–420.

Rogers, Peg. "*In re Rights to Use Water in the Big Horn River,* 753 P.2d 76 (Wyo. 1988)." *Natural Resources Journal* 30 (1990): 439.

Smith, Mark E. "Conservation Reserve Enhancement Program: Early Results from a Federal-State Partnership." *Agricultural Outlook* AO-277 (November 2000): 16–20.

Thorson, John E. "Proceedings on the Symposium on Settlement of Indian Water Rights Claims." *Environmental Law* 22 (1992): 1009.

Williams, Susan. "The *Winters* Doctrine on Water Administration." *Rocky Mountain Mineral Law Institute* 36 (1990): 24-1.

"The Zuni Experience: Floodplains, Wetlands, and Intertwined Spiritual Traditions." *Arizona Flood Management Association Newsletter,* July 2000, 8.

Reports

Ad Hoc Group on Indian Water Rights, Western Governors' Association. *Questions and Answers Regarding the Domenici Amendment to the Budget Act.* Denver, Colorado, April 24, 2001.

"Assured Water Supply Requirement—Legal Availability of Central Arizona Project Water or Colorado River Water Leased from an Indian Community." R 12-15-703.01 in *Ariz. Admin. Reg.* 7, no. 28 (July 13, 2001): 3038.

Central Valley Water Use Study Committee, *Irrigation Water Use in the Central Valley of California*. Division of Agriculture and Natural Resources, University of California and California Department of Water Resources, 1987.

Chambers, Reid P., and John F. Echohawk. *Implementing Winters Doctrine Indian Reserved Water Rights: Producing Indian Water and Economic Development without Injuring Non-Indian Water Users?* Occasional Papers Series. Boulder: Natural Resources Law Center, University of Colorado, 1991.

Driver, Bruce. *Western Water: Tuning the System*. Denver: Western Governors' Association, 1986.

Hamlet, Alan F., Dennis P. Lettenmaier, Edward Miles, and Philip Mote. *Preparing for Climate Change in the Pacific Northwest: A Discussion of Water Resources Adaptation Pathways*. Preparatory White Paper for Climate and Water Policy Meeting, Skamania, Washington, July 2001. Seattle: Climate Impacts Group, University of Washington.

Intergovernmental Panel on Climate Change. *Water: The Potential Consequences of Climate Variability and Change for the Water Resources of the United States*. National Assessment of the Potential Consequences of Climate Variability and Change, IPCC, Geneva, Switzerland, 2000.

McCool, Daniel. "Indian Water Right Settlements: Negotiating Tribal Claims to Water." www.ucowr.siu.edu/updates/pdf/v107_A5.pdf (visited July 2, 2004).

Montana Reserved Water Rights Compact Commission. "Compacts." www.dnrc.state.mt.us/rwrcc/ (visited February 24, 2003).

———. *Historical Report for the Northern Cheyenne–Montana Compact*. Missoula, Mont.: Compact Commission, December 1990.

———. *Land and Water Resources of the Northern Cheyenne Indian Reservation*. Commission Staff Technical Report. Missoula, Mont.: Compact Commission, July 1990.

National Academy of Sciences. *Endangered and Threatened Fishes in the Klamath River Basin: Causes of Decline and Strategies of Recovery*. Washington D.C.: NAS, 2004.

Scientific Evaluation of Biological Opinions on Endangered and Threatened Fishes in the Klamath River Basin: Interim Report. Washington, D.C.: NAS, 2002.

National Agricultural Statistical Service. *1998 Farm and Ranch Irrigation Survey*. AC97 SP-1. Washington, D.C.: U.S. Department of Agriculture, 1999.

New Mexico Office of the State Engineer. "Navajo Irrigation Project Can Go Forward." *Water Line*, winter 2000. Available at www.seo.state.nm.us/publications/waterlines/wl-winter-2000/navajo.html (visited July 4, 2004).

Roncalio, Teno. *Report Concerning Reserved Rights Claims by and on Behalf of the Wind River Indian Reservation, In re Rights to Use Water in the Big Horn River*. (Wyo. 5th Dist., December 15, 1982.)

———. *Wyoming's Petition for a Writ of Certiorari to the Supreme Court of Wyoming*, appendix H. August 19, 1988.

Searchinger, Timothy. *Suggestions to States Interested in Developing Conservation Reserve Enhancement Programs*. Washington, D.C.: Environmental Defense, 1997.

Solley, W.B., R.R. Pierce, and H.A. Perlman. "Estimated Use of Water in the United States in 1995." In *Survey Circular 1200*. Reston, Va.: U.S. Geological Survey, Department of the Interior, 1998.

U.S. Department of Commerce, Bureau of the Census. *Statistical Brief: Housing of American Indians on Reservations*. Washington, D.C.: Bureau of the Census, 1995.

U.S. Department of the Interior. "Final Report and Recommendations of the Working Group on the Endangered Species Act and Indian Water Rights." *Federal Register* 65 (2000): 41709.

U.S. Fish and Wildlife Service. *Final Biological Opinion for the Animas–La Plata Project, Colorado and New Mexico*. Washington, D.C.: U.S. Fish and Wildlife Service, October 25, 1991.

U.S. House. *To Approve the Fort Hall Indian Water Rights Settlement, and for Other Purposes*. 101st Cong., 2d sess., H Rep. 5308, July 18, 1990.

U.S. National Water Commission. *Water Policies for the Future*. Final Report to the President and to the Congress of the United States. Port Washington, N.Y.: Water Information Center, 1973.

Yardes, David. "Restoring Endangered Ecosystems: The Truckee-Carson Water Rights Settlement." *Natural Resource Law Notes*, January 1992.

Conference Papers and Presentations

Connor, Michael. "Congressional Outlook for Funding for Indian Water Rights Settlements." Indian Water Rights Settlement Conference, Native American Rights Fund and Western States Water Council, St. George, Utah, October 10–12, 2001.

Cottingham, Susan. Keynote address on Settling Indian Water Rights Claims at the Western Governors' Association Environmental Summit on the West II, Salt Lake City, Utah, April 24–26, 2002.

Echohawk, John. Speaker on Settling Indian Water Rights Claims at the Western Governors' Association Environmental Summit on the West II, Salt Lake City, Utah, April 24–26, 2002.

Ely, Joe. "Pyramid Lake Negotiated Settlement: Overview and Perspectives." Paper presented at the Innovations in Western Water Law and Management Conference, Natural Resources Law Center, University of Colorado, Boulder, 1991.

Fasset, Jeff. "Big Horn Adjudication." Settlement of Indian Water Rights, symposium sponsored by the Native American Rights Fund and the Western States Water Council, Albuquerque, New Mexico, September 1–3, 1992.

Gover, Kevin. "Disciplinary Values and Perspectives in Approaching Interstate Water Conflicts: Tribal Rights." Presentation at the First Utton Center Conference on Law, Science and Water, Snowbird, Utah, October 10–12, 2002.

Hayes, David. Speaker on Settling Indian Water Rights Claims at the Western Governors' Association Environmental Summit on the West II, Salt Lake City, Utah, April 24–26, 2002.

McGrath, Shaun. Speaker on Indian Water Rights. Indian Water Rights Settlement Conference, Native American Rights Fund and Western States Water Council, St. George, Utah, October 10–12, 2001.

Morsette, Jim. Speaker on Settling Indian Water Rights Claims at the Western Governors' Association Environmental Summit on the West II, Salt Lake City, Utah, April 24–26, 2002.

State of Washington Water Research Center. Indian Water Rights Conference. Bellevue, Wash.: Super Ferro Dynamic, 1981. Sound recording.

Stewart, Margaret. Speaker on Indian Water Rights Settlements. Indian Water Rights Settlement Conference, Native American Rights Fund and Western States Water Council, St. George, Utah, October 10–12, 2001.

Whiting, Jeanne. Speaker at Natural Resources Law Center annual conference, University of Colorado School of Law, Boulder, Colorado, June 2001.

Williams, Susan. "Big Horn Adjudication." Paper presented at Settlement of Indian Water Rights, symposium sponsored by the Native American Rights Fund and the Western States Water Council, Albuquerque, New Mexico, September 1–3, 1992.

———. "Acquiring Water for Tribes." Paper presented at the Two Decades of Water Law Policy and Reform: A Retrospective and Agenda for the Future, Natural Resources Law Center, University of Colorado, Boulder, June 13–15, 2001.

Theses

Eden, Susana. "Negotiation and the Resolution of Water Allocation Disputes." Master's thesis, University of Arizona, 1988.

Jacobson, Judith. "A Promise Made: The Navajo Indian Irrigation Project." Cooperative Thesis 119, University of Colorado and National Center for Atmospheric Research, 1989.

AUTHORS AND CONTRIBUTORS

George Britton is deputy city manager in Modesto, California, and was deputy city manager in Phoenix, Arizona, from 1986 to 2001, and was responsible for both water and wastewater activities for the city. Before that, he was executive assistant for then-governor Bruce Babbitt and was responsible for natural resources activities from 1980 to 1986.

Sarah Britton is an attorney practicing with the public defender in Sacramento, California. She graduated from the University of Arizona James E. Rogers College of Law in spring 2003. Prior to law school, Sarah lived in Port-au-Prince, Haiti, working for USAID, as well as serving as a criminal defense investigator in Washington, D.C.

Carmen Carrion is a graduate research assistant at the University of Arizona. She has a M.S. degree from Ohio State University and is from Mexico.

Bonnie G. Colby is professor of Agricultural and Resource Economics at the University of Arizona, where she has been a faculty member since 1983. Colby's Ph.D. is from the University of Wisconsin. Her expertise is in the economics of natural resource policy and disputes over water, public lands, and environmental regulation. Colby is the author of over one hundred published articles and book chapters and three previous books.

Jeffrey Cordova is a member of the Taos Pueblo Tribe from Taos, New Mexico. He is studying hydrology and water resources at the University of Arizona. He is employed as a student hydrologic technician at the United States Geological Survey Water Resources Division, where he has worked for three years. Upon completing his education, he plans to work with American Indian tribes to manage and develop their water resources.

Nelson J. Cordova is a tribal councilman at Taos Pueblo. He has served in various capacities at the tribal level, including governor of Taos Pueblo in 2001 and war chief in 1999. Currently, he is serving as a tribal water rights coordinator and oversees the adjudication of the Pueblo's water rights in the *New Mexico v. Abeyta* water adjudication suit. Cordova was appointed to the New Mexico Water Trust Board and serves on the Department of the Interior's Joint Federal-Tribal Water Rights Funding Task Force. He is a graduate of New Mexico State University and Pennsylvania State University.

Barbara Cosens is an assistant professor at the University of Idaho School of Law, Moscow, Idaho. She also is the mediator for the Walker River negotiations in Nevada. Barbara served as legal counsel to the Montana Reserved Water Rights Compact Commission from 1991 to 2001. During that time, she served as chief legal counsel for the commission in the settlement of reserved water rights for ten areas, including the Rocky Boy's and Fort Belknap Indian Reservations; three units of the U.S. Fish and Wildlife Service; and five units of the National Park Service. She completed an LL.M. in environmental and natural resource law at Northwestern School

of Law, Lewis and Clark College, in Portland, Oregon. Barbara received her J.D. from the University of California, Hastings College of the Law, in 1990.

John Echohawk is executive director of the Native American Rights Fund, located in Boulder, Colorado. A Pawnee, John was the first graduate of the University of New Mexico's special program to train Indian lawyers, and was a founding member of the American Indian Law Students Association while in law school. John has been with NARF since its inception in 1970 and has served continuously as executive director since 1977. He has been recognized as one of the one hundred most influential lawyers in America by the *National Law Journal*.

George Frisvold received his Ph.D. in agricultural and resource economics in 1989 from the University of California, Berkeley. In 1995–1996, Dr. Frisvold served on the senior staff of the President's Council of Economic Advisers, with responsibility for agricultural, natural resource, and international trade issues. Currently, he is a professor and extension specialist in the Department of Agricultural and Resource Economics at the University of Arizona. His research interests include transboundary water management and the impacts of public policy on agriculture and the environment.

David H. Getches is dean of the University of Colorado School of Law and has served as the Raphael J. Moses professor of natural resources law. Author of a significant number of books, he was the founding executive director of the Native American Rights Fund, and from 1983–1987, served as executive director of the Colorado Department of Natural Resources under Governor Richard D. Lamm. Getches has consulted widely concerning water policy and national policies concerning indigenous peoples with governmental agencies and nongovernmental organizations throughout the United States and in several foreign countries.

Robert J. Glennon is the Morris K. Udall professor of law and public policy at the University of Arizona James E. Rogers College of Law, and has served on the faculty of the law school since 1985. He holds a Ph.D. in history from Brandeis University, and a J.D. from Boston College Law School. Glennon serves on the advisory boards of Southwest Rivers and the *Western Water Law & Policy Reporter* and is a trustee of the Rocky Mountain Mineral Law Foundation. Professor Glennon is the author of *Water Follies: Groundwater Pumping and the Fate of America's Fresh Waters* (Washington, D.C.: Island Press, 2002).

David J. Hayes is a partner in Latham & Watkins's Washington, D.C., office, where his practice focuses on environmental, energy, and natural resources matters. Hayes has an extensive background in EPA-related regulatory matters: contaminated sites, chemical regulation, air and water pollution issues; and in natural resource–related matters: water rights and allocation, Endangered Species Act implementation, energy project permitting, land conservation projects, and Indian-related matters.

Ramsey Laursoo Kropf is a shareholder with Patrick, Miller & Kropf, P.C., a Colorado law firm with its practice limited to water issues. She also serves as the special master for the fifth judicial district court in Wyoming's Bighorn River general adjudication, acting as a judicial officer and conducting hearings in the adjudication. Kropf received her joint J.D./M.B.A. degree from the University of Colorado in 1991. She is admitted to the state bar in Arizona, Wyoming, and Colorado.

Scott B. McElroy is an attorney with the law firm of Greene, Meyer & McElroy, P.C., of Boulder, Colorado. He received his J.D. from the University of Toledo College of Law in 1974. His practice is limited to the representation of Indian tribes and their members, concentrating on the litigation and negotiation of natural resource disputes. Prior to his entry into private practice, McElroy practiced with the Department of Justice and the Department of the Interior, as well as the Native American Rights Fund. While at Justice, McElroy tried *Arizona v. California II*.

James P. Merchant is vice-president of Dornbusch Associates in Berkeley, California. He holds J.D. and M.B.A. degrees from Stanford University. He specializes in water resource issues, including water transfers, planning for municipal and agricultural projects, and water rights disputes. He has testified as an expert economist in several water rights controversies and has participated in eight of the completed Indian water rights settlements. Over the years, he has worked on water issues for more than forty Indian tribes.

Lucy Moore is a nationally recognized practitioner in the field of environmental and public policy dispute resolution, with a particular emphasis on cross-cultural disputes. She is president of Lucy Moore & Associates in Santa Fe, New Mexico, and has over twenty years of experience working as a mediator and facilitator on a wide variety of issues involving tribal governments and communities.

Michael C. Nelson retired (2003) as the presiding judge of the superior court of Apache County, Arizona, a position he had held since 1989. In 1994, Judge Allen Minker appointed Nelson to be the settlement judge in the Little Colorado stream adjudication. In 2000, he was appointed settlement judge in the Gila River adjudication. Nelson is presently acting as the mediator in *New Mexico ex rel. State Engineer v. Aamodt, et al.* in the federal district court in New Mexico. He has published a number of articles on or related to Indian water rights, Indian tribal law, and tribal-state relations. He received his B.A. from Stanford in 1970 and his J.D. from The University of Arizona in 1977.

Stephen E. Snyder is a mediator, attorney, and consultant in conflict management who resides in Corrales, New Mexico. He has conducted several workshops on mediation, alternative dispute resolution, and collaborative problem solving for judges, special masters, mediators, and litigants in water rights adjudications throughout the western United States. In July 2000—one year before the Klamath water crisis—Snyder and a colleague conducted a workshop on interest-based negotiation for the stakeholders in the Klamath basin alternative dispute-resolution process. In 2004, he was appointed special master for three adjudications in New Mexico.

John E. Thorson served as special master for Arizona's general stream adjudications from 1990 until 2000. He is now an administrative law judge for the California Public Utilities Commission. While in Arizona, Thorson heard cases in adjudications that comprise approximately 77,000 water rights claimed by 27,000 parties. He is cofounder of Dividing the Waters, an education and communications project for judges who are involved in water rights litigation in fifteen western states. A native of New Mexico, Thorson received his law degree from Boalt Hall, University of California at Berkeley, and his doctorate in public administration from the University of Southern California. He is a member of the Arizona, California, Montana, and New Mexico state bars, as well as the bar of the United States Supreme Court.

Beth S. Wolfsong is an attorney with Southern Arizona Legal Aid, where she represents domestic violence survivors in various civil and criminal proceedings. Wolfsong received a J.D. from the University of Arizona James E. Rogers College of Law in 2002, where she devoted most of her time to studying environmental and federal Indian law. In her free time, she volunteers with a nonprofit environmental justice group and continues to research and explore contemporary issues affecting indigenous nations and the environment.

M. Evelyn Woods has practiced federal Indian law and water law since receiving her degree from the University of Colorado School of Law in 1995. She has represented a variety of western tribes in litigation and transactional work with the Boulder law firms Fredericks, Pelcyger, Hester and White, L.L.C., and Whiteing & Smith. Woods is currently special counsel to the Shivwits Band of Southern Paiutes, near St. George, Utah, implementing its recent reserved water rights settlement, and teaches seminars in Indian law and Indian water rights as an adjunct professor at Denver University School of Law. She is a member of the Cherokee Nation of Oklahoma and is past president of the Colorado Indian Bar Association.

INDEX